Presented to the McCormick Library
in fond memory of
Cathryn Hintze

By the
HACC Live Action Role Playing Club
Spring 2010

Bram Stoker's
Notes for *Dracula*

Bram Stoker's Notes for *Dracula*

A Facsimile Edition

BRAM STOKER

Annotated and Transcribed by
ROBERT EIGHTEEN-BISANG *and*
ELIZABETH MILLER

Foreword by MICHAEL BARSANTI

McFarland & Company, Inc., Publishers
Jefferson, North Carolina, and London

Library of Congress Cataloguing-in-Publication Data

Stoker, Bram, 1847–1912.
Bram Stoker's notes for Dracula : a facsimile edition / Bram Stoker ;
annotated and transcribed by Robert Eighteen-Bisang and
Elizabeth Miller ; foreword by Michael Barsanti.
p. cm.
Includes bibliographical references and index.

ISBN 978-0-7864-3410-7
library binding : 50# alkaline paper ♾

1. Stoker, Bram, 1847–1912 — Notebooks, sketchbooks, etc.
2. Stoker, Bram, 1847–1912 — Manuscripts.
3. Stoker, Bram, 1847–1912. Dracula.
I. Eighteen-Bisang, Robert.
II. Miller, Elizabeth, 1939–
III. Title.
PR6037.T617Z46 2008 823'.8 — dc22 2008019450

British Library cataloguing data are available

Manufactured in the United States of America

McFarland & Company, Inc., Publishers
Box 611, Jefferson, North Carolina 28640
www.mcfarlandpub.com

To
Stephanie Moss:

for her enthusiasm as a teacher,
her inspiration as a scholar
and her support as a friend.

— Elizabeth Miller

To
Matilda:

My wife, my muse, my Mina.

— Robert Eighteen-Bisang

Acknowledgments

Richard Dalby, Joel Emerson, Clive Leatherdale, Walter Sinclair, David J. Skal and Sylvia Starshine have all played important parts in the creation of this book. Their expertise and their friendship are deeply appreciated. The staff of the Rosenbach Museum & Library was extremely helpful when we went to Philadelphia to examine the Notes in September of 2006. Thanks are due to Elizabeth Fuller for helping to put a final polish on the manuscript. Michael Barsanti, Derick Dreher and Greg Giuliano deserve special mention for, without their contributions, this book would not have been possible.

Table of Contents

Foreword by Michael Barsanti

Bram Stoker's Notes for *Dracula* are one of the greatest treasures in the Rosenbach Museum & Library — a small house that has been converted into a museum and rare-book library on a shady, residential street in the center of Philadelphia. The Notes are kept in a specially-made box in company with manuscripts by Stoker's fellow Dubliners Oscar Wilde and James Joyce, as well as Joseph Conrad, Lewis Carroll, and other famous writers.

The Rosenbach was once the home of two brothers, Abraham and Philip Rosenbach. The brothers ran a company that bought and sold paintings, prints, picture frames, silver, antiques, and of course, rare books and manuscripts. At its peak, about 1920 to 1940, the Rosenbach Company sold some of the greatest books the world had to offer, thanks to the genius of younger brother Abraham — also known as "the Doctor." As a dealer, Dr. Rosenbach helped establish many of the greatest libraries in the United States, but he couldn't help but keep some of the best prizes for himself. The brothers eventually decided to turn their home into a museum and to give their collections to the public.

The *Dracula* Notes were not, however, purchased by the brothers. The museum acquired them from Philadelphia bookseller Charles Sessler in 1970, but how they got there is not completely known. They were originally sold at Sotheby's by Stoker's widow, Florence, in 1913 — a year after his death — to a New York book dealer named James Drake for 2£, 2s. Then in the 1930s and 1940s, they were in the inventory of Charles Scribner's Sons in New York, and from there the trail goes cold again until the Rosenbach purchase. The museum purchased the Notes because they are an extraordinary record of the construction of an extraordinary novel. (Coincidentally, the museum also holds a very rare booklet bought by Dr. Rosenbach — a 1488 pamphlet from Nuremberg, Germany, about Vlad Dracula.)

When the notes were first sold, they were mounted in an album. The album leaves were highly acidic, however, and in 1997 the notes were removed and conserved. The individual leaves of the manuscript were paginated while in the album, and the museum has retained that pagination for the sake of consistency. Clearly the pagination does not imply any kind of chronological order.

The following is a description of the contents of the notes:

> Manuscript and typescript notes, photographs, and a newspaper clipping, comprising both background research and an outline for the book. The first section consists of 49 leaves of manuscript: a list of characters, notes on vampires, outlines for the whole book and for most chapters (all 7 chapters for each of books 1–3 and ch. 26–27), chronologies, and miscellaneous notes on characters and events. The second section consists of 30 manuscript leaves, 2 photographs, and a clipping: reading notes on vampires and werewolves; and shipwrecks, weather, geography, and language in the area of Whitby, North Yorkshire, where part of the story takes place. The last section consists of 37 leaves of typescript notes with manuscript corrections, being reading notes on various works about the history and geography of the Carpathians, dream theory, and tombstones at Whitby.

Among the many achievements of Robert Eighteen-Bisang and Elizabeth Miller in this book is a new arrangement of these pages in a sequence that reflects the order and nature of their composition. This must have been an easy task, however, next to the incredible difficulty of deciphering Stoker's handwriting! We are greatly pleased to be associated with their work, which will introduce the complexity and genius of Stoker's method to a wide audience, and begin a new era in *Dracula* scholarship.

M.B. • *October 2007*

Michael Barsanti is the former associate director of the Rosenbach Museum & Library

Introduction

"Bram Stoker's Original Foundation Notes & Data for His 'Dracula'" (hereafter, the "Notes") outline the development of the plot from early, often unrecognizable pastiches of people, places and events to a nine-page calendar of events that includes most of the familiar story that has been told and retold for more than a century. These papers, which are housed in the Rosenbach Museum & Library in Philadelphia, are an indispensable resource for anyone who is interested in the genesis and composition of *Dracula.*

Outlines of the plot, research documents and interlineations in the typed pages are scribbled in Stoker's cramped, often hurried hand. Before these papers were "discovered," his claim to fame as the author of the world's foremost vampire novel was open to question, for this dark, erotic fantasy soars far above any of his other works. Anthony Boucher began his introduction to the Limited Editions Club's edition of *Dracula* by asking, "How did the most successful horror novel in the English (and possibly in any) language come to be written by a man whose first published book was entitled *The Duties of Clerks of Petty Sessions in Ireland*?" (v), while H. P. Lovecraft claimed to have known "an old lady who almost had the job of revising 'Dracula' back in the 1890s — she saw the original ms., & says it was a fearful mess. Finally someone else (Stoker thought her price for the work was too high) whipped it into such shape as it now possesses" (24).

There are many misconceptions about the origin and contents of the novel. Claims that the fifteenth-century warlord Vlad the Impaler was *the* model for the literary Count Dracula, that Jonathan Harker's imprisonment in Castle Dracula was inspired by Oscar Wilde's time in Reading Gaol, that "Dracula's Guest" was not part of the novel from the beginning, or that this story was once the *first* chapter of the book leave no doubt that the people who made them did not study the Notes. This is not surprising, for until we obtained permission from the Rosenbach to publish an annotated transcription of this material, only a handful of its 124 pages had been published. The primary intention of this book is to make every page of the Notes available to anyone who is interested in them.

Few people knew that the Notes existed until Professors Raymond McNally and Radu Florescu — who had co-authored the pioneering study *In Search of Dracula* in 1972 — came upon them fortuitously when they travelled to the Rosenbach to see a fifteenth-century pamphlet about the Impaler. Their surprise and joy are evident in the introduction to *The Essential Dracula* (1979):

> Then, like a bolt from the blue, the archivist asked us a startling question: might we also be interested in seeing the original notes that Stoker made while creating the novel *Dracula*?
>
> At first we could not believe our ears. No scholar had ever found Stoker's notes. In fact no one knew where they were. We quizzed the archivist who told us that the notes had not been catalogued at the Rosenbach Foundation.

> We were paralyzed with amazement. Here was the single most important find concerning the origins of the novel. What an opportunity! And how curiously often it happens that some great find like this turns up by accident while one is engaged in an entirely different quest.
>
> After we had pored over the Stoker notes, we looked at each other in triumph. We knew that we were at last witnessing the birth of *Dracula* in the mind of Bram Stoker [17].

The first reference to the Notes appeared in Raymond McNally's anthology *A Clutch of Vampires* in 1975 (163) as part of his introduction to a newspaper article from 1896 titled "Vampires in New England" (which was clipped into Stoker's Notes and is included here as page 85). Two years later, Joseph Bierman undertook the first comprehensive study of these documents. He summarizes them as follows:

> ... handwritten and typewritten notes, dated and undated, about numerous subjects of central or tangential interest to a writer who was thinking of settings, characters, and plot for a story of the supernatural; descriptions of topography, landscape and customs from the work of contemporary travellers in Danubian countries; notes on a theory of dreams; transcriptions of tombstone inscriptions; accounts of conversations with old sailors and coastguardsmen; and notes for the novel itself [52].

Bierman determined that the earliest dated Note was written on 8 March 1890 (negating the widely-held belief that the author did not begin writing *Dracula* until 1895); the novel was originally set in Styria, but this province in Austria was soon changed to Transylvania; the Notes neither prove nor disprove the rumor that the Hungarian professor Arminius Vambery furnished Stoker with any information about Dracula or Transylvania. Bierman's most important discovery, however, may be that Stoker probably found the name "Dracula" in the public library in Whitby while on vacation with his wife, Florence, and their son, Noel, in the summer of 1890—months after he began writing the novel.

McNally and Florescu published their annotated edition of *Dracula* (*The Essential Dracula*) two years later. They drew heavily on the Notes for annotations to the first three chapters, which are full of details about Transylvanian history, geography and customs. However, they continued to cling to their well-known claim that Vlad the Impaler was "the basis of the legend" (15) despite evidence in the Notes that challenges this assertion.

Christopher Frayling has conducted the most detailed examination of the Notes to date. His vampire anthology, *Vampyres: Lord Byron to Count Dracula* (1991), includes a scholarly and erudite overview of the Notes, accompanied by excerpts from several of Bram Stoker's research sources. His study focuses on the material that shaped the first three chapters of the novel for, in his words, "Not only are these by far the best-known chapters of *Dracula*— they reappear in all the major screen adaptations — but they are also the chapters for which Bram Stoker did the most interesting research" (303).

Over the ensuing years, a handful of authors have used the Notes in ingenious ways. In *Bram Stoker* (1982), Phyllis Roth uses highlights from them to review *Dracula*, "Dracula's Guest" and other works. Clive Leatherdale's *The Origins of Dracula* (1987) reprints material from several of Stoker's research sources, with extensive excerpts from William Wilkinson, Sabine Baring-Gould, Major E. C. Johnson and Emily Gerard. David J. Skal's study of *Dracula*'s progress from novel to stage and screen found that "The Dracula notes, with their abundance of overlapping characters, offer one of the few tangible insights into Stoker's working methods" (*Hollywood Gothic* 1990, 22). The Rosenbach Museum & Library's *Bram Stoker's Dracula: A Centennial Exhibition* (1997) includes photographs of several pages of Notes with brief explanations of their contents. Two of Elizabeth Miller's books —*Dracula: Sense & Nonsense* (2000 [revised 2006]) and *Bram Stoker's Dracula: A Documentary Volume* (2005)— draw heavily on the Notes to challenge widespread misconceptions about the novel. Bram Stoker's Notes have even inspired a novel. In *The Un-Dead: The Dracula Novel Rewritten to Include Stoker's Deleted Characters and Events* (2007), Joel Emerson imagines what *Dracula* would look like if the characters and events that Stoker hinted at in the notes were reinserted into the text.

Bram Stoker's Notes for Dracula is the first comprehensive examination and analysis of all of the Notes. We believe that these papers are an invaluable resource. Their richness reflects the depth and diversity of the novel, while both of these texts yield a multitude of meanings and interpretations.

Methodology

The original copy of "Bram Stoker's Original Foundation Notes & Data for His 'Dracula'" is divided into three sections: handwritten plot notes, handwritten research notes, and typewritten research notes. The arbitrary order in which these documents are arranged is often confusing but, before we could place them in a logical and readable sequence, we were confronted by the challenge of transcribing the handwritten material.

Transcribing the Notes

As Stoker himself confessed, "I seldom wrote, in working times, less than fifty letters a day. Fortunately — for both myself and the readers, for I write an extremely bad hand — the bulk of them were short" (*Personal Reminiscences of Henry Irving* v1.42).

We were able to decipher most of his script without difficulty, but particular words, phrases and lines of text resisted our initial efforts. Parallel passages in other parts of the Notes, in sources cited in these Notes and in the text of *Dracula*, helped us solve many of these puzzles. When both of us were confident we had found the best possible reading, we inserted our solution in the transcript and presented any viable alternative in a footnote. Patience and perseverance enabled us to transcribe most of the handwritten material, but a number of expressions refused to yield their secrets to us.

We designated unreadable text with "xxx" and enclosed the author's original deletions in triangular brackets <TEXT>. (Hence, any illegible deletion is rendered as <xxx>.) We also took the liberty of correcting spelling errors and amending the author's idiosyncratic abbreviations and punctuation marks. Finally, we inserted a white dot —º— to indicate any pause the author seems to have ignored or taken for granted. For instance, "Seward's diary wants a cat" is rendered "Seward's diary º wants a cat." These conventions allowed us to transcribe the text page by page, line by line and word by word.

The accompanying photofacsimiles of the handwritten documents allow readers to judge the success of our efforts and, if they wish, to try to unravel the mysteries of Bram Stoker's penmanship, the meaning of obscure phrases and the original (or best possible) order of the text.

Categories of Notes

We divided Sections I and II of the Rosenbach Notes into handwritten outlines of the plot and handwritten research notes. This strategy enables readers to concentrate on the development of plot, which is the most interesting and important part of these documents. In their publication, *Bram Stoker's Dracula*, the Rosenbach refers to the first three pages of Section II as a "list of vampire characteristics, [written] between 1890 and 1896" (22). However, we found that these pages — i.e., 38a, 38b and 38c — contain only four lines of research and, by our criteria, belong in our Part I. We arranged the handwritten research material in Section II in a more logical order, but left the typewritten notes in Section III as is.

Sequence of Pages

Our next task was to determine the proper sequence of the plot notes. We would like to have been able to present them in the same order in which they had been written, but this proved to be impossible. Many pages contain revisions that were made at a later, unknown date (or dates). Hence, it is impossible to determine what the first draft said. Dated pages and other clues allowed us to group pages together in rough chronological order: early outlines of the plot, chapter-by-chapter drafts of the entire novel, a calendar of events which contains a new version of the plot of the novel, and various outlines for the final part of the book.

After a great deal of trial and error, we found that the key was how the position of each page in these groups affects the "flow" of the text. Our final decisions were often more art than science.

It was not necessary to determine the initial sequence of the research material in Parts II and III. In fact, we found that any attempt to do so created more problems than it solved.

Method of Presentation

Facsimiles of the Notes are accompanied by transcriptions of the text on the facing pages. When supplemental material that is not part of the original notes or transcriptions is presented, the material is separated by the following designation: ❧ ❧ ❧.

Every transcription is headed by our page number and its original (or Rosenbach) page number. Other relevant details follow this information or are presented in footnotes. In Parts II and III, we provide standard bibliographical information for each source from which Stoker took notes.

Our explanatory text and footnotes contain four types of references:

1. The original page numbers are referred to as the "Rosenbach" numbers.
2. The page numbers we assigned to our transcription are referred to as "pages" in the text but (p.) in citations.
3. Quotations from *Dracula* give the chapter and page number in Archibald Constable's text of 1897. Hence, "I am Dracula; and I bid you welcome, Mr. Harker, to my house" (2:17) refers to chapter 2, page 17.
4. Quotations from other sources give the author's or editor's name (or the title) followed by the appropriate page number.

We then summarize our findings about the Notes and examine them from different perspectives. Three of the appendices present the reader with a bird's eye view of the Notes. Appendix I gives the original order and number of each page, followed by the new number we have assigned it. Appendix VIII is a précis of important themes and events in *Dracula* in which material that is *not* in the Notes is highlighted in italics. In contrast, Appendix IX presents characters and events that appear in the Notes but do not play a part in the novel.

Limitations of the Notes

1. It is not possible to determine if "Bram Stoker's Original Foundation Notes & Data for his 'Dracula'" includes all of his preliminary Notes. Given his habit of jotting ideas on any scrap of paper that was readily available and the inevitable passage of time, some additional pages may have been lost.

2. It is not possible to determine when most of the Notes were written.

3. It is not possible to determine when the revisions were made.

4. It is not possible to determine when Stoker read the sources he cites.

5. In most cases, we do not know where the Notes were written.

6. Various lines, paragraphs and pages are scored through with a single stroke. These marks seem to indicate that Stoker had finished with sections of the Notes, but we do not know what purpose they serve or when they were made.

7. Almost half the events in the novel are not mentioned in the Notes. Most of the interactions between human beings and vampires from chapters 16 to 27 are missing.

8. The Notes are not a substitute for the novel.

9. The Notes are just one stage in the development of the text. The typescript is the next known pre-textual document, but it is highly unlikely that Stoker moved directly from the Notes to the typescript. He probably bridged the gap between them with one or more lost drafts of the novel.

10. Finally, the Notes do not obviate the importance of three post-textual documents: the play, *Dracula: or, the Un-Dead,* which was created from proof copies of the novel; the preface to the Icelandic edition of *Dracula* of 1901; and the abridged edition of *Dracula* which was published in 1901. Each of these documents provides unique and important insights into their author's immortal masterpiece.

Bram Stoker's Notes for Dracula presents our effort to bring a semblance of order to the Notes and to explain them to ourselves and to others. We could not have accomplished this without the help of many other people. Of course, we take full responsibility for any faulty transcriptions or other errors we have made.

Bram Stoker's Original Foundation Notes & Data for His "Dracula"

Part I

Handwritten Notes on the Plot

This remarkable book, which has already run into nine editions,[1] has been aptly described as "the very weirdest of weird tales."[2]

1. Archibald Constable's final edition of *Dracula* claims that it is the "Eighth edition" of "1904." When William Rider & Son assumed the rights to the novel in 1912 they designated their first printing the "Ninth Edition."

2. The widespread description of *Dracula* as "the very weirdest of weird tales" originated in a review of *Dracula* that appeared in *Punch* on 26 June 1897.

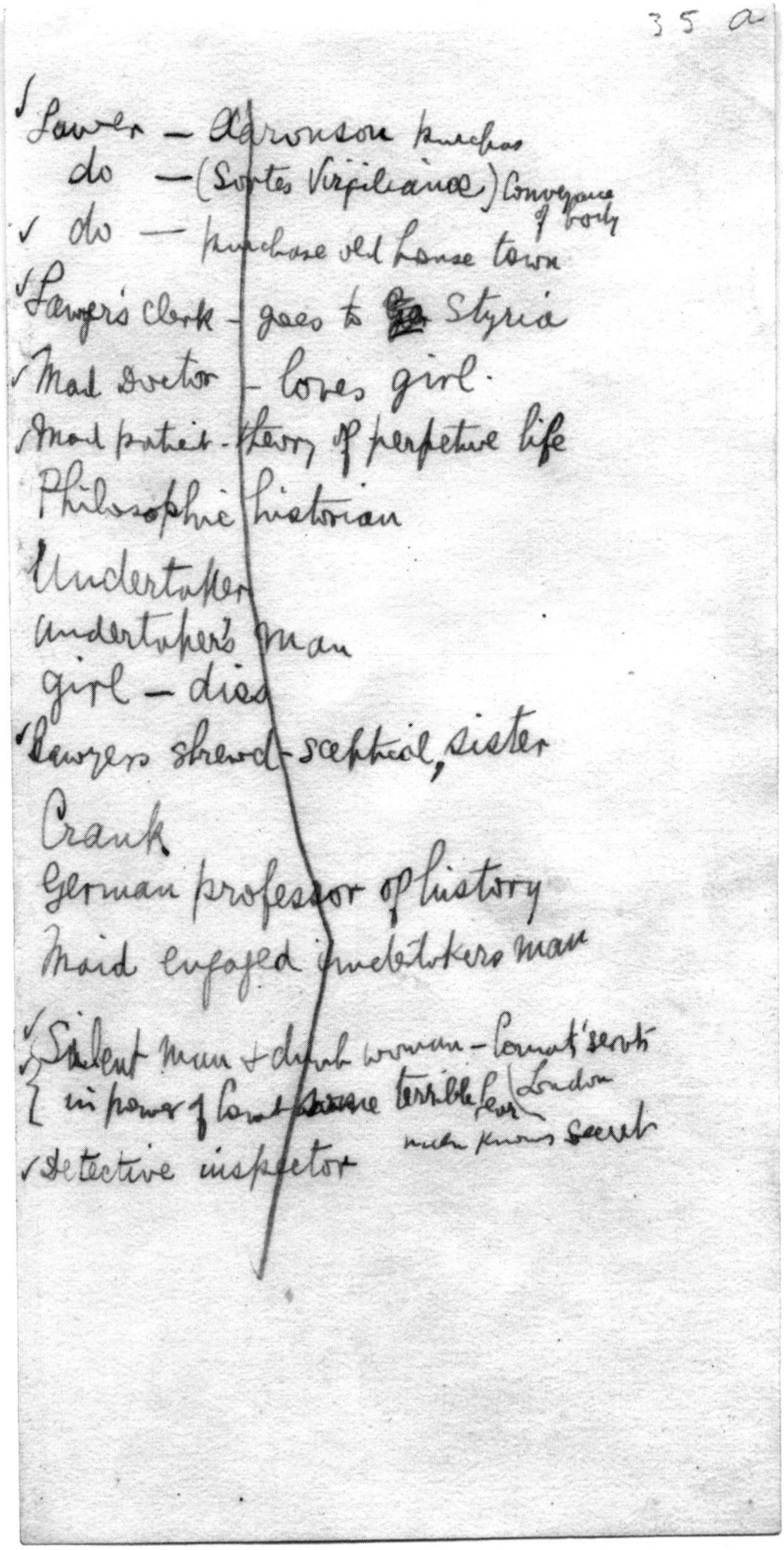

35 a

√Lawyer — Aaronson purchase
do — (Sortes Virgilianae) Conveyance of body
√ do — purchase old house town
√Lawyer's Clerk — goes to ~~Sty~~ Styria
√Mad Doctor — loves girl.
√Mad patient — theory of perpetuating life
Philosophic historian
Undertaker
undertaker's man
girl — dies
√Lawyers shrewd — sceptical, sister
Crank
German professor of history
Maid engaged undertakers man
√Silent man & dumb woman — Count's servts
{ in power of Count because terrible fear London
man knows secret
√Detective inspector

Page 1. Rosenbach #35a. Size (in inches): 6 × 3.

Lawyer[3]—Aaronson purchase[4]
[ditto]—(Sortes Virgilianae)[5] conveyance of body
[ditto]—purchase old house town
Lawyer's clerk—goes to <Ge> Styria[6]
Mad Doctor—loves girl
Mad patient[7]—theory of perpetual life[8]
Philosophic historian
Undertaker
Undertaker's man
Girl—dies
Lawyer's shrewd, sceptical sister
Crank
German professor of history
Maid engaged undertaker's man
Silent man & dumb woman—Count's[9] servants London ° in power of Count ° some terrible fear—man knows secret[10]
Detective inspector[11]

3. In *Dracula*, the protagonists include Jonathan Harker, "a full-blown solicitor" (2:16) who remarks that the Count "would have made a wonderful solicitor" (3:31) and Abraham Van Helsing who is "a lawyer as well as a doctor" (13:166). Although Bram Stoker never practiced law, he was called to the bar at the Inner Temple in London on 30 April 1890.

4. Aaronson is purchasing a house in London for a foreign client.

5. "Sortes Virgilianae" is Latin for Virgilian lots, a form of divination that uses words or phrases from Virgil as guides to future events.

6. It looks as if the author started to write "Germany," but quickly replaced "Ge" with "Styria," the state in southeastern Austria where Joseph Sheridan Le Fanu's vampire story "Carmilla" is set.

7. The "Mad Doctor" and his "Mad patient" form a dyad from the beginning.

8. The madman will become R. M. Renfield, who tries to extend his life by eating flies, spiders and birds.

9. Hence, Bram Stoker's literary creation was a "Count" *before* he was named Dracula or lined his coffin with soil from Transylvania.

10. Whom does this refer to, and what does he know?

11. Christopher Frayling believes that the "Philosophic historian" was combined with the "German professor of history" and the "Detective inspector" to forge the redoubtable Professor Abraham Van Helsing (305). The first list of characters also includes antecedents of Peter Hawkins (Aaronson), Jonathan Harker (lawyer's clerk), Dr. John Seward (mad doctor), Lucy Westenra (his beloved) and Renfield (mad patient).

35v a

8/3/90 Letter to Presdt. Incorporated Law Society

I Letter from do to Abraham Aaronson Solicitor enclosing copy of reply

Letter to Aaronson from Count — Styria asking to come or send trustworthy person who does not speak German etc.

Letters from latter to his principal with inter alia letters to his pal

(In this series of letters is told visit to Castle Munich Dead house — people in train knowing address

this uncle him — met at station storm arrive old Castle — left in courtyard

driver disappears Count appears — describe old dead man made alive waxen

colour dead dark eyes — what fire in them not human — hell fire — stay in

Castle no one but old man but no pretence of being alone — old man in waking

trance — young man goes out sees girls one tries to kiss him not on lips but throat

Old Count interferes — rage & fury diabolical — This man belongs to me I want him.

A prisoner for a time — looks at books — English — law directory sortes Virgilianae

Central place marked with point of knife. Instructed to buy property — requirement

Conservative Club in grounds — near river

Page 2. Rosenbach #35 verso a. Size: 3 × 6. Landscape.

8/3/90[12]

Letter to President Incorporated Law Society[13]
Letter from [ditto] to Abraham Aaronson solicitor º enclosing copy of reply
Letter to Aaronson from Count ___[14] Styria asking to come or send trustworthy law [sic][15] who does not speak German[16]
Letters from latter to his principal with *inter alia*[17] letters to his pal [sic][18]
(In this series of letters is told visit to Castle[19]—Munich Dead house[20]—people on train knowing address[21] dissuade him—met at station º storm º arrive old castle—left in courtyard º driver disappears º Count appears—describe old dead man made alive º waxen colour º dead dark eyes—what fire in them—not human—hell fire—Stay in castle. No one but old man but no pretence of being alone[22]—old man in waking trance—Young man goes out º sees girls º one tries to kiss him not on lips but throat[23] º Old Count interferes—rage & fury diabolical—This man belongs to me I want him.[24] A prisoner for a time[25]—looks at books—English law directory º sortes Virgilianae º central place marked with point of knife.[26] Instructed to buy property—requirement consecrated church on grounds[27]—near river[28]

12. Dates are written as day, month and year. Hence, 8/3/90 means 8 March 1890.

13. These entries indicate that Stoker intended to tell his story through a series of letters, diaries and other forms of communication from the beginning.

14. Stoker used "Count," "Count" followed by a blank space, a straight line or "Wampyr" as markers before he found the name "Dracula."

15. "[L]aw" is an abbreviation for "lawyer."

16. This prohibition made sense when the story was set in Styria where German is the national language. In Munich ["Dracula's Guest"] Jonathan Harker complains, "There was just enough of English mixed with the German for me to understand the drift of his talk ... but it was difficult to argue with a man when I did not know his language" (2–3) yet, in Klausenburgh [*Dracula*], he found his "smattering of German very useful" (1:1).

17. "[I]nter alia" is Latin for "among other things."

18. "[P]al" is an abbreviation for "principal."

19. Like many fairy-tale villains, the Count lives in a castle.

20. The words "Munich Dead house" are inserted into the text. Note that in the nineteenth century, a "dead house" was a mortuary rather than a mausoleum.

21. I.e., upon learning he is off to see the vampire.

22. "No one but old man but no pretence of being alone" must have been written hastily, for this phrase contradicts itself.

23. Jonathan Harker confides, "Lower and lower went her head as the lips went below the range of my mouth and chin and seemed to fasten on my throat" (3:39).

24. "But the Count! Never did I imagine such wrath and fury, even to the demons of the pit. His eyes were positively blazing. The red light in them was lurid, as if the flames of hell-fire blazed behind them....

"'How dare you touch him, any of you? How dare you cast eyes on him when I had forbidden it? Back, I tell you all! This man belongs to me!'" (3:40).

25. "The castle is a veritable prison, and I am a prisoner!" (2:27).

26. Did Dracula choose his law firm by stabbing a knife into a law directory, or decide on the location of his new home by thrusting a knife into a map? The vampire's use of divination is in keeping with the supposition that he is a sorcerer.

27. As Frayling points out, "This is the earliest example of Bram Stoker extending the 'rules' of the vampire genre: the Count, it seems, has to rest in consecrated earth" (305).

28. This paragraph lays the foundation for chapters 2 and 3. Note that the abrupt ending combined with the absence of a closing parenthesis mark seems to indicate a break in Stoker's line of thought.

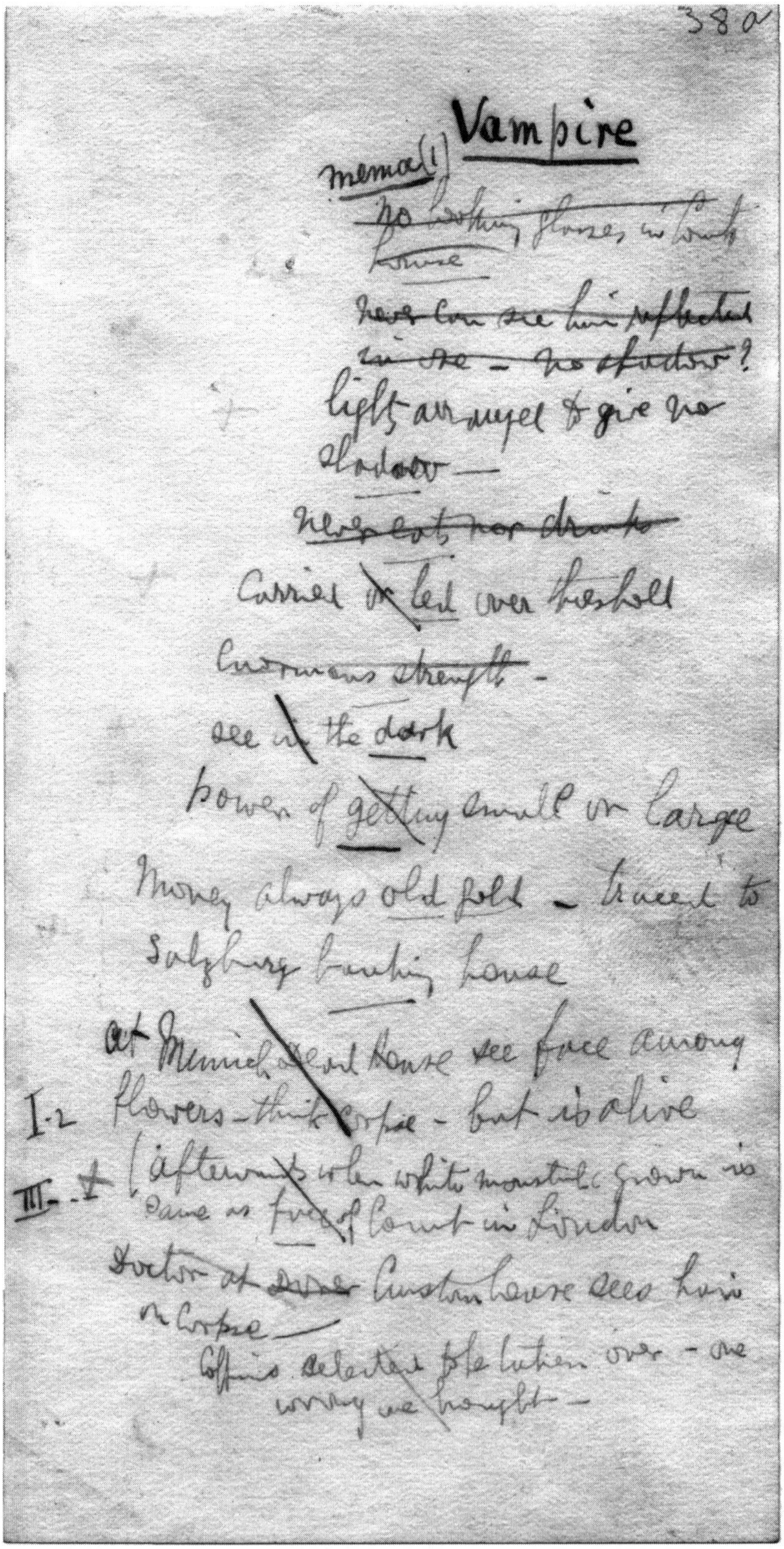
380a

Vampire

memo (1)

~~no looking glasses in Counts house~~

~~never can see his reflection in one — no shadow~~?

light arranged to give no shadow —

~~never eats nor drinks~~

carried or led over threshold

~~enormous strength~~ -

see in the dark

power of getting small or large

Money always old gold — traced to Salzburg banking house

at Munich dead house see face among

I-2 flowers — think corpse — but is alive

III-1 (afterwards when white moustache grown is same as face of Count in London

Doctor at ~~Dover~~ Customhouse sees him or corpse

Coffins selected to be taken over — one wrong one brought —

Page 3. Rosenbach #38a. Size: 6 × 3.

Vampire[29]

Memo (1)[30]

no looking glasses in Count's house[31]
never can see him reflected in one[32]— no shadow?
lights arranged to give no shadow
never eats nor drinks[33]
carried or led over threshold
enormous strength[34]
see in the dark
power of getting small or large[35]
money always old gold[36]— traced to Salzburg[37] banking house
I-2[38] At Munich Dead House see face among flowers — think corpse — but is alive
III Afterwards when white moustache grown is same as face of Count in London[39]
Doctor at Dover Custom house[40] sees him or corpse
Coffins selected to be taken over — one wrong one brought[41]

---

29. Memos 1, 2 and 3 appear to have been composed at the same time, soon after page 2 was written.
30. The first memo continues to explore the "rules" of vampirism, provides details about the castle and begins the process of transforming the "old dead man made alive" (p. 2) into a vampire.
31. As Jonathan Harker puts it, "[I]n none of the rooms is there a mirror. There is not even a toilet glass on my table, and I had to get the little shaving glass from my bag before I could either shave or brush my hair" (2:20).
32. "I had hung my shaving glass by the window, and was just beginning to shave. Suddenly I felt a hand on my shoulder, and heard the Count's voice saying to me, 'Good morning.' I started, for it amazed me that I had not seen him, since the reflection of the glass covered the whole room behind me.... The whole room behind me was displayed; but there was no sign of a man in it, except myself" (2:26).
33. "It is strange that as yet I have not seen the Count eat or drink. He must be a very peculiar man!" (2:27).
34. "When the caleche stopped the driver [Dracula] jumped down, and held out his hand to assist me to alight. Again, I could not but notice his prodigious strength. His hand actually seemed like a steel vice that could have crushed mine if he had chosen" (2:15).
35. All of these abilities are literary inventions.
36. Dracula has "gold of all kinds, Roman, and British, and Austrian, and Hungarian, and Greek and Turkish money, covered with a film of dust, as though it had lain long in the ground" (4:48).
37. The fact that Salzburg is in Austria gives credence to the idea that Memo 1 is part of an early draft.
38. "I-2" and "III" are book and chapter numbers, which may have been added later.
39. When the Harkers see Dracula in London, Jonathan exclaims, "It is the man himself!" (13:176). In the typescript, the words "man in the Munich Dead House!" are crossed out, and "himself" is inserted in pen (272).
40. Before he was seduced by the charms of Whitby, the author assumed that his vampire would enter England via Dover, which was the most common portal to London.
41. No such incident occurs in the novel.

Vampire

Mema (2)

II . . . Zoological garden — wolves hyenas cowed — rage of eagle & lion &c

II. III goes through fog by instinct

I. II white teeth &c

\+ Crosses river & running water at exact slack or flood of tide —

II + influence over rats

II + painters cannot paint him — their likenesses always like some one else —

II insensibility to music

II absolute despisal of death & the dead

II. III + Attitude with regard to religion — only moved by relics older than own real date of century —

I. II. III + power of Creating evil thoughts or banishing good ones in others present

\+ Could not Codak him — come out black or like skeleton corpse &c.

Page 4. Rosenbach #38b. Size: 6 × 3.

Vampire

Memo (2)[42]

II	Zoological garden — wolves hyenas cowed — rage of eagle & lion
II. III	goes through fog by instinct
I. II	white teeth
	crosses river & running water at exact slack or <full> flood of tide
II	influence over rats
II	painters cannot paint him — their likenesses always like some one else
II	insensibility to music
II	absolute despisal of death & the dead
II. III	attitude with regard to religion — only moved by relics older than own real date[43] — <xxx> century[44]
I. II. III	power of creating evil thoughts or banishing good ones in others present
	Could not codak[45] him — come out black or like skeleton corpse[46]

42. Many of the ideas on this page are reworked on (our) page 6.

43. "Instinctively I moved forward with a protective impulse, holding the crucifix and wafer in my left hand. I felt a mighty power fly along my arm; and it was without surprise that I saw the monster cower back before a similar movement made spontaneously by each one of us" (23:315).

44. It seems as if Stoker had not yet decided when, i.e., in what century, his vampire would be born.

45. "[C]odak" is a figure of speech for "photograph." Jonathan Harker shows Dracula photographs of his new estate: "I have taken with my kodak views of it [Carfax] from various points" (2:24).

46. According to Peter Haining, Elizabeth Grey's "The Skeleton Count; or, The Vampire Mistress" was serialized in *The Casket*" in 1828, making it "without question, the earliest vampire serial story" (*Vampire Omnibus* 10).

38C

Vampire

memo (3)

IV

The dinnerparty at the
Mad doctor's.
Thirteen – each has a number.
Each asked to tell something
strange – order of numbers
makes the story complete – at
the end the Count comes in –

The divisional surgeon, being sick the
doctor is asked to see man in coffin –
restores him to life

Page 5. Rosenbach #38c. Size: 6 × 3.

Vampire

Memo (3)[47]

IV The dinner party[48] at the mad doctor's[49]
thirteen — each has a number
Each asked to tell something strange[50] — order of numbers makes the story complete[51] — at the end the Count comes in[52]
The divisional surgeon being sick the doctor[53] is asked to see man in coffin[54] — restores him to life[55]

---

47. None of the events on this page are found in the novel. The theme of a dinner party with thirteen guests appears again on page 7 but is deleted on page 8.

48. Joel Emerson muses, "The concept that Dracula would attend a dinner with his victims actually made it into one of the movie adaptations — the 1979 version of *Dracula* starring Frank Langella" (491 n.116). Stoker originally intended a larger role for the Count, who had more interaction with the human characters. In the novel, once Dracula arrives in England, he emerges from the shadows briefly and unpredictably. Every appearance is laden with menace. Gail B. Griffin points out that he becomes "a pervasive presence, a force rather than a 'character.' He is more dangerous when incorporeal than when visible" (137).

49. On pages 1 and 5, we have an unnamed "mad doctor." On page 7, this character becomes "Doctor of Madhouse <xxx> Seward." This discrepancy raises the question of whether Seward was originally as insane as his "mad patient."

50. This fragment echoes the celebrated literary gathering at the Villa Diodati, where a ghost-story contest led to the creation of Shelley's *Frankenstein*, Byron's "A Fragment" and, eventually, Polidori's "The Vampyre." In her preface to the first edition of *Frankenstein* in 1818, Mary Shelley explains, "I passed the summer of 1816 in the environs of Geneva. The season was cold and rainy, and in the evenings we crowded around a blazing wood fire, and occasionally amused ourselves with some German stories of ghosts, which happened to fall into our hands. These tales excited in us a playful desire of imitation. Two other friends ... and myself agreed to write each a story, founded on some supernatural experience" (47).

51. "[O]ne guest starts a 'strange' story that is continued by the next guest, and so on, until every guest has added to the tale" (*Bram Stoker's Dracula* 22).

52. Early drafts include a parody of the Last Supper, with the Count fulfilling the role of the anti-Christ.

53. Doctors play important parts in *Dracula*. Three of Bram's brothers were doctors: William Thornley was a pioneer in the field of brain surgery; Richard was a surgeon with the Indian Army in Nepal, Tibet and Afghanistan; and George served with the Red Crescent Ambulance in the Balkans.

54. The "man in coffin" seems to be the "face among flowers" (p. 3).

55. The motif of bringing a corpse back to life through sorcery is a crucial part of many vampire tales that pre-date *Dracula*. Here, the question of who restored life to whom and how this was accomplished is one of the most baffling dead ends in the Notes.

4

Goes through fog by instinct
at Zoo rage of lion – eagle &c
Crosses running water at exact flood or slack of tide
influence over rats
painters cannot reproduce him – like one or else
insensible to music
absolute despisal of death or the dead. Can tell if dead even more [illegible] dead
[illegible]
Power of creating evil thoughts – or destroying will
could not photograph – came out like corpse or black &c
Has to be brought or helped over threshold
Can see in the dark
Can grow small or large
Immortalizable – Gladstone

Long thorny branch of wild rose on coffin to prevent Vampire leaving it
Swallow – golinella lui Dieu, [fowl of the ?] is lucky
Crow unlucky specially when flying over one's head
St. George's Day 24 April – on May 6 eve of 24 night of 23 (ie Witches Sabbath)

Page 6. Rosenbach #4. Size: 8 × 5.[56]

goes through fog by instinct[57]
at Zoo — rage of Lion[58] — eagle
crosses running water at exact flood or slack of tide
influence over rats
painters can't reproduce him — like someone else
insensible to music
absolute despisal of death & the dead. Can tell if dead — sees man seemingly dead
says 'no'[59]
power of creating evil thoughts — & destroying will[60]
could not photograph — come out like corpse or black
has to be brought or helped over threshold[61]
can see in the dark
can get small or large
Immortaliable [sic][62] — Gladstone[63]
long thorny branch of wild rose on coffin to prevent vampire leaving it[64]
swallow — galinelle lui Dieu — fowl of the Lord — is lucky
Crow unlucky — especially when flying over one's head
St. George's Day 24 April — our May 6 — even. of 24 night of 23 is Witches' Sabbath[65]

56. This is the first of two pages that have the embossment "Lyceum Theatre" on the bottom verso of the page, upside-down.

57. Many vampire characteristics are discarded, but others work their way into Van Helsing's lecture in chapter 18.

58. "We Szekelys have a right to be proud, for in our veins flows the blood of many brave races who fought as the lion fights, for lordship" (3:29).

59. The conceit that Dracula can tell at a glance if a body is dead or alive is not found in the novel.

60. Mina confesses, "I was bewildered, and, strangely enough, I did not want to hinder him" (21:295).

61. When he arrives at the castle, Jonathan Harker recalls, "He [Dracula] made no motion of stepping to meet me, but stood like a statue, as though his gesture of welcome had fixed him into stone. The instant, however, that I had stepped over the threshold, he moved impulsively forward, and holding out his hand grasped mine...." (2:16).

62. "[I]mmortaliable" — which Frayling transcribes as "immortality" (308) — refers to the belief that the human soul is immortal.

63. Stoker uses a similar word, "immortaliability," in a letter to former Prime Minister William Gladstone.

64. The last four lines may have been appended to the text, with the final three coming from Emily Gerard's "Transylvanian Superstitions."

65. Evil forces were believed to be more powerful on the eves of certain saints' days.

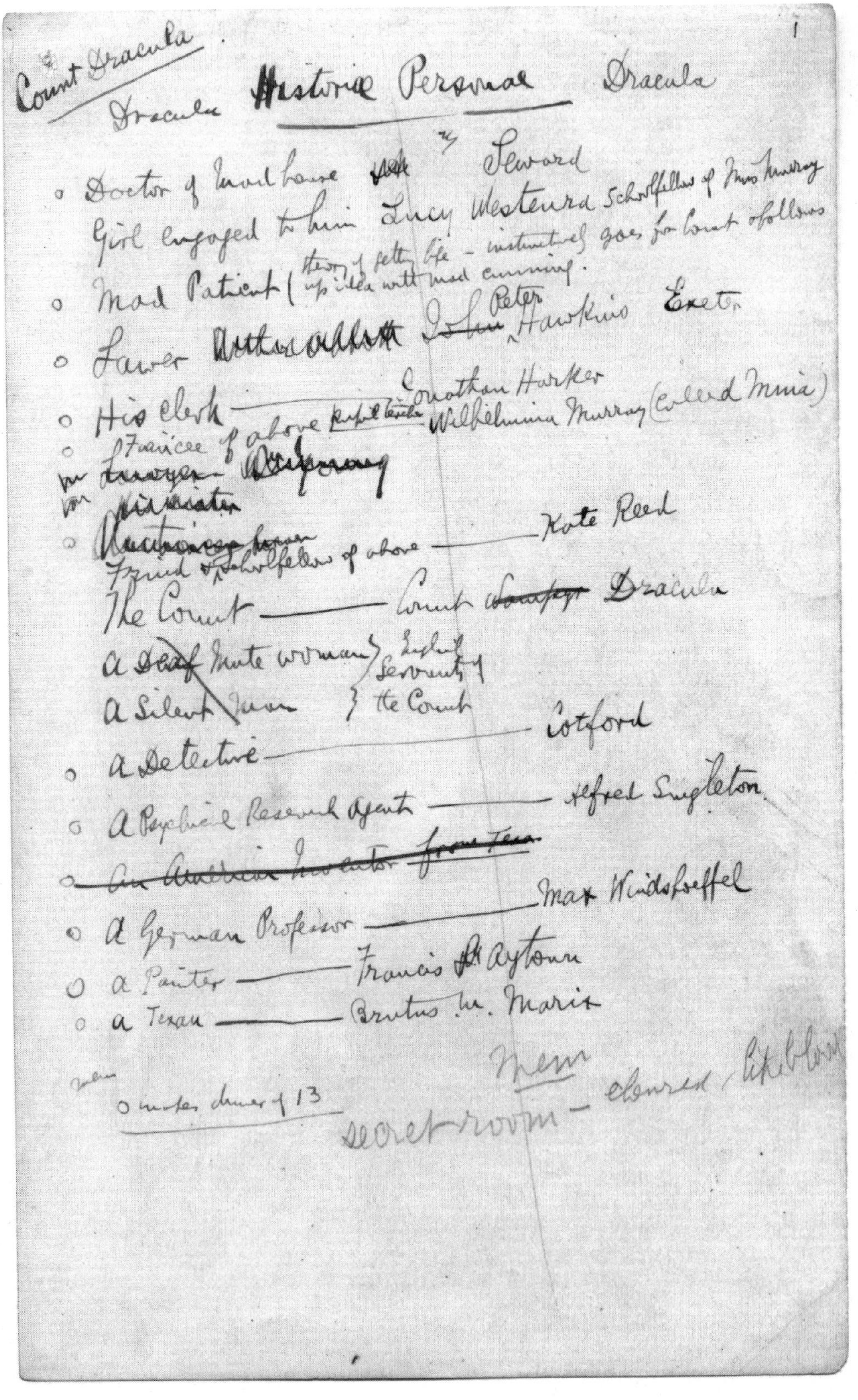

Count Dracula

Dracula ~~Historiae~~ Personae Dracula 1

o Doctor of Mad house ~~[illegible]~~ Seward

Girl engaged to him Lucy Westenra Schoolfellow of Miss Murray

o Mad Patient (theory of getting life – instinctively goes for Count & follows up idea with mad cunning.

o Lawyer ~~Arthur Abbott~~ ~~John~~ Peter Hawkins Exeter

o His clerk — Jonathan Harker

o Fiancée of above ~~pupil teacher~~ Wilhelmina Murray (called Mina)

~~lawyer~~ ~~[illegible]~~

~~[illegible]~~

o ~~[illegible]~~ Friend & Schoolfellow of above — Kate Reed

The Count — Count ~~Vampyre~~ Dracula

A ~~Deaf~~ Mute woman } English Servants of the Count

A Silent Man }

o A Detective — Cotford

o A Psychical Research Agent — Alfred Singleton

o ~~An American Inventor from Texas~~

o A German Professor — Max Windshoeffel

o A Painter — Francis ~~[illegible]~~ Aytown

o A Texan — Brutus M. Marix

Mem

o makes dinner of 13

secret room – cleared / like blood

Page 7. Rosenbach #1. Size: 8 × 5.

Count Dracula ... Dracula ... Dracula.[66]

Historiae Personae[67]

Doctor of madhouse <xxx> Seward
Girl engaged to him ° Lucy Westenra[68] ° schoolfellow of Miss Murray
Mad patient[69] — theory of getting life — instinctively goes for Count & follows up idea with mad cunning
Lawyer <Arthur Abbott>[70] <John> Peter Hawkins[71] ° Exeter[72]
His clerk ___ Jonathan Harker
Fiancée of above ° pupil teacher Wilhelmina Murray (called Mina)
<Lawyer — Wm. Young>
<His sister>
<Auctioneer>
Friend & former schoolfellow of above ___ Kate Reed[73]
The Count ___ Count <Wampyr> Dracula[74]
<A Deaf Mute Woman>
<A Silent Man> English servants of the Count[75]
A Detective ___ Cotford
A Psychical Research Agent ___ Alfred Singleton
<An American Inventor from Texas>[76]
A German Professor ___ Max Windshoeffel
A Painter ___ Francis <A> Aytown
A Texan ___ Brutus M. Marix[77]
Mem. makes dinner of 13[78]
Mem. secret room — coloured like blood[79]

---

66. "Count Dracula" is underlined in the top left-hand corner of the page, while "Dracula" is scribbled on both sides of the heading. Stoker may have been savoring the sound of this word as a possible name for his anti-hero.

67. "Historiae Personae" is Latin for "The Characters of the Story." This list, which expands and names many of the characters on page 1, was created in two or more stages.

68. This is the first appearance of the name "Westenra." In contrast to the novel, Lucy is engaged to John Seward.

69. The name "Renfield" does not appear in the Notes. According to John McLaughlin, "a blank space [is] reserved [in the typescript] for the later insertion of his name." Eventually, he is called the "Flyman" or "Renfold," but his name is used "only in the latter portions of the novel" (n.p.).

70. Frayling transcribes this name as "William Abbott" (307).

71. Abraham Aaronson's transformation into Arthur Abbott, then John and, finally, Peter Hawkins testifies to a minimum of three revisions. Eventually, Stoker bestowed his given name, "Abraham," on Professor Van Helsing and christened Lucy's victorious suitor "Arthur."

72. Hawkins, like Harker, resides in Exeter.

73. Kate Reed will rise from the grave of literary obscurity to become an ongoing character in Kim Newman's *Anno Dracula* series.

74. Stoker began to use the name "Dracula" during or shortly after the summer of 1890.

75. Both the deaf mute woman and the silent man are Dracula's servants.

76. The "inventor" will become "Brutus M. Marix." As David J. Skal points out, the author's "working imagination seem[s] to spontaneously clone, merge and shuffle fictional identities, as if testing the possibilities" (22).

77. In 1985, Clive Leatherdale interpreted this name as "Moris" (*Novel & Legend* 235 n.31); five years later, Skal transcribed it as "Marix" (10).

78. The preceding list contained nineteen characters but six of them were crossed out, leaving thirteen.

79. "Mem" and the contents of the memo are added in pencil. In the novel, there is no such room in any of the Count's houses.

14/3/90 2

Book I. ~~Styria~~ to London

Chap 1 — The lawyers letters &c
" 2 — (~~Clerk~~ Clerk visit ~~Styria~~ Transylvania) Munich
" 3 — the journey — ~~wolves~~ — blue flame &c
4 { 4 — arrive the Castle
" { ~~5~~ — Loneliness the kiss "this man belongs to me".
5 Dr Seward's diary
" 6 — old Chapel — carrying earth — Sortes Virgilianae (notes in letter)
" 7 — ~~The purchase of London Estate~~ Dr Seward's Diary — fly patient — Load down

Book II Tragedy

Chap 1 ~~The auctioneer~~ Whitby — argument inquiring things
" 2 ~~The Doctor~~ Whitby — the storm — ship arrives
" 3 ~~The Lawyers~~ Clerk Whitby. Lucy walks in sleep — Lucy —
" 4 ~~A night of terror~~ — London Mina's wedding
" 5 ~~A medical impasse~~ A night of terror (wolf visit) Dracula visits asylum
" 6 ~~The Tragedy~~ A medical impasse — Lucy dies
" 7 ~~The Vow~~ Opening vault. The Vow

Book III Discovery

Chap 1 The Suspicion — Harker's Diary
" 2 Inquiries — the dinner — re Vampires
" 3 ~~D...~~ Mina's letter Dracula Transylvania left Transylvania
" 4 On the track Texan in Transylvania
" 5 — Strange clues — Count's house searched blood red worm
" 6 — A test of sanity (?)
" 7 — Conviction Harker sees the Count. Disappearance ~~of the Count~~

Chap 1 (?) ~~A Dinner of Thirteen~~
" 2 A Vigilante Committee

Book IV Punishment

" 3 Disappearance
" 4 A choice of dwellings
" 5 Closing the net (removing earth
" 6 Back to ~~Styria~~ Transylvania
" 7 A Tourists Tale — one killed by wolf (which?)

Bring in the Texan

28 2/6/90 1/5/6

Page 8. Rosenbach #2. Size: 8 × 5.[80]

14/3/90[81]

Book I: <Styria> Transylvania[82] to London

chap 1 — The lawyers' letters
2 — (<lawyer> clerk visits <Styria> Transylvania) Munich[83]
3 — the journey — <wolves> ᵒ blue flames[84]
4 — arrive the Castle
Loneliness ᵒ the Kiss — "this man belongs to me."
5 — Dr. Seward's Diary
6 — old chapel — carting[85] earth. Sortes Virgilianae (notes in letter)
7 — <the purchase of London estate>
Dr. Seward's Diary — fly patient — bound down[86]

Book II: Tragedy[87]

chap 1 <The auctioneer> Whitby — argument uncanny things
2 <The Doctor> Whitby — the storm — ship arrives
3 <The lawyer's clerk> Whitby. Lucy walks in sleep — bloody
4 <A night of terror> London ᵒ Mina's wedding
5 <A medical impasse> A night of terror (wolf missing)[88] ᵒ Dracula visits asylum
6 <The Tragedy> A medical impasse — Lucy dies
7 <The Vow> Opening vault. The vow[89]

Book III: Discovery

chap 1 The Suspicion — Harker's Diary
2 Inquiries — the Dinner — re Vampires
3 <Discoveries> Mina suspects Dracula[90] ᵒ Texan to go to Transylvania[91]

notes continue on page 31

---

80. This is the second of two pages that have the embossment "Lyceum Theatre," which appears on the bottom verso of the page, upside-down.
81. The first draft of page 8 is dated 14/3/90, six days after page 2, but references to "Transylvania," "Dr. Seward's diary" and "Whitby" indicate that this page was later revised.
82. Exactly when Transylvania trumped Styria as the vampire's homeland remains a mystery, but there is no doubt that this decision was made *after* 14/3/90.
83. This line was revised at least twice.
84. The belief that, on St. George's Eve, a blue flame appears over any place where treasure has been buried can be found in Emily Gerard's "Transylvanian Superstitions."
85. We say "carting," McNally and Florescu say "covering" (*Essential Dracula* 27).
86. We read the last two words as "bound down" (i.e., restrained) but McNally and Florescu see them as "loved doom" (27) while Frayling paraphrases them as "in love with death" (306).
87. At some point, the entire first draft of Book II was deleted.
88. In the novel, a wolf escapes from the zoological gardens in chapter 11.
89. The "vow" refers to the vampire hunters' pact: "to find out the author of all this our sorrow and to stamp him out" (16:222).
90. Mina, who has assumed some of the duties of the "detective inspector" in the first list of characters, is wondering whether Count Dracula could be the vampire who murdered Lucy.
91. This is the first of many indications that the Texan, Quincey P. Morris, once played a more significant part in the novel. In *Buffalo Bill's America*, Louis S. Warren points out that "*Dracula*, although a novel set in the world's largest city, is essentially also, crucially, a frontier tale" (304).

Lyceum Theatre (circa 1895), where Stoker was the business manager between 1878 and 1902.

4 On the track — Texan in Transylvania
5 Strange clues — Count's house searched ° blood red room[92]
6 a test of sanity (?)
7 Conviction ° Harker sees the Count

Book IV: Punishment

chap 1(?) <A Dinner of thirteen> <Disappearance of the Count>
2 A Vigilante Committee[93]
3 Disappearance
4 a choice of dwellings[94]
5 closing the net (removing earth)
6 Back to <Styria> Transylvania
7 a Tourist's Tale — one killed by wolf (wehr?)[95]

Bring in the Texan

<28 26 6000 156,000>[96]

92. In *The Essential Dracula*, McNally and Florescu render this as "evening" rather than "room" (27).
93. "Vigilante" is an Americanism.
94. In addition to his stronghold in Carfax, near Purfleet, Dracula has one hideaway at "197, Chicksand Street, Mile End New Town" (20:267); another at "Jamaica Lane, Bermondsey" (20:267); and a house at "347, Piccadilly" (20:280) that he paid for in cash under the alias "Count de Ville."
95. There is a werewolf in "Dracula's Guest," but not in the novel.
96. Stoker is estimating the length of the novel if it were to contain 26–28 chapters with 6000 words each.

5

Book I

Chapter 1

Letter 1. Sir Robert Parton Prest. I.L.S. to Peter Hawkins Cathedral Place Exeter, stating letter rec.d from Count Wampyr

" 2. Count ~~Wampyr~~ Dracula Transylvania to Peter Hawkins, asking him to purchase estate.

" 3 Peter Hawkins to Count Wampyr – replying & saluting him but he will send Harker. asking some kind of idea of place required

" 4 Count ~~Wampyr~~ Dracula to Peter Hawkins. giving information required

" 5. Peter Hawkins to Count ~~Wampyr~~ Dracula. place secured in official enclosing copies (2) of letters from Harker re estate at Purfleet

" 6 Kate Reed to Lucy Westenra telling of Harker's visit to the school to see Mina Murray. & of Mina's confidence & her story. with postscript telling how she thought afterwards it would be well to ask Mina's permission before telling her story. — she knows it all dear long ago: & that she goes to stay with her on summer holiday at Whitby.

8 Telegram Dracula to Hawkins to let Harker start for Munich

Page 9. Rosenbach #5. Size: 8 × 5.

Book I[97]

Chapter 1[98]

Letter 1. Sir Robert Parton Pres. I. L. S. to Peter Hawkins Cathedral Place Exeter stating letter rec. from Count Wampyr

2. Count <Wampyr> Dracula o Transylvania to Peter Hawkins asking him to purchase estate.

3. Peter Hawkins to Count Wampyr — replying & stating has gout but will send Harker[99] o asking some kind of idea of place required

4. Count <Wampyr> Dracula to Peter Hawkins giving information required

5. Peter Hawkins to Count <Wampyr> Dracula. Place secured on approval o enclosing copies (2) of letters from Harker re estate at Purfleet[100]

6. Kate Reed[101] to Lucy Westenra telling of Harker's visit to the school to see Mina Murray & of Mina's confidence & her story — with postscript telling how she thought after writing it would be well to ask Mina's permission before telling her story — she knows it all over long ago & that she goes to stay with her on summer holiday at Whitby[102]

8. Telegram o Dracula[103] to Hawkins to let Harker start for Munich

97. The following pages expand on page 8, which is dated 14/3/90. The use of "Count Wampyr" shows that this page was started before Stoker's vacation in Whitby and eventually revised.

98. "The outlines for Chapters 1 and 2 summarize the purchase of the Count's property in England and recount the experiences of Jonathan Harker as he travels to Styria, stopping in Munich to view a performance of Wagner's *The Flying Dutchman*" (*Bram Stoker's Dracula* 18).

99. A remnant of Peter Hawkins' letter can be found in chapter 2: "I much regret that an attack of gout, from which malady I am a constant sufferer, forbids absolutely any travelling on my part for some time to come; but I am happy to say I can send a sufficient substitute, one in whom I have every possible confidence" (2:18).

100. Purfleet, in Essex, is east of London on the north bank of the Thames.

101. Kate Reed is probably the unnamed messenger Lucy alludes to when she says, "Some one has evidently been telling tales" (5:56). McNally and Florescu believe that "Mrs. Westenra seems to have taken [Kate Reed's] place ... in the novel" (26).

102. Frayling renders "over" as "dead." However, either wording supports his conclusion that Kate Reed had "some 'story' which is of interest to Mina" and the fact "that 'it is all dead long ago'" allows them "to remain friends." He then wonders, "Could it possibly have been a romance with Jonathan?" (312).

103. In contrast to letters 4 and 5, "Dracula" is not a substitute for "Wampyr." The absence of letter number 7 implies that this name was added later.

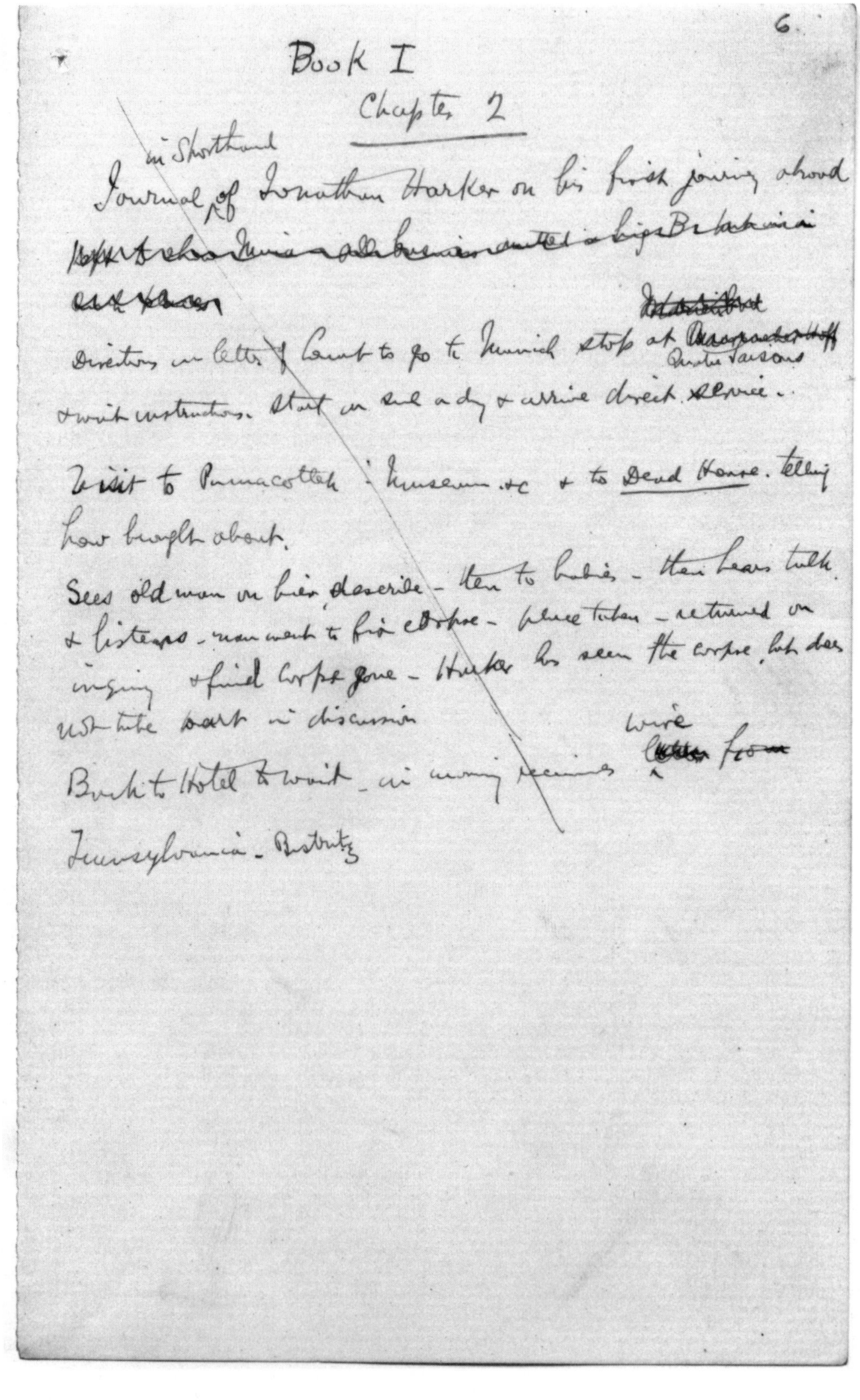

6.

Book I

Chapter 2

Journal ^in Shorthand^ of Jonathan Harker on his first journey abroad

~~[illegible]~~

Directions in letter of Count to go to Munich stop at ~~[illegible]~~ Quatre Saisons & wait instructions. Start on such a day & arrive direct. Service.

Visit to Pinacothek – Museum &c & to Dead House. telling how brought about.

Sees old man on bier, describe – then to babies – then hears talk & listens – man went to fix corpse – place taken – returned on ringing & find corpse gone – Harker has seen the corpse, but does not take part in discussion

Back to Hotel to wait – in morning receives ^wire^ ~~letter~~ from

Transylvania – Bistritz

Page 10. Rosenbach #6. Size: 8 × 5.

Book I

Chapter 2

Journal in shorthand[104] of Jonathan Harker on his first journey abroad <kept to show Mina — all business omitted xxx xxx in such places>[105]

Directions in letter of Count to go to Munich stop at <Auracher Hoff> <Marienbad> Quatre Saisons[106] & wait instructions. Start on same day & arrive direct service.

Visit to Pinnacothek [sic] museum[107] & to Dead House — telling how brought about.

Sees old man on bier[108] o describe — then to babies — then hears talk & listens — man went to fix corpse — place taken — returned on inquiry & find corpse gone — Harker has seen the corpse but does not take part in discussion

Back to hotel to wait — in morning receives <letter> wire[109] from Transylvania — Bistritz[110]

104. Stoker incorporated up-to-date methods of communication from the beginning.

105. As Jonathan writes, "I shall enter here some of my notes, as they may refresh my memory when I talk over my travels with Mina" (1:2).

106. Baedeker's *Southern Germany and Austria, Including Hungary and Transylvania* (1887) lists a "Four Seasons" hotel "near the Hof-Theater" (121) in Munich. The "Marienbad" is further from the center of the city. "Dracula's Guest" opens, "When we started for our drive the sun was shining brightly on Munich, and the air was full of the joyousness of early summer. Just as we were about to depart, Herr Delbruck (the maitre d'hotel of the Quatre Saisons [Four Seasons]), where I was staying...." (1).

107. "Pinakothek" is Greek for "repository of pictures" (Baedeker 138).

108. This scene was dropped from the novel, but it may have been reworked as an incident in "Dracula's Guest" where the narrator sees "a beautiful woman with rounded cheeks and red lips, seemingly sleeping on a bier" (11). In the novel, the "old man on bier" may become Dracula in his coffin.

109. As Baedeker's *London and its Environs* (1898) informs us, "The whole telegraph system of Great Britain, with the sole exception of wires for the private use of the railway-companies, belongs to the Government.... Telegrams are received at all railway-stations and almost all post offices throughout the country. They may also be posted in any pillar-box or post office and are, in that case, if properly prepaid, dispatched as soon as possible after the box is cleared. London and its suburbs contain 300 telegraph-offices, open from 8 A.M. to 8 P.M." (qtd. in Glennis Byron 452).

110. The last four paragraphs raise important questions about the order and content of early, deleted chapters.

7

Book I

Chapter 3

Jonathan Harker's ~~Diary~~ Journal (Continued)

The Journey to Bistritz Stop at Hotel. Have known they sent on telegram &c.—When hear destination all very sad & mysterious. Give strange gifts (see XIX Century.)

At Borgo Pass—~~alone~~ left by diligence—alone—solitude—comfort (?) of driver—Arrival of carriage drunk man muffled—the journey wolves howl & surround—blue flames—driver stops & take them &c strange sounds—mist—thunder—dogs & wolves howl—midnight Arrival at Castle—describe—left alone—enter Count supper—to bed—describe room &c

Page 11. Rosenbach #7. Size: 8 × 5.

Book I

Chapter 3[111]

Jonathan Harker's <Diary> Journal—(Continued)

The journey to Bistritz <with> stop at hotel.[112] Name known.[113] They sent on telegram. When hear destination all very sad & mysterious. Some strange gifts[114] ° (see XIX Century)[115]

At Borgo Pass.[116] <arrive> left by diligence[117]—alone—solitude—comfort (?) of driver—arrival of carriage ° driver man muffled[118]—the journey ° wolves howl & surround—blue flames—driver stops[119]—knife thrown—strange sounds—mist—thunder—dogs wolves howl—midnight arrival at castle—describe—left alone—enter Count ° supper—to bed—describe room[120]

---

111. Hence, the first chapter of the novel was once the third chapter.

112. In the novel, Count Dracula directs Jonathan Harker to a hotel in Bistritz called the "Golden Krone." Baedeker (259) lists a "Goldne Krone" hotel in Salzburg, across from the house where Mozart was born.

113. The innkeepers do not call Jonathan Harker by name; they ask if he is "The Herr Englishman?" (1:4).

114. Harker was moved when "She then rose and dried her eyes, and taking a crucifix from her neck offered it to me. I did not know what to do, for, as an English Churchman, I have been taught to regard such things as in some measure idolatrous.... She saw, I suppose, the doubt in my face, for she put the rosary round my neck and said, 'For your mother's sake,' and went out of the room" (1:5).

115. "XIX Century" refers to *The Nineteenth Century*, the magazine that published "Transylvanian Superstitions."

116. This is the first reference to the "Borgo Pass," which has been immortalized as the location of Dracula's Castle. Stoker may have found it in Baedeker (407) or in Charles Boner's *Transylvania: Its Products and Its People*. Both books include maps that feature the pass. Despite many claims to the contrary, neither Vlad the Impaler nor any member of his family had a castle in the Borgo Pass.

117. A "diligence" is a small, speedy coach.

118. According to Jonathan Harker, "[The] horses were ... driven by a tall man, with a long brown beard and a great black hat, which seemed to hide his face from us. I could only see the gleam of a pair of very bright eyes, which seemed red in the lamplight, as he turned to us" (1:10).

119. "All at once the wolves began to howl as though the moonlight had had some peculiar effect on them.... How he came there, I know not, but I heard his voice raised in a tone of imperious command.... As he swept his long arms, as though brushing aside some impalpable obstacle, the wolves fell back and back further still" (1:13–14).

The coachman [Dracula], resembles Count Azzo von Klatka in "The Mysterious Stranger" (1853): "As soon as the stranger appeared the wolves gave over their pursuit, tumbled over each other, and set up a fearful howl. The stranger now raised his hand, appeared to wave it, and the wild animals crawled back into the thickets" (42).

120. "It was a welcome sight; for here was a great bedroom well lighted and warmed with another log fire, which sent a hollow roar up the wide chimney" (2:17).

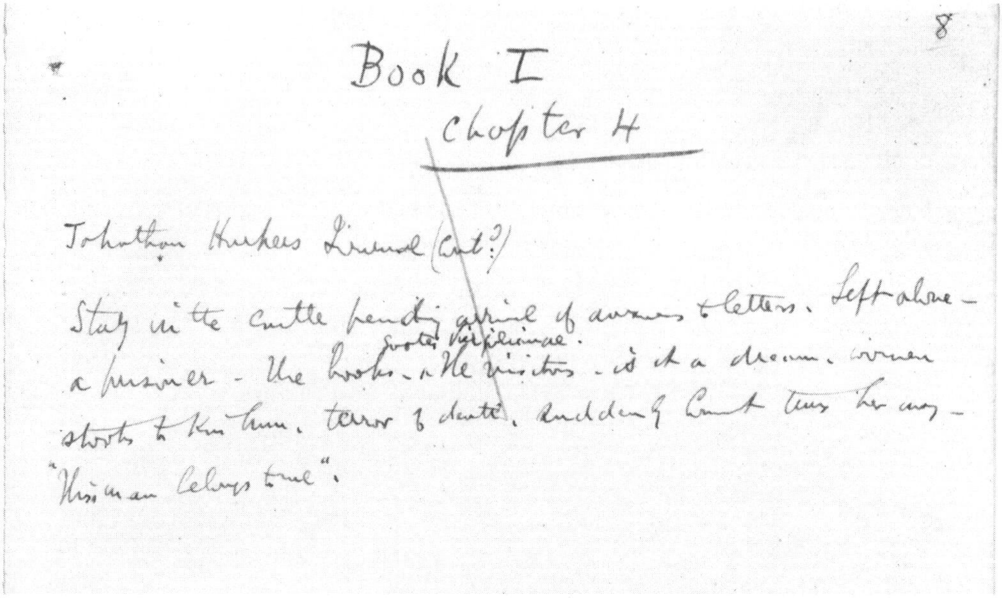

8

Book I
Chapter 4

Jonathan Harker's Journal (cont?)

Stay in the castle pending arrival of answers to letters. Left alone — a prisoner — the books — the visitors — is it a dream. women stoop to kiss him. terror of death. suddenly Count turns her away — "this man belongs to me".

Illustration for Stoker's story "The Castle of the King" (from *Under the Sunset*, 1882).

Page 12. Rosenbach #8. Size: 8 × 5.

Book I

Chapter 4

Jonathan Harker's Journal Cont.

Stay in the castle pending arrival of answers to letters. Left alone — a prisoner — the books — sortes Virgilianae — the visitors — is it a dream — woman[121] stoops to kiss him[122] — terror of death — suddenly Count turns her away — "This man belongs to me."[123]

121. Here there is just one woman. Elsewhere, there are an unspecified number of "women." In the novel, Jonathan Harker recalls, "In the moonlight opposite me were three young women, ladies by their dress and manner" (3:38).

122. Harker continues: "One said, 'Go on! You are first, and we shall follow: yours is the right to begin.'"

"The other added, 'He is young and strong. There are kisses for us all.' I lay quiet, looking out from under my eyelashes in an agony of delightful anticipation. The fair girl advanced and bent over me till I could feel the movement of her breath upon me. Sweet it was in one sense, honey-sweet, and sent the same tingling through the nerves as her voice, but with a bitter underlying the sweet, a bitter offensiveness, as one smells in blood.

"I was afraid to raise my eyelids, but looked out and saw perfectly under the lashes. The fair girl went on her knees, and bent over me, fairly gloating. There was a deliberate voluptuousness which was both thrilling and repulsive, and as she arched her neck she actually licked her lips like an animal, till I could see in the moonlight the moisture shining on the scarlet lips and on the red tongue as it lapped the white sharp teeth. Lower and lower went her head as the lips went below the range of my mouth and chin and seemed about to fasten on my throat" (3:39).

123. "With a fierce sweep of his arm, he hurled the woman from him, and then motioned to the others, as though he were beating them back; it was the same imperious gesture that I had seen used to the wolves. In a voice which, though low and almost in a whisper, seemed to cut through the air and then ring round the room as he said,

"'How dare you touch him, any of you? How dare you cast eyes on him when I had forbidden it? Back, I tell you all! This man belongs to me! Beware how you meddle with him, or you'll have to deal with me'" (3:40).

9

Book I

Chapter 5

Dr. Sewards Diary

Letter Lucys letter to Mina Murray

Page 13. Rosenbach #9. Size: 8 × 5.

Book I

Chapter 5

Dr. Seward's Diary[124]

Letter[125] ∘ Lucy's letter to Mina Murray[126]

124. Dr. Seward introduces us to his patient in chapter 5: "R. M. Renfield, aetat 59.— Sanguine temperament; great physical strength; morbidly excitable; periods of gloom ending in some fixed idea which I cannot make out" (5:62). While we never learn the cause of Renfield's breakdown, it has no connection with Dracula.

125. In the fifth chapter, letters between Mina and Lucy return us to the mundane world: "There is no greater jolt in *Dracula* than this abrupt transition from horror to domestic happiness" (David Seed 66).

126. Lucy boasts to Mina, "My dear, it never rains but it pours. How true the old proverbs are. Here am I, who shall be twenty in September, and yet I never had a proposal till to-day, not a real proposal, and to-day I have had three. Just fancy! THREE proposals in one day! Isn't it awful! I feel sorry, really and truly sorry, for two of the poor fellows. Oh, Mina, I am so happy that I don't know what to do with myself. And three proposals! ...

"Well, my dear, number One came just before lunch. I told you of him, Dr. John Seward, the lunatic-asylum man, with the strong jaw and the good forehead. He was very cool outwardly, but was nervous all the same. He had evidently been schooling himself as to all sorts of little things, and remembered them; but he almost managed to sit down on his silk hat, which men don't generally do when they are cool, and then when he wanted to appear at ease he kept playing with a lancet in a way that made me nearly scream. He spoke to me, Mina, very straightforwardly. He told me how dear I was to him, though he had known me so little, and what his life would be with me to help and cheer him. He was going to tell me how unhappy he would be if I did not care for him, but when he saw me cry he said that he was a brute and would not add to my present trouble. Then he broke off and asked if I could love him in time; and when I shook my head his hands trembled, and then with some hesitation he asked me if I cared already for any one else.... I felt it a sort of duty to tell him that there was some one....

"Well, my dear, number two came after lunch. He is such a nice fellow, an American from Texas, and he looks so young and so fresh that it seems almost impossible that he has been to so many places and has had such adventures.... Mr. Quincey P. Morris found me alone.... I must tell you beforehand that Mr. Morris doesn't always speak slang — that is to say, he never does so to strangers or before them, for he is really well educated and has exquisite manners — but he found out that it amused me to hear him talk American slang....

"Well, he did look so good-humoured and so jolly that it didn't seem half so hard to refuse him as it did poor Dr. Seward" (5:57–60).

10

Book I

Chapter 6

Jonathan Harker's Diary Cont[d]

attempt to get away from Castle. Wolves. wehrwolf old chapel – cutting earth. shrieks from grave – agony of terror re falling senseless. found by Count.

Is it all a dream back to London

Letter from Hawkins to be made partner or London agent

Choose London.

Page 14. Rosenbach #10. Size: 8 × 5.

Book I

Chapter 6

Jonathan Harker's Diary Cont.

Attempt to get away from castle — Wolves[127] — wehr wolf— old chapel — carting earth — shrieks from grave — sights of terror & falling senseless — found by Count[128]

Is it all a dream ° back to London[129]

Letter from Hawkins ° to be made partner or London agent

Chooses London[130]

127. When Harker asks "Why may I not go to-night?" (4:50), the Count replies, "You English have a saying which is close to my heart, for its spirit is that which rules our *boyars*: 'Welcome the coming, speed the parting guest.' Come with me, my dear young friend. Not an hour shall you wait in my house against your will, though sad am I at your going, and that you so suddenly desire it. Come!' With a stately gravity, he, with the lamp, preceded me down the stairs and along the hall. Suddenly he stopped. 'Hark!'"

Then Harker hears the wolves:

"As the door began to open, the howling of the wolves without grew louder and angrier; their red jaws, with champing teeth, and their blunt-clawed feet as they leaped, came in through the opening door.... [o]nly the Count's body stood in the gap. Suddenly it struck me that this might be the moment and means of my doom; I was to be given to the wolves, and at my own instigation. There was a diabolical wickedness in the idea great enough for the Count, and as a last chance I cried out,

"'Shut the door! I shall wait till morning' and covered my face with my hands to hide my tears of bitter disappointment" (4:50–51).

128. Given that there are no shrieks from the grave in *Dracula*, and no one falls senseless or is found by the Count, we can only wonder what the author intended.

129. Most of *Dracula* is set in London — Piccadilly, Green Park, the British Museum, the London Zoo, Spaniard's Inn, Hampstead, Mile End, Bermondsey, King's Cross, Fenchurch St., etc. The use of familiar landmarks is a departure from traditional Gothic novels with remote and foreign locales. As Glennis Byron observes, "*Dracula* is, like such other late-Victorian Gothics as *Jekyll and Hyde*, *Dorian Gray*, *The Island of Dr. Moreau*, very much of its time, very much a late-Victorian text, soon leaving the strange and alien world of Transylvania to land firmly in the urban centre of Victorian London" (13–14).

130. This offer does not take place in the novel.

11

Book I

Chapter 7

Dr. Seward's Diary.

Development of Study – Lucy visits asylum – her effect on mad patient with flies. Curiosity concerning Closed estate. Peeps over wall &c. Seward promises to get leave to show it her. ~~the board down~~. the notice board down – Mystery

Page 15. Rosenbach #11. Size: 8 × 5.

Book I

Chapter 7

Dr. Seward's Diary.

Developments of study—Lucy visits asylum[131]—her effect on mad patient with flies[132]—curiosity concerning closest estate. Peeps over wall. Seward promises to get leave to show it to her. <the blood room> The notice board down—Mystery

Sir Henry Irving.

131. In the novel, Mina, not Lucy, visits Renfield in his cell.

132. In "Lombroso's Criminal Man and Stoker's *Dracula*," Ernest Fontana claims, "The characterization of Renfield ... is also derived from Lombroso. His excitability, his susceptibility to paroxysms, and, more specifically, his consumption of live animals all are symptoms of what Lombroso identifies as the epileptic-criminal type....

"The contrast between Renfield's zoöphagus and raging paroxysms on the one hand and, on the other hand, his scientific and philosophical sophistication, which he shows in Chapter 18, is, for Lombroso, also characteristic of the epileptic-criminal" (161–162).

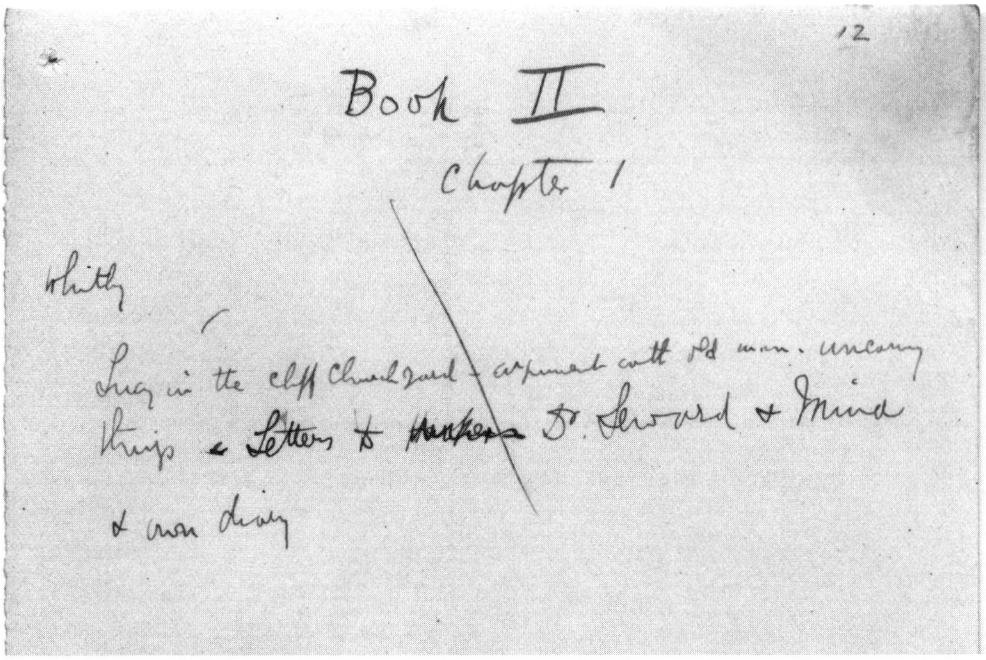
12

Book II

Chapter 1

Whitby

Lucy in the cliff Churchyard — argument with old man. uncanny things — Letters to ~~Harker~~ Dr. Seward & Mina & own diary

Whitby, abbey with graves (courtesy Barbara Zapffe Vielma).

Page 16. Rosenbach #12. Size: 8 × 5.

Book II

Chapter 1

Whitby[133]

Lucy in the cliff church yard — argument with old man[134] — uncanny things — Letters to <Harker> Dr. Seward & Mina & own diary

The Stoker family, drawing by George du Maurier (*Punch*, 11 September 1886).

133. The sixth chapter opens with an entry from Mina Murray's Journal: "24 July. Whitby.— Lucy met me at the station, looking sweeter and lovelier than ever, and we drove up to the house at the Crescent in which they have rooms. This is a lovely place. The little river, the Esk, runs through a deep valley, which broadens out as it comes near the harbour. A great viaduct runs across, with high piers, through which the view seems somehow further away than it really is. The valley is beautifully green, and it is so steep that when you are on the high land on either side you look right across it, unless you are near enough to see down. The houses of the old town — the side away from us — are all red-roofed, and seem piled up one over the other anyhow, like the pictures we see of Nuremberg. Right over the town is the ruin of Whitby Abbey ... a most noble ruin, of immense size, and full of beautiful and romantic bits; there is a legend that a white lady is seen in one of the windows. Between it and the town there is another church, the parish one, round which is a big graveyard, all full of tombstones. This is to my mind the nicest spot in Whitby, for it lies right over the town, and has a full view of the harbour and all up the bay to where the headland called Kettleness stretches out into the sea. It descends so steeply over the harbour that part of the bank has fallen away, and some of the graves have been destroyed.... There are walks, with seats beside them, throughout the churchyard; and people go and sit there all day long" (6:64).

134. The old man becomes "Mr. Swales" who, Mina says, "is a funny old man. He must be awfully old, for his face is all gnarled and twisted like the bark of a tree. He tells me that he is nearly a hundred, and that he was a sailor in the Greenland fishing fleet when Waterloo was fought" (6:65). In the novel, Lucy rebukes Mr. Swales for making light of the inscriptions on the headstones.

13

Book II

Chapter 2

Whitby ~~Letters Lucy to Dr. Seward & Mina~~

The Storm Mina away on business. Newspaper report

~~Stran~~ Strange sail - seeming derelict - runs into harbour

and aground - no one on board - bodies washed up on shore -

Lucy writes to Mina & Dr. Seward's Diary Red Eyes in Sunset

Same night Lucy on cliff sunset sees strange man amongst

tombs - describe - they talk - he reads inscription on tomb.

Fisherman talk - ship full of clay - coffin found aboard -

local {attorney / merchant} his instructions to claim cargo & forward to

London Care Harker - Mina (diary) leaves name - shall ask Jonathan

later.

Page 17. Rosenbach #13. Size: 8 × 5.

Book II

Chapter 2

Whitby <Letter — Lucy to Dr. Seward & Mina>

The Storm[135] o Mina away on business — Newspaper report <arrive>

Strange sail — seeming derelict — runs into harbour and aground[136] — no one on board — bodies washed up on shore.[137] Same night Lucy on cliff sunset — Lucy writes to Mina — Dr. Seward's Diary — Red eyes in sunset[138] — sees strange man amongst tombs — describe — they talk — he reads inscription on tomb. Fishermen talk — ship full of clay[139] — coffin found aboard — local attorney/merchant has instructions to claim cargo & forward to London care Harker[140] — Mina (diary) hears name — shall ask Jonathan later.

135. "Then without warning the tempest broke. With a rapidity which, at the time, seemed incredible, and even afterwards is impossible to realise, the whole aspect of nature at once became convulsed. The waves rose in growing fury, each overtopping its fellow, till in a very few minutes the lately glassy sea was like a roaring and devouring monster" (7:78–79).

136. "The wind suddenly shifted to the northeast, and the remnant of the sea-fog melted in the blast; and then, *mirabile dictu*, between the piers, leaping from wave to wave as it rushed at headlong speed, swept the strange schooner before the blast, with all sail set, and gained the safety of the harbour" (7:80).

137. In the novel, most of the crew members disappear whilst the "Demeter" is en route to England, leaving the reader to imagine their fate. Eventually, the first mate commits suicide by jumping overboard and, when the Captain's body is found, it is lashed to the wheel of the ship.

138. "'His red eyes again! They are just the same.' ... [Lucy] appeared to be looking over at our own seat, whereon was a dark figure seated alone. I was a little startled myself, for it seemed for an instant as if the stranger had great eyes like burning flames; but a second look dispelled the illusion" (8:96–97).

139. "She is almost entirely in ballast of silver sand, with only a small amount of cargo — a number of great wooden boxes filled with mould" (7:82).

140. This cargo was consigned to Dracula's solicitor in Whitby, "Mr. S. F. Billington of 7, The Crescent..." (7:82).

14

Book II

Chapter 3

(Letters Lucy & Mina)

Whitby ~~Mina~~ Lucy's ~~dream & walks in sleep~~ finds strange brooch on shore & puts it on — she becomes fond of dreaming & walks in sleep (renewing old habit) Lucy's dream. Mina wakes suddenly & misses her — goes in pursuit sees something white & something dark in moonlight in old churchyard on cliff — seems like man — then wolf — then seems to fly. Follows — finds Mina in sleep on bench — wound in ~~throat~~ & brooch covered with blood. "I must have pricked myself in ~~my~~ my sleep putting it on".

Page 18. Rosenbach #14. Size: 8 × 5.

Book II

Chapter 3

(Letters Lucy & Mina)

Whitby <Mina's> Lucy's <dream>—<walks in sleep> finds strange brooch on shore & puts it on—she becomes fond of dreaming & walks in sleep (renewing old habit)[141] o Lucy's dream. Mina wakes suddenly & misses her—goes in pursuit sees something white something dark in moonlight in old churchyard on cliff—seems like man—then wolf—then seems to fly[142]—follows—finds Mina in sleep on bench[143]—wound in throat & brooch covered with blood. "I must have pricked myself in my sleep putting it on."[144]

141. "Lucy ... has lately taken to her old habit of walking in her sleep. Her mother has spoken to me about it, and we have decided that I am to lock the door of our room every night" (6:74). In *On the Truths Contained in Popular Superstitions with an Account of Mesmerism*, Herbert Mayo points out that "the patient is most frequently a girl" (69).

142. "[T]here, on our favourite seat, the silver light of the moon struck a half-reclining figure, snowy white. The coming of the cloud was too quick for me to see much, for shadow shut down on light almost immediately; but it seemed to me as though something dark stood behind the seat where the white figure shone, and bent over it. What it was, whether man or beast, I could not tell" (8:93).

143. The author is confusing Lucy with Mina.

144. Instead of having Lucy seem to prick herself with a mysterious brooch, the novel has Mina blame herself for the marks on her friend's throat: "I fastened the shawl at her throat with a big safety-pin; but I must have been clumsy in my anxiety and pinched or pricked her with it..." (8:94).

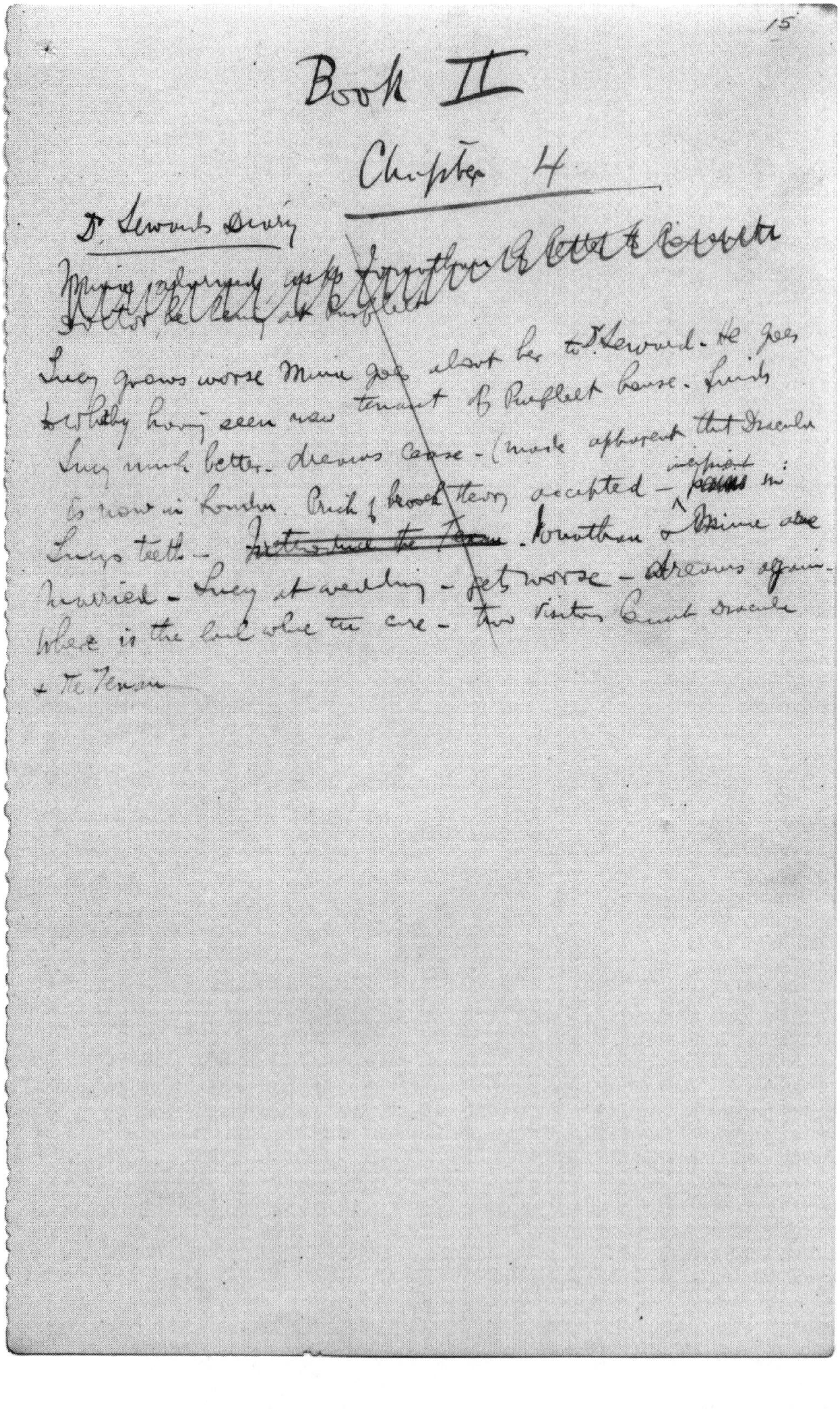

15

Book II

Chapter 4

Dr. Sewards Diary

~~Mina [illegible] to Jonathan [illegible]~~
~~Doctor [illegible] at Purfleet~~

Lucy grows worse Mina goes about her to Dr. Seward. He goes to Whitby having seen new tenant of Purfleet house. Finds Lucy much better. dreams cease. (made apparent that Dracula is now in London. Proof of blood theory accepted — incipient points in Lucy's teeth — ~~introduce the Texan~~. Jonathan & Mina are married — Lucy at wedding — gets worse — dreams again. Where is the [illegible] where the cure — two visitors Count Dracula & the Texan

Page 19. Rosenbach #15. Size: 8 × 5.

Book II

Chapter 4

Dr. Seward's Diary

<Mina alarmed — asks Jonathan by letter to consult doctor re living at Purfleet>

Lucy grows worse ° Mina goes about her to Dr. Seward.[145] He goes to Whitby having seen new tenant of Purfleet house[146]—finds Lucy much better — dreams cease — (made apparent that Dracula is now in London). Prick of brooch theory accepted — <pain> incipient in Lucy's teeth[147] — <Introduce the Texan>[148] — Jonathan & Mina are married — Lucy at wedding[149] — gets worse — dreams again. Where is the evil where the cure — two visitors Count Dracula & the Texan[150]

THE TWO GREAT WESTERN SHOWMEN.
HENRY: "Yes, Bill, nobody knows better than I the value of the 'puff preliminary.' "
BILL: "Henry, you've made business boom for me over here, and I guess I'll do you the same good turn when I get back among the boys."

Buffalo Bill and Henry Irving (*Illustrated Bits*, 21 May 1887).

145. In the novel, Arthur rather than Mina, contacts Dr. Seward about Lucy's illness.

146. The "new tenant" is obviously Count Dracula, but no such visit occurs in the novel.

147. "Her open mouth showed the pale gums drawn back from the teeth, which thus looked positively longer and sharper than usual" (12:156).

148. Warren argues convincingly that "Clearly, William Cody was the inspiration for Quincey Morris. The similarities between the fictional character and the historical Cody are extensive.... Both are hunters ... and both have been hunting guides to the aristocracy.... Morris's origins as a Texan are likely an attempt to locate him 'out West' more than anything specific. But ... the earlier version of the character in the short story 'The Squaw' hailed from Cody's home state of Nebraska. Finally and most important, by the time Stoker began to write *Dracula* in the 1890s the ubiquity of Buffalo Bill's Wild West show would have made it practically impossible for Stoker to conjure up a western character without thinking of Buffalo Bill" (331).

149. In the book, the wedding takes place in Budapest and Lucy is not in attendance.

150. Franco Moretti suggests that Morris may have been in league with Dracula: "Lucy dies — and then turns into a vampire — immediately after receiving a blood transfusion from Morris. Nobody suspects ... [when] Morris leaves the room to take a shot — missing naturally — at the big bat ... or, when, after Dracula bursts into the household, Morris hides among the trees ... loses sight of Dracula and invites the others to call off the hunt for the night.... So long as things go well for Dracula, Morris acts like an [his] accomplice. As soon as there is a reversal of fortunes, he turns into his staunchest enemy" (96).

16.

Book II

Chapter 5

Lucy's Diary

a night of Terror

(Main attempts of Count Dracula to get in to Lucy's room in various ways – bird & beast & dark ~~mist~~ mass – scratching out window pane – threatening – finally comes glass with mass of blood – ~~he~~ seems to throw it out of hands – she is guarded by some spell (?) placed accidentally [describe before hand] Dracula's rage – insensibility – recovery.

Dr. Seward's Diary

Dracula visits asylum. stumbles on threshold &c – Effect on madman with fly theory.

Mem wolf missing from Zoological gardens – has scaled [illegible] (this at beginning of chapter) at last made manifest wolf captured in neighbourhood – of Lucy's house – dogs killed &c

Page 20. Rosenbach #16. Size: 8 × 5.

Book II

Chapter 5

Lucy's Diary

A Night of Terror

Mem. attempts of Count Dracula to get into Lucy's room in various ways — bird & beast & dark <xxx> mass — scratching out window pane — threatening —finally covers glass with mass of blood —<then> seems to throw it out of bounds — she is guarded by some spell (?) placed accidentally (describe before hand)[151] o Dracula's rage — insensibility — recovery.

Dr. Seward's Diary

Dracula visits asylum. Stumbles on threshold[152] — Effect on madman with fly theory.

Mem. Wolf missing from Zoological Gardens[153] — has escaped outwards — [this at beginning of chapter] at end made manifest wolf captured in neighbourhood of Lucy's house — dogs killed[154]

151. The conceit of Lucy being protected by a spell was abandoned.

152. In the novel, Dracula does not stumble on the threshold. According to Renfield, "He came up to the window in the mist, as I had seen him often before; but he was solid then — not a ghost, and his eyes were fierce like a man's when angry....

"And then a red cloud, like the colour of blood, seemed to close over my eyes; and before I knew what I was doing, I found myself opening the sash and saying to Him, 'Come in, Lord and Master!'" (21:286–287).

153. One of the keepers at the Zoological Gardens notes that, prior to the wolf's disappearance, he had seen a strange man at the wolf's cage: "a tall, thin chap, with a 'ook nose and a pointed beard ... a 'ard, cold look and red eyes" (11:140).

154. The day after Dracula landed in Whitby in the form of a dog (or wolf) that leaped from the wreck of the "Demeter," we learn that "Early this morning a large dog, a half-bred mastiff belonging to a coal merchant close to Tate Hill Pier, was found dead in the roadway opposite its master's yard. It had been fighting, and manifestly had had a savage opponent, for its throat was torn away, and its belly was slit open as if with a savage claw" (7:83).

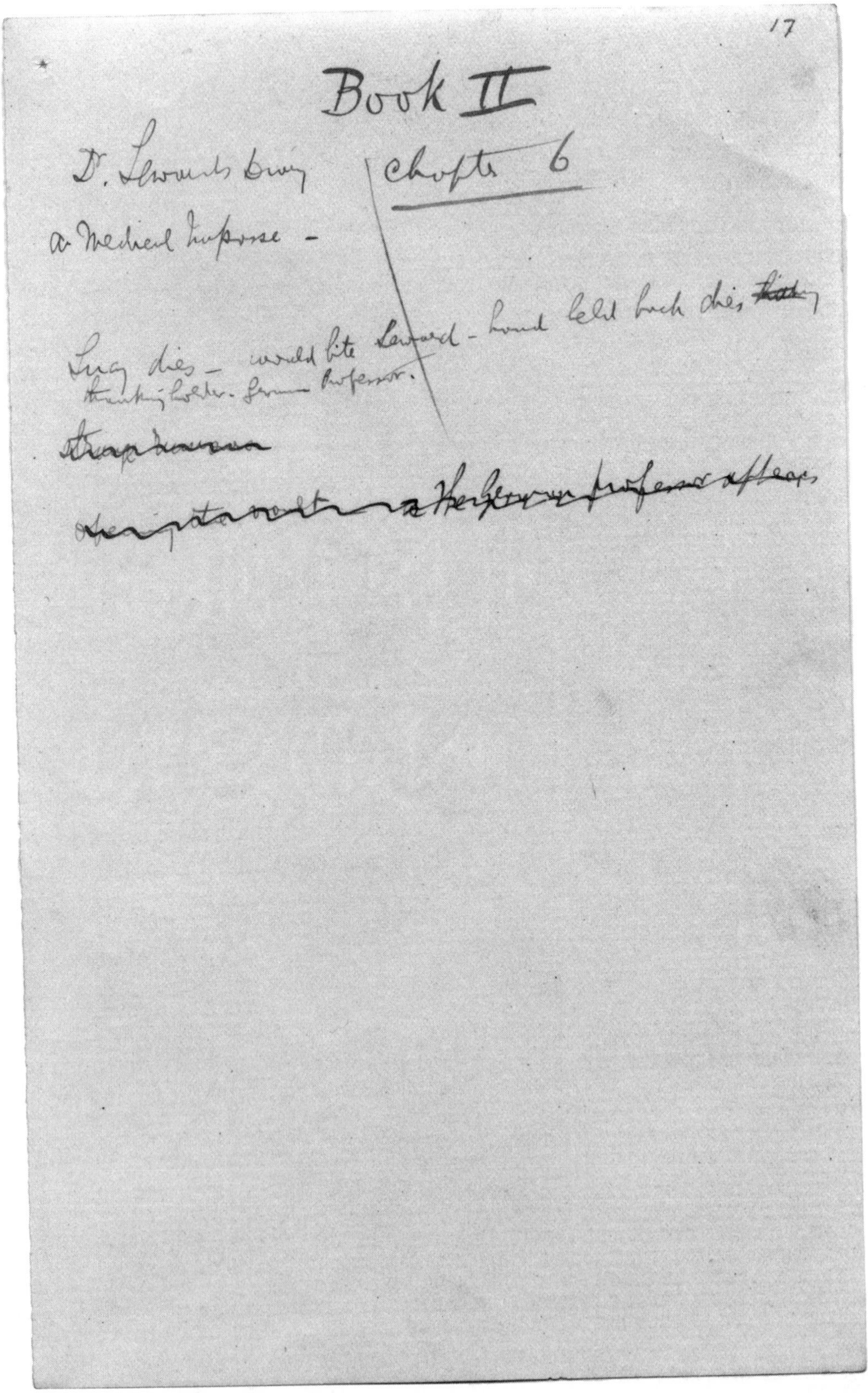
17

Book II

Dr. Seward's Diary | Chapter 6

a Medical Impasse –

Lucy dies – would bite Seward – hand held back dies ~~thinking~~
thinking better – German Professor.

~~[illegible]~~

~~[illegible] German professor appears~~

Page 21. Rosenbach #17. Size: 8 × 5.

Book II

Chapter 6

Dr. Seward's Diary

A Medical Impasse —[155]

Lucy dies — would bite Seward[156]— hand held back[157] o dies —<thinking> thanking holder — German Professor[158]

<strange rumours>

<opening the vault — the German Professor appears>[159]

155. *Dracula* scholar William Hughes observes that "Lucy's descent into vampirism is structured as a medical case, the progress of her 'illness' being observed and investigated by a variety of participant characters including the patient herself" (142).

156. In the current draft Lucy Westenra is still engaged to John Seward. Arthur Holmwood has not yet joined the cast of characters.

157. "'Arthur! Oh, my love, I am so glad you have come! Kiss me!' Arthur bent eagerly over to kiss her; but at that instant Van Helsing, who, like me, had been startled by her voice, swooped upon him, and catching him by the neck with both hands, dragged him back with a fury of strength which I never thought he could have possessed, and actually hurled him across the room.

"'Not for your life!' he said; 'not for your living soul and hers!' And he stood between them like a lion at bay" (12:164).

158. "Very shortly after she opened her eyes in all their softness, and putting out her poor pale, thin hand, took Van Helsing's great brown one; drawing it to her, she kissed it. 'My true friend,' she said, in a faint voice, but with untellable pathos, 'My true friend, and his! Oh, guard him, and give me peace!'" (12:164). Note that the Rider edition of 1912 ends this passage with "give him peace!" (173).

159. Hence, the Dutchman, Abraham Van Helsing, was originally of German origin.

18

Book II

Chapter 7

Dr. Seward's Diary

~~[illegible] Revenge~~
The Vow

Strange Rumours

The Professor's ~~opinion~~ advice

Opening the Vault

Horror

The Professors Opinion

The Vow

Page 22. Rosenbach #18. Size: 8 × 5.

Book II

Chapter 7

Dr. Seward's Diary

<a dinner of revenge>
<the vow>

Strange rumours[160]
The Professor's <opinion> advice
Opening the Vault

Horror
The Professor's opinion
The Vow

160. This may be a harbinger of newspaper reports about a mysterious woman: "The neighbourhood of Hampstead is just at present exercised with a series of events which seem to run on lines parallel to those of what was known to the writers of headlines as 'The Kensington Horror,' or 'The Stabbing Woman,' or 'The Woman in Black.' During the past two or three days several cases have occurred of young children straying from home or neglecting to return from their playing on the Heath. In all these cases the children were too young to give any properly intelligible account of themselves, but the consensus of their excuses is that they had been with a 'bloofer lady.' It has always been late in the evening when they have been missed, and on two occasions the children have not been found until early in the following morning" (13:180). Of course, the "bloofer lady" is Lucy Westenra, who has returned from the grave as a beautiful un-dead ogre.

19

Book III

Chapter I

Jonathan Harker's Diary
re Visit from Dr. Seward. To help to find out mystery.

Jonathan & Mina talk together

Expect a clue re Cargo of earth.

Baffled

Page 23. Rosenbach #19. Size: 8 × 5.

Book III

Chapter 1

Jonathan Harker's Diary

re Visit from Dr. Seward — to help to find out mystery.
Jonathan & Minna [sic][161] talk together
Expect a clue re cargo of earth.
Baffled

161. At times, Stoker spells "Mina" with two n's.

20

Book III

Chapter 2

Suspicion

Dr. Seward's Diary

Consult the Texan

Consult the Professor

a little dinner & a Conversation re Vampires

The Count suspected

Page 24. Rosenbach #20. Size: 8 × 5.

Book III

Chapter 2

Suspicion

Dr. Seward's Diary

Consult the Texan
Consult the Professor
A little dinner & a conversation re Vampires[162]
The Count suspected

---

162. This becomes Van Helsing's lecture on vampires in chapter 18. In the course of the novel, Dracula is endowed with an arsenal of supernatural powers:

he is potentially immortal
he can survive indefinitely on the blood of mortals
he has the strength of twenty men
he has more than mortal cunning
he can shape-shift into the form of a wolf or a bat
he can appear as mist or elemental dust
he can appear at will
he can grow and become small
he can command the dead
he can direct the elements
he can control the meaner things
he can vanish at will
he can grow younger
he can see in the dark
he has no reflection in a mirror
he casts no shadow
he can hypnotize and seduce his victims
he can transform his victims into vampires

However, his powers are offset by crippling limitations:

he may not enter a household unless he is invited in
he loses his supernatural powers during the daytime
he must sleep on the soil of his native land
he cannot cross running water except at the slack or the flood of the tide
he can change shape only at noon or at exact sunrise or sunset
he is repelled by garlic and holy symbols (crucifix, holy wafer)
he can be destroyed by driving a stake through his heart, decapitating his body and burning it to ashes
a branch of wild rose on his coffin will trap him
a sacred bullet fired into his coffin will kill him

21

Book III

Chapter 3

~~Dr~~ Jonathan Harker's diary (kept by Mina)

Clues. Mina suspects Dracula — asks Jonathan about him he shews old diary — she is certain he is the man — Jonathan assents — "if there is any such person" result of inquiries. all strange things known of him brought together.

Dr Seward told

Texan offers to go to Transylvania

Page 25. Rosenbach #21. Size: 8 × 5.

Book III

Chapter 3

Jonathan Harker's Diary (Kept by Minna [sic])

clues — Minna [sic] suspects Dracula — asks Jonathan about him ° he shows old diary — she is certain he is the man — Jonathan assents — "If there is any such person" ° result of inquiries all strange things known of him brought together

Dr. Seward told

Texan offers to go to Transylvania[163]

163. Contrary to popular opinion, *Dracula* was not the first vampire tale to be set in "The Land Beyond the Forest." Alexandre Dumas' *Les Mille et un Fantômes* (1849) includes a story about a pale-faced lady who haunts the Carpathians. In "The Mysterious Stranger" (1853), the un-dead Count Azzo terrorizes a family in this region. Marie Nizet's *Capitaine Vampire* (1879) concludes in Transylvania, while Jules Verne's romantic adventure, *The Castle of the Carpathians* (1892) takes place there.

22

Book III

Chapter 4

Texan's letter visit to Transylvania

Page 26. Rosenbach #22. Size: 8 × 5.

Book III

Chapter 4

Texan's letter — visit to Transylvania[164]

164. Before leaving for Transylvania, Jonathan Harker conducts some preliminary research: "Having some time at my disposal when in London, I had visited the British Museum, and made search among the books and maps in the library regarding Transylvania; it had struck me that some foreknowledge of the country could hardly fail to have some importance in dealing with a noble of that country. I find that the district he named is in the extreme east of the country, just on the borders of three states, Transylvania, Moldavia, and Bukovina, in the midst of the Carpathian mountains; one of the wildest and least known portions of Europe....

"In the population of Transylvania there are four distinct nationalities: Saxons in the south, and mixed with them the Wallachs, who are the descendants of the Dacians; Magyars in the west, and Szekelys in the east and north. I am going among the latter, who claim to be descended from Attila and the Huns. This may be so, for when the Magyars conquered the country in the eleventh century they found the Huns settled in it. I read that every known superstition in the world is gathered into the horseshoe of the Carpathians, as if it were the centre of some imaginative sort of whirlpool" (1:1–2).

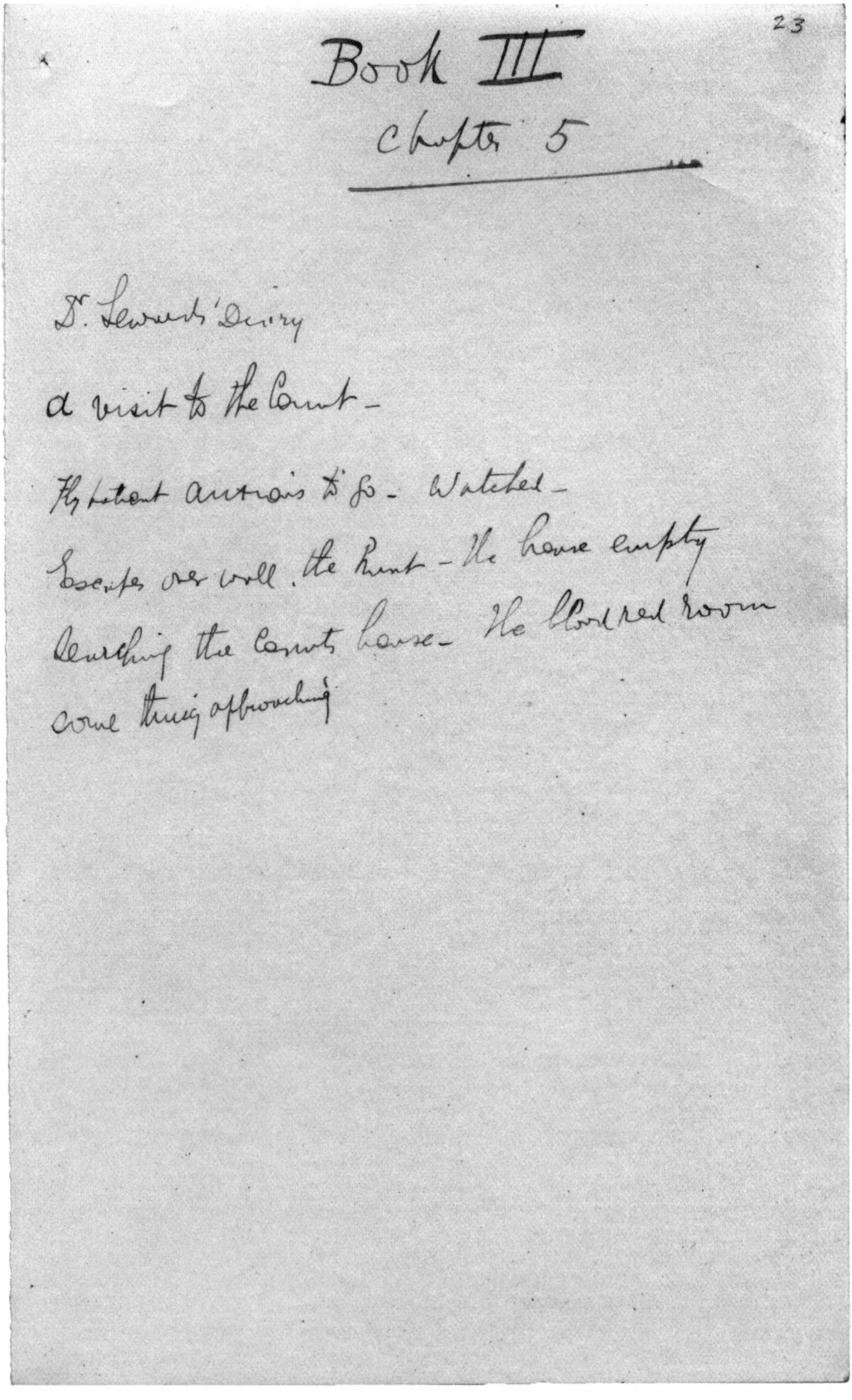

23

Book III

Chapter 5

Dr. Seward's Diary

A visit to the Count –

The patient anxious to go – Watched –

Escapes over wall. the hunt – the house empty

Searching the Count's house – the blood red room

Some thing approaching

Page 27. Rosenbach #23. Size: 8 × 5.

Book III

Chapter 5

Dr. Seward's Diary

a visit to the Count —
Fly patient anxious to go — watched —
Escapes over wall — the hunt — the house empty
Searching the Count's house[165] — the blood red room
some thing approaching

165. In the novel, the vampire hunters break into two of Dracula's lairs. First, they enter his residence at Carfax: "The whole place was thick with dust. The floor was seemingly inches deep, except where there were recent footsteps, in which on holding down my lamp I could see marks of hobnails where the dust was caked. The walls were fluffy and heavy with dust, and in the corners were masses of spiders' webs whereon the dust had gathered till they looked like old tattered rags as the weight had torn them partly down....

"[T]he place was small and close, and the long disuse had made the air stagnant and foul. There was an earthy smell, as of some dry miasma, which came through the fouler air. But as to the odour itself, how shall I describe it? It was not alone that it was composed of all the ills of mortality and with the pungent, acrid smell of blood, but it seemed as though corruption had become itself corrupt. Faugh! it sickens me to think of it. Every breath exhaled by that monster seemed to have clung to the place and intensified its loathsomeness....

"[W]e saw a whole mass of phosphorescence, which twinkled like stars. We all instinctively drew back. The whole place was becoming alive with rats....

"They seemed to swarm over the place all at once, till the lamplight, shining on their moving dark bodies and glittering, baleful eyes, made the place look like a bank of earth set with fireflies.... The rats were multiplying in thousands, and we moved out" (19:256–259).

When they searched Dracula's lair in Piccadilly they found, among other things, "a clothes brush, a brush and comb, and a jug and basin — the latter containing dirty water which was reddened as if with blood" (22:309).

24

Book III

Chapter 6

A test of Sanity

The return of Count Dracula — His anger at intrusion — Explained by capture of the patient. Patient's conduct and attitude to Count. Count attempts to prove in his way of patient sane — proves it. Lunatic killed matters explained — Patient to be discharged — Harker

Page 28. Rosenbach #24. Size: 8 × 5.

Book III

Chapter 6

A test of Sanity

The return of Count Dracula. His anger at intrusion[166]— Explained by capture of fly patient. Patient's conduct and attitude to Count.[167] Count offers to prove in his way if patient sane— proves it[168] ° suspicions lulled ° matters explained— Patient to be discharged

Harker

166. "Two of the most infamous creatures of the night—Jack the Ripper and Bram Stoker's Count Dracula—stalked the foggy, gas-lit streets of Victorian England, shed their victims' blood, took their lives and vanished into the night. More than a century later, their stories continue to fascinate and repel us.

"In the autumn of 1888 an unknown number of prostitutes in Whitechapel, a maze of squalid tenements in London's East End, were murdered by a serial killer (or killers) who came to be known as 'Jack the Ripper.' The wanton brutality of these crimes, combined with the fiend's blood-curdling pseudonym and the lingering mystery of his (her or their) identity has intrigued generations of policemen, reporters and amateur detectives. Jack's 'trade name' is taken from two taunting messages that were written in red ink and crayon and mailed to the press. A letter with the salutation 'Dear Boss' arrived on September 27, 1888. After chuckling about attempts to catch him, the author warned there would be more atrocities. 'I am down on whores,' he wrote, 'and I shant [sic] quit ripping them till I do get buckled... How can they catch me now. [sic]' It was signed with the immortal phase: 'Yours truly / Jack the Ripper.' The first letter was followed by a postcard in the same handwriting. A few weeks later, George Lusk received a battered cardboard box that contained an anonymous note with the return address 'From hell' and half of a kidney which was said to have been torn from the fiend's most recent victim. Its author claimed to have fried and eaten the other piece. These messages were reproduced in newspapers and posted in police stations in the hope that someone would recognize the handwriting but, in spite of their crucial role in the history and myth of the Ripper, they were probably hoaxes by enterprising journalists....

"When the vampire hunters confront the Count at his house in Piccadilly, Harker slashes at him with his knife. Dracula is forced to flee again but, once he is safe, he turns to the men and taunts them: 'My revenge is just begun! I spread it over centuries, and time is on my side. Your girls that you all love are mine already' (23:315). This threat against women combined with the boast that he cannot be stopped bears an uncanny resemblance to the infamous 'Dear Boss' letter. Its intentions are similar and it is delivered in a broken but compelling grammar and rhythm.

"Just as the murders in Whitechapel exposed the rift between socially sanctioned morality and private vices, Dracula's threats suggest that the maidens the heroes have sworn to protect could become whores. The fact that this exchange takes place on October 3rd, a scant six days after Jack's first letter, is [an] example of how the novel follows the timing of the murders" (Robert Eighteen-Bisang 3, 10).

167. "As I got through the belt of trees I saw a white figure scale the high wall which separates our grounds from those of the deserted house.

"I ran back at once, told the watchman to get three or four men immediately and follow me into the grounds of Carfax, in case our friend might be dangerous. I got a ladder myself, and crossing the wall, dropped down on the other side. I could see Renfield's figure just disappearing behind the angle of the house, so I ran after him. On the far side of the house I found him pressed close against the old iron-bound oak door of the chapel. He was talking, apparently to some one, but I was afraid to go near enough to hear what he was saying, lest I might frighten him, and he should run off. Chasing an errant swarm of bees is nothing to following a naked lunatic, when the fit of escaping is upon him! After a few minutes, however, I could see that he did not take note of anything around him, and so ventured to draw nearer to him, the more so as my men had now crossed the wall and were closing him in. I heard him say:

"'I am here to do your bidding, Master. I am Your slave, and You will reward me, for I shall be faithful. I have worshipped You long and afar off. Now that You are near, I await Your commands, and You will not pass me by, will You, dear Master, in Your distribution of good things?'

footnotes continue on page 73

25

Book III

Chapter 7

Return of the Texan — new light on Dracula — the professors lecture on history — garlic & other accidents. Count uneasy — ~~a sudden disappearance~~ — "~~The~~ Harker sees the Count — out of him ~~the~~ man pointing out: "the man" of the Munich Dead-house

Page 29. Rosenbach #25. Size: 8 × 5.

Book III

Chapter 7[169]

return of the Texan — new light on Dracula — the Professor's lecture in history[170] — garlic[171] & other accidents ° Count uneasy — <a sudden disappearance> — Harker sees the Count — met him going out — the man of the Munich Dead-house

---

"He is a selfish old beggar anyhow. He thinks of the loaves and fishes even when he believes he is in a Real Presence. His manias make a startling combination. When we closed in on him he fought like a tiger. He is immensely strong, and he was more like a wild beast than a man. I never saw a lunatic in such a paroxysm of rage before; and I hope I shall not again. It is a mercy that we have found out his strength and his danger in good time. With strength and determination like his, he might have done wild work before he was caged. He is safe now, at any rate. Jack Sheppard himself couldn't get free from the strait-waistcoat that keeps him restrained, and he's chained to the wall in the padded room. His cries are at times awful, but the silences that follow are more deadly still, for he means murder in every turn and movement" (8:104–105).

168. The fact that this idea was discarded leaves us wondering what the Count's way was and what proof he could have supplied.

169. The chapter summaries end abruptly, which suggests the beginning of a new phase in the construction of the plot.

170. As Professor Van Helsing explains, "I have asked my friend Arminius of Buda-Pesth University, to make his record; and, from all the means that are, he tell me of what he [Dracula] has been. He must, indeed, have been that Voivode Dracula who won his name against the Turk, over the great river on the very frontier of Turkey-land. If it be so, then was he no common man; for in that time, and for centuries after, he was spoken of as the cleverest and most cunning, as well as the bravest of the sons of the 'land beyond the forest.' That mighty brain and that iron resolution went with him to his grave, and are even now arrayed against us. The Draculas were, says Arminius, a great and noble race, through now and again were scions who were held by their coevals to have had dealings with the Evil One. They learned his secrets in the Scholomance, amongst the mountains over Lake Hermanstadt, where the devil claims the tenth scholar as his due. In the records are such words as 'stregoica'— witch, 'ordog,' amd 'pokol'— Satan and hell; and in one manuscript this very Dracula is spoken of as 'wampyr,' which we all understand too well" (18:246). With the exception of the reference to the Voivode Dracula who pursued the Turks, this account is fiction, not history.

In chapter 23 he continues: "I have studied, over and over again since they came into my hands, all the papers relating to this monster; and the more I have studied, the greater seems the necessity to utterly stamp him out.... [H]e was in life a most wonderful man. Soldier, statesman, and alchemist — which latter was the highest development of the science-knowledge of his time. He had a mighty brain, a learning beyond compare, and a heart that knew no fear and no remorse. He dared even to attend the Scholomance, and there was no branch of knowledge of his time that he did not essay" (23:310–311). Again, this "history" is fictional.

171. From ancient times garlic was believed to have supernatural powers but, in popular culture, it is used like a crucifix to repel vampires.

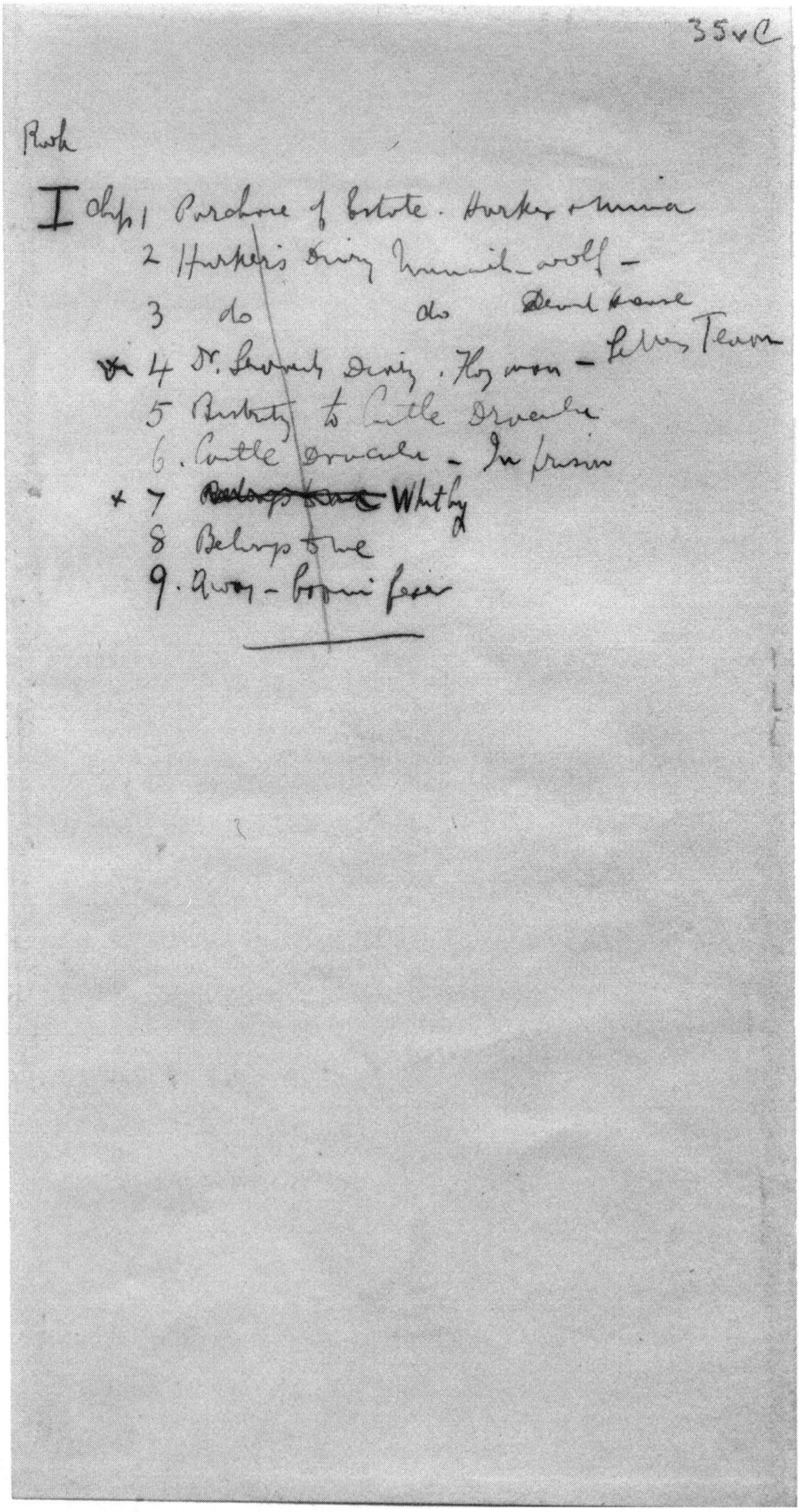

35vC

Book

I Chap 1 Purchase of Estate. Harker & Mina
2 Harker's Diary Munich–wolf –
3 do do Dead House
x 4 Dr. Seward's Diary. Fly man – Letters Texan
5 Bistritz to Castle Dracula
6. Castle Dracula – In prison
x 7 ~~[illegible]~~ Whitby
8 Belongs to me
9. Away – brain fever

Page 30. Rosenbach #35 verso c. Size: 6 × 3¼.

Book I[172]

chap. 1 Purchase of Estate. Harker & Mina
2 Harker's Diary ° Munich — wolf—
3 [ditto] — Dead House[173]
4 Dr. Seward's Diary. Fly man — letters[174] Texan
5 Bistritz to Castle Dracula
6 Castle Dracula — In prison
7 <belongs to me> Whitby
8 Belongs to me
9 Away[175] — brain fever[176]

---

172. The revised plot on this page and on the two following pages culminates in the outline of 29 February 1892. Pages 30 and 31 shift from four books with seven chapters each to three books with nine chapters each.

173. *The Atlantic Monthly* described the Munich Dead House in January 1877: "There is a curious burial custom at Munich. The law requires that every man, woman, and child who dies within city limits shall lie in state for three days in the Leichenhaus (dead house) of the Gottesacker, the southern cemetery, outside the Sendling Gate. This is to prevent any chance of premature burial, an instance of which many years ago gave rise to the present provision. The Leichenhaus is comprised of three large chambers or salons, in which the dead are placed upon raised couches and surrounded by flowers. A series of wide windows ... affords the public an unobstructed view of the interior. The spectacle is not so repellant as one might anticipate. The neatly-kept, well-lighted rooms, the profusion of flowers, and the scrupulous propriety which prevails in all the arrangements, make the thing as little terrible as possible. On the Sunday of our visit to the Gottesacker, the place was unusually full of bodies awaiting interment, old men and women, young girls, and infants. Some were like exquisite statues, others like wax-figures, and all piteous. Attached to the hand of each adult was a string or wire connected with a bell in the custodian's apartment. It would be difficult to imagine a more startling sound than would be the sudden kling-kling of one of those same bells" ("From Ponkapog to Pesth" n.p.).

174. Quincey's only written contribution to the novel consists of his note to Arthur: "We've told yarns by the camp-fire in the prairies; and dressed one another's wounds after trying a landing at the Marquesas; and drunk healths on the shore of Titicaca. There are more yarns to be told, and other wounds to be healed, and another health to be drunk. Won't you let this be at my camp-fire tomorrow night? I have no hesitation in asking you, as I know a certain lady is engaged to a certain dinner-party, and that you are free. There will only be one other, our old pal at the Korea, Jack Seward. He's coming, too, and we both want to mingle our weeps over the wine-cup, and to drink a health with all our hearts to the happiest man in all the wide world, who has won the noblest heart that God has made and the best worth winning. We promise you a hearty welcome, and a loving greeting, and a health as true as your own right hand. We shall both swear to leave you at home if you drink too deep to a certain pair of eyes. Come!" (5:63).

175. Hence, Jonathan's adventure in Transylvania and the events leading up to it were spread out over nine chapters.

176. In Victorian times, it was believed that too much excitement could cause "brain fever" which, in turn, could lead to insanity or death.

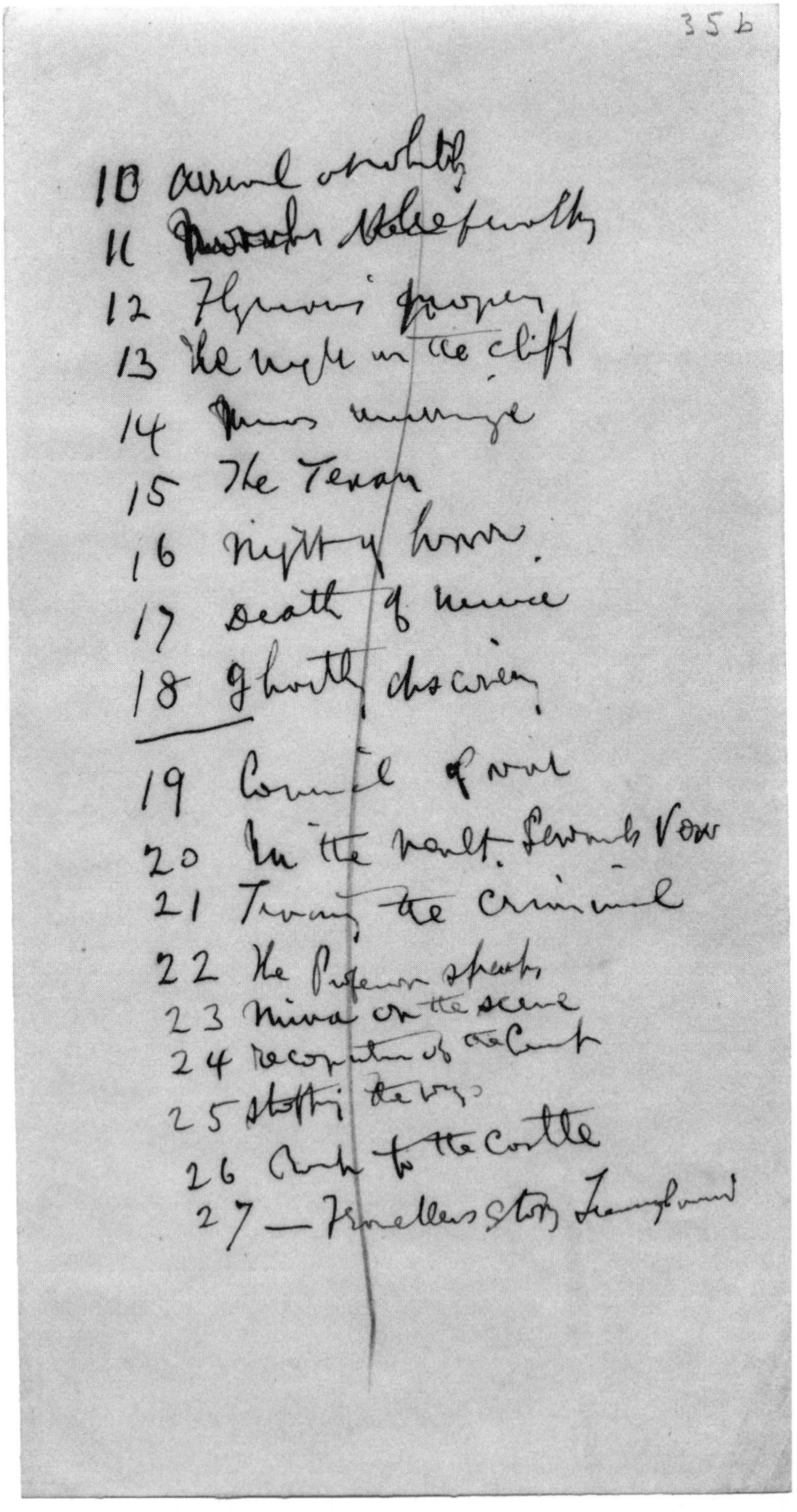
35b

10 Arrival at Whitby
11 ~~[illegible]~~ Whole family
12 Flymans progress
13 The night on the cliff
14 ~~Mina's~~ marriage
15 The Texan
16 Night of horror.
17 Death of Lucy
18 Ghostly discovery.

19 Council of war
20 In the vault. Sewards Vow
21 Tracing the criminal
22 The Professor speaks
23 Mina on the scene
24 Recognition of the Count
25 Stopping the ways
26 Rush to the Castle
27 — Travellers Story Transformed

Page 31. Rosenbach #35b. Size: 6 × 3¼.

10 Arrival at Whitby
11 xxx sleepwalking
12 Flyman's property
13 the night on the cliff
14 Mina's marriage
15 the Texan
16 night of horror
17 Death of Mina[177]
18 ghastly discovery
19 Council of war
20 In the vault. Seward's Vow
21 Tracing the criminal
22 The Professor speaks
23 Mina on the scene
24 recognition of the Count
25 shipping the earth
26 Back to the castle
27 Traveller's Story Transylvania

The Beefsteak Room in the Lyceum Theatre (*English Illustrated Magazine*, September 1890).

177. This line confuses Lucy with Mina again for, six lines later, we find "Mina on the scene."

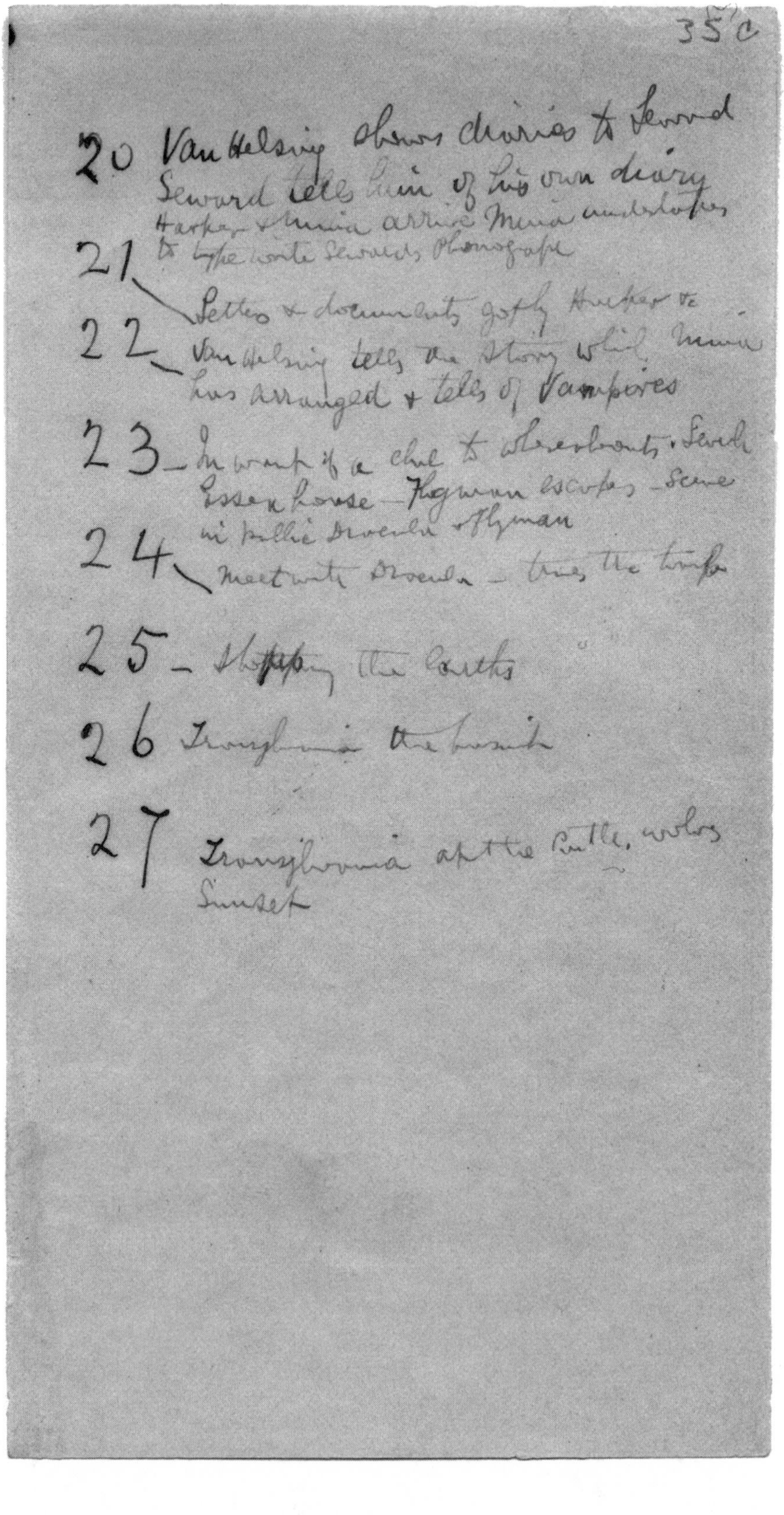

35 C

20 Van Helsing shows diaries to Seward
Seward tells him of his own diary
Harker & Mina arrive Mina undertakes
21 to typewrite Seward's Phonograph
Letters & documents got by Harker &c
22 Van Helsing tells the story which Mina
has arranged & tells of Vampires
23 In want of a clue to whereabouts. Search
Essex house — Flyman escapes — Scene
in which Dracula & Flyman
24 Meet with Dracula — tries the trap
25 Shipping the Earths
26 Transylvania the search
27 Transylvania at the Castle, wolves
Sunset

Page 32. Rosenbach #35c. Size: 6 × 3¼.

20 Van Helsing shows diaries to Seward[178]
Seward tells him of his own diary
Harker and Mina arrive—Mina undertakes to typewrite Seward's phonograph[179]
21 Letters & documents got by Harker
22 Van Helsing tells the story which Mina has arranged[180] & tells of vampires[181]
23 In want of a clue to whereabouts—Search Essex house—Flyman escapes—Scene in public ° Dracula & Flyman
24 Meet with Dracula[182]—tries the tomb
25 shipping the earth
26 Transylvania ° the pursuit
27 Transylvania ° at the castle ° wolves ° Sunset

---

178. This page reworks parts of the previous page.

179. Dr. Seward's Diary is "Kept in phonograph." Thomas Edison invented the phonograph in 1877; by the time Stoker began writing *Dracula*, it was being used for clinical note-taking.

180. Seed suggests, "Since understanding Dracula is a necessary precondition to defeating him, the exchange and accumulation of information literally is resistance to him. Characters become proportionately less vulnerable the more they act together, and the more they act together the more conscious they become of recording" (73). Mina, who collates, copies and distributes the documents, emerges as a catalyst in the pursuit and defeat of Dracula.

181. In *The Living Dead,* James B. Twitchell maintains, "The story of Stoker's *Dracula* is this: a band of boys, a gang if you will, under the direction of a wise father-figure/priest/doctor must destroy a demon who has been ravaging their women" (134).

182. Was Professor Van Helsing to meet with Dracula?

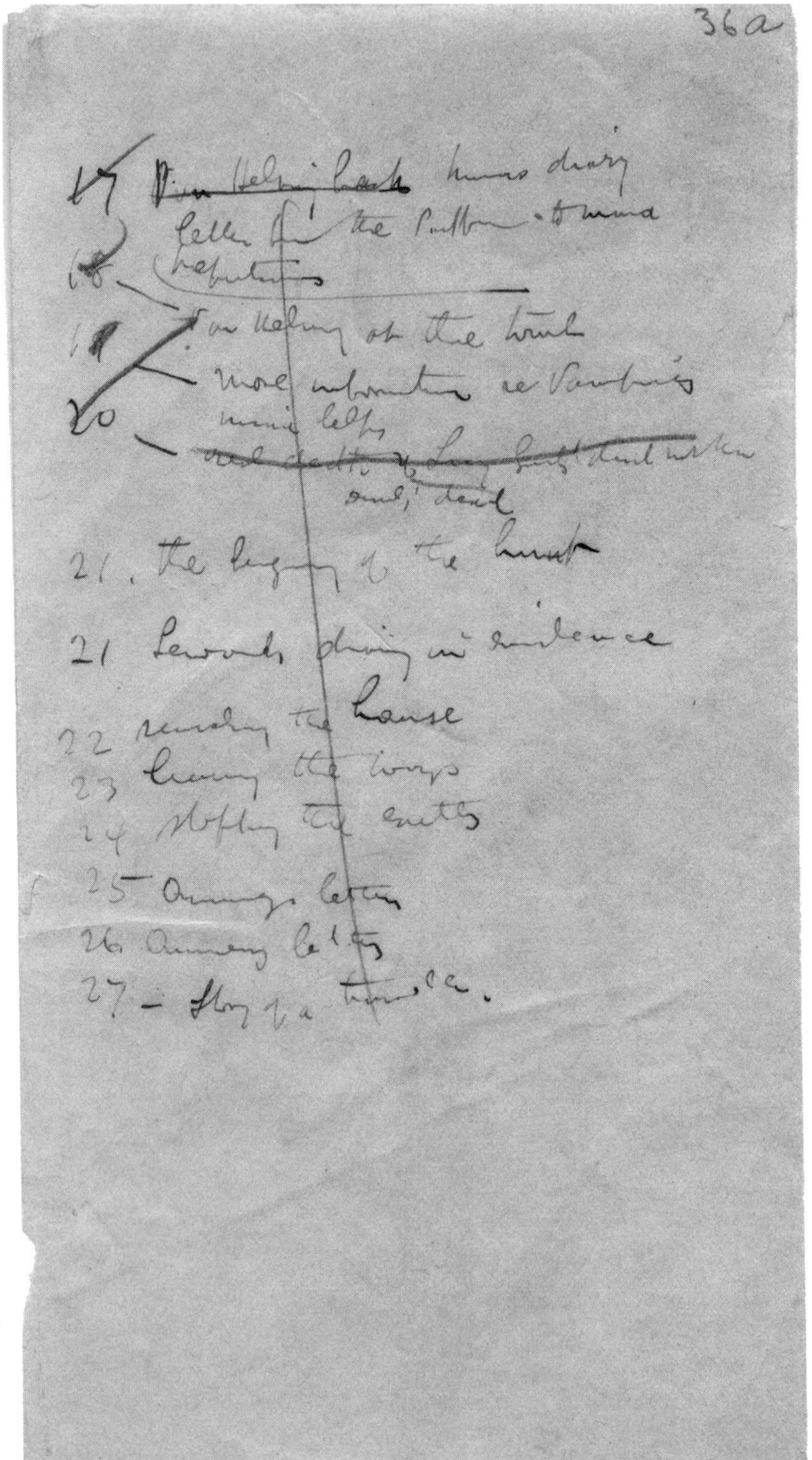
36a

17 ~~Van Helsing back~~ Mina's diary
Letter from the [illegible] to Mina
18 [illegible]
19 Van Helsing at the tomb
more information re Vampires
20 [illegible]
~~[illegible]~~
[illegible]
21. the beginning of the hunt
21 Renfield's doings in evidence
22 searching the house
23 clearing the boxes
24 stopping the earths
25 Arminius letter
26. Arminius letter
27 — story of a [illegible]

Page 33. Rosenbach #36a. Size: 6 × 3½.

17 <Van Helsing back> Mina's diary
letter from the Professor to Mina — preparations
18 Van Helsing at the tomb
19 More information re vampires — Mina helps
20 <real death — Lucy finds dead mother> xxx dead[183]
21 the beginning of the hunt
21 Seward's diary in evidence
22 searching the house
23 learning the ways
24 shifting the earth
25 Quincey's letter
26 Quincey's letter
27 story of a traveller

183. "On the bed lay two women, Lucy and her mother. The latter lay farthest in, and she was covered with a white sheet, the edge of which had been blown back by the draught through the broken window, showing the drawn, white face with the look of terror fixed upon it. By her side lay Lucy, with face white and still more drawn. The flowers which had been round her neck we found upon her mother's bosom, and her throat was bare, showing the two little wounds which we had noticed before, but looking horribly white and mangled" (12:149).

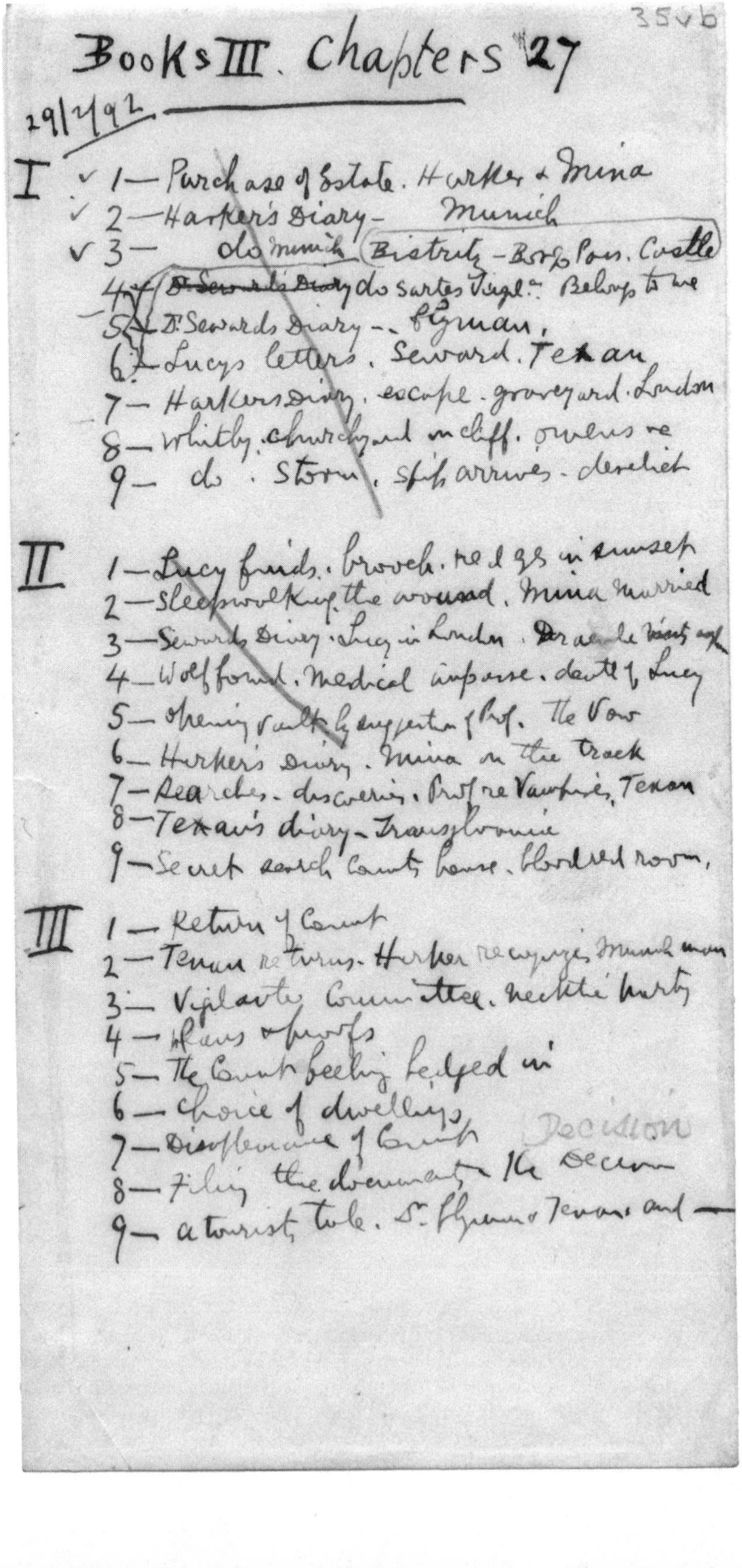
35vb

Books III. Chapters 27

29/2/92

I
✓ 1 — Purchase of Estate. Harker & Mina
✓ 2 — Harker's Diary — Munich
✓ 3 — do Munich (Bistritz — Borgo Pass. Castle)
4 — ~~Dr Seward's Diary~~ do Sartes Vigil.ce Belongs to me
5 — Dr Seward's Diary — Flyman
6 — Lucy's letters. Seward. Texan
7 — Harker's Diary. escape — graveyard. London
8 — Whitby. churchyard on cliff. owners re
9 — do. Storm. Ship arrives — derelict

II
1 — Lucy finds. brooch. red eyes in sunset
2 — Sleepwalking. the wound. Mina married
3 — Seward's Diary. Lucy in London. ~~Dracula visits asyl~~
4 — Wolf found. Medical impasse. death of Lucy
5 — Opening vault by suggestion of Prof. The Vow
6 — Harker's Diary. Mina on the track
7 — Searches — discoveries. Prof re Vampire. Texan
8 — Texan's diary — Transylvania
9 — Secret search Count's house. Blood red room.

III
1 — Return of Count
2 — Texan returns — Harker recognizes Munich man
3 — Vigilante Committee. Necktie party
4 — Plans & proofs
5 — The Count feeling hedged in
6 — Choice of dwellings
7 — Disappearance of Count
8 — Filing the documents. The Decision Decision
9 — A tourist's tale. Dr Seward & Texan and —

Page 34. Rosenbach #35 verso b. Size: 6 × 3.

Books III. Chapters 27[184]

29/2/92

I

1 Purchase of Estate. Harker & Mina
2 Harker's Diary — Munich
3 [ditto] Munich — Bistritz — Borgo Pass. Castle
4 <Dr. Seward's Diary> [ditto] Sortes Virgil — belongs to me
5 Dr. Seward's Diary — flyman
6 Lucy's letters. Seward. Texan
7 Harker's Diary — escape — graveyard London
8 Whitby ° churchyard on cliff. Omens
9 [ditto] storm — ship arrives — derelict

II

1 Lucy finds brooch — red eyes in sunset
2 sleepwalking ° the wound. Mina married
3 Seward's Diary. Lucy in London. Dracula visits asylum
4 Wolf found — medical impasse — death of Lucy
5 Opening vault by suggestion of Prof. The Vow
6 Harker's Diary. Mina on the track
7 Searches — discoveries — Prof. re Vampires — Texan
8 Texan's diary — Transylvania
9 Secret search Count's house — blood red room

III

1 Return of Count
2 Texan returns. Harker recognizes Munich man
3 Vigilante Committee — necktie party[185]
4 Plans & proofs
5 The Count feeling hedged in
6 Choice of dwellings
7 Disappearance of Count. Decision
8 Filing the documents — the decision
9 A tourist's tale[186] ° flyman[187] & Texan and ___

184. This outline revises and summarizes several pages of chapter notes.

185. "[N]ecktie party" is another term from the American frontier.

186. The "tourist's tale" becomes Jonathan Harker's closing note: "In the summer of this year we made a journey to Transylvania, and went over the old ground which was, and is, to us so full of vivid and terrible memories. It was almost impossible to believe that the things which we had seen with our own eyes and heard with our own ears were living truths. Every trace of all that had been was blotted out" (27:389).

187. The reference to the "flyman" here is surprising. Emerson toys with the idea that "Quincey was killed by Renfield, who is now a vampire (which is of course the only way Renfield *could* be involved in the ending anyway, seeing as he 'died' back in Purfleet many chapters earlier)" (497 n.196).

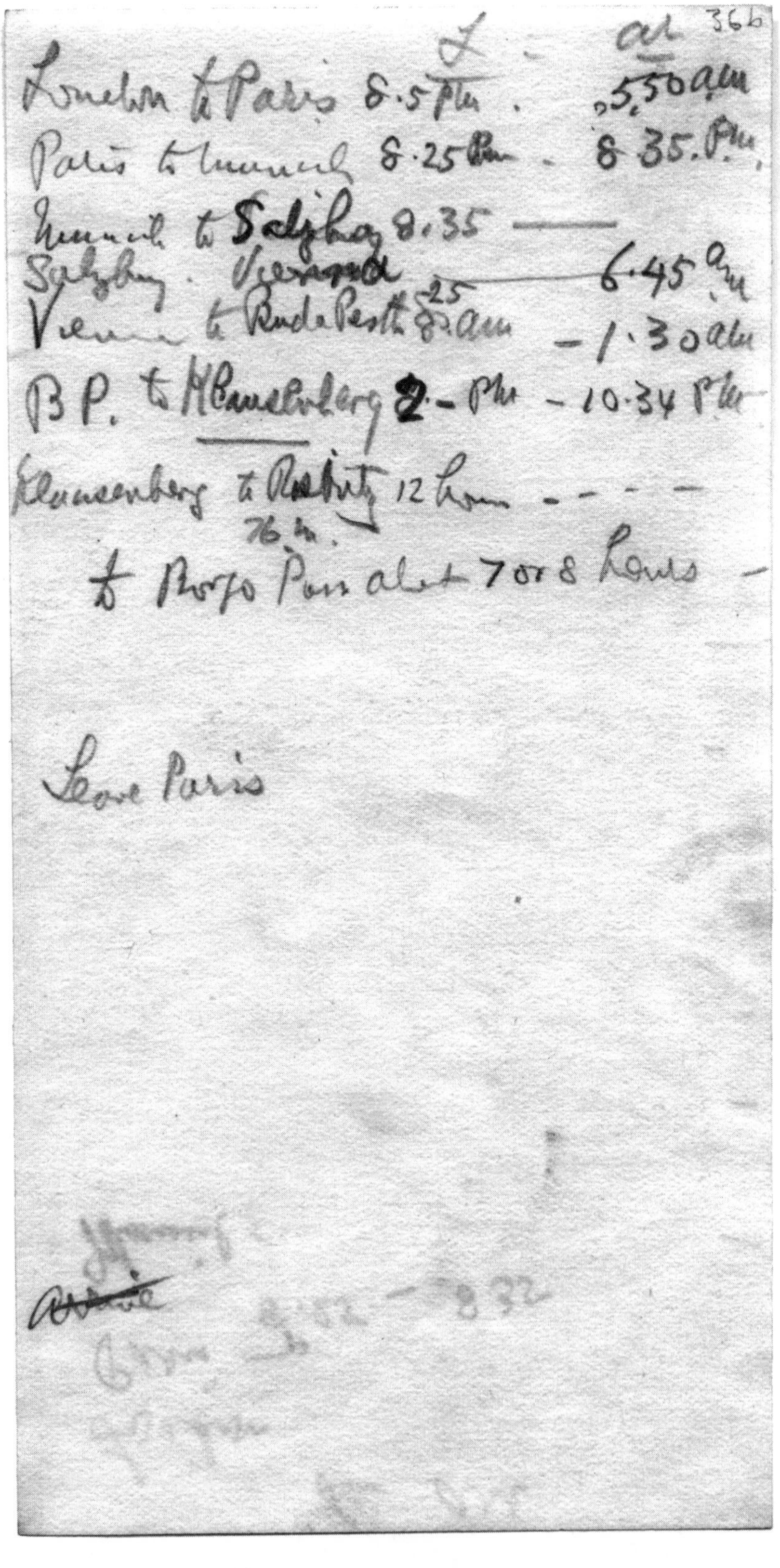
£ — at 36b

London to Paris 8.5 pm. — 5.50 am

Paris to Munich 8.25 pm — 8.35 pm.

Munich to Salzburg 8.35 ——

Salzburg. ~~Vienna~~ —— 6.45 am

Vienna to Buda Pesth 8.25 am — 1.30 pm

B.P. to Klausenburg 2 - pm — 10.34 pm

Klausenburg to Bistritz 12 hours ----
76 m.

to Borgo Pass about 7 or 8 hours —

Leave Paris

~~Arrive~~

Page 35. Rosenbach #36b. Size: 6 × 3.

	Leave	Arrive[188]
London to Paris	8.5 PM	5.50 AM
Paris to Munich	8.25 AM	8.35 PM
Munich to Salzburg	8.35	
Salzburg — Vienna		6.45 AM
Vienna to Buda-Pesth	8.25 AM	1.30 AM
BP to Klausenberg	2 PM	10.34 PM

Klausenberg to Bistritz[189] ° 12 hours — 76 m.
to Borgo Pass ° about 7 or 8 hours —

Leave Paris

<Arrive>

Irving and Stoker at the Lyceum (*The Tatler*, 9 October 1901).

188. For the sake of clarity, we have replaced "L" and "Ar" with "Leave" and "Arrive," and set the departure and arrival times in columns. As McNally and Florescu point out, "Most modern readers may not realize it, but the train schedules in the novel are accurate" (*Essential Dracula* 18). Arrival in Budapest was likely meant to be 1:30 P.M.; today, a train trip from Vienna to Budapest takes about three hours.

189. At the time *Dracula* was written, Hungarian was the official language of Transylvania. However, Stoker (like Baedeker) uses German spellings for Transylvanian cities.

36c

Leave Klausenburg 3 May morg. (arr. eve. Bistritz)
arrive. Bistritz — 4 May eve
Leave Bistritz 5 May

Page 36. Rosenbach #36c. Size: 6 × 3.

leave Klausenberg ° 3 May morning ° (arr evening Bistritz)[190]
arrive Bistritz — 4 May evening
leave Bistritz — 5 May

190. Victor Sage notes that "The opening of Maturin's *Melmoth the Wanderer* provides us with what has become the paradigm of the horror-plot: the journey from the capital ... to the provinces" (*Horror Fiction in the Protestant Tradition* 8). *Dracula* opens, "3 May. Bistritz.— Left Munich at 8.35 P.M. on 1st May, arriving at Vienna early next morning; should have arrived at 6.46, but train was an hour late. Buda-Pesth seems a wonderful place, from the glimpse which I got of it from the train and the little I could walk through the streets. I feared to go very far from the station, as we had arrived late and would start as near the correct time as possible. The impression I had was that we were leaving the West and entering the East; the most Western of splendid bridges over the Danube, which is here of noble width and depth, took us among the traditions of Turkish rule.

"We left in pretty good time, and came after nightfall to Klausenburgh. Here I stopped for the night at the Hotel Royale....

"I had to hurry breakfast, for the train started a little before eight, or rather it ought to have done so, for after rushing to the station at 7.30 I had to sit in the carriage for more than an hour before we began to move. It seems to me that the further East you go the more unpunctual are the trains. What ought they to be in China?

"All day long we seemed to dawdle through a country which was full of beauty of every kind. Sometimes we saw little towns or castles on the top of steep hills such as we see in old missals; sometimes we ran by rivers and streams which seemed from the wide stony margin on each side of them to be subject to great floods.... At every station there were groups of people, sometimes crowds, and in all sorts of attire. Some of them were just like the peasants at home or those I saw coming through France and Germany, with short jackets and round hats and home-made trousers; but others were very picturesque. The women looked pretty, except when you got near them, but they were very clumsy about the waist.... The strangest figures we saw were the Slovaks, who are more barbarian than the rest, with their big cowboy hats, great baggy dirty-white trousers, white linen shirts, and enormous heavy leather belts, nearly a foot wide, all studded over with brass nails....

"It was on the dark side of twilight when we got to Bistritz, which is a very interesting old place. Being practically on the frontier — for the Borgo Pass leads from it into Bukovina — it has had a very stormy existence, and certainly shows marks of it" (1:1–3).

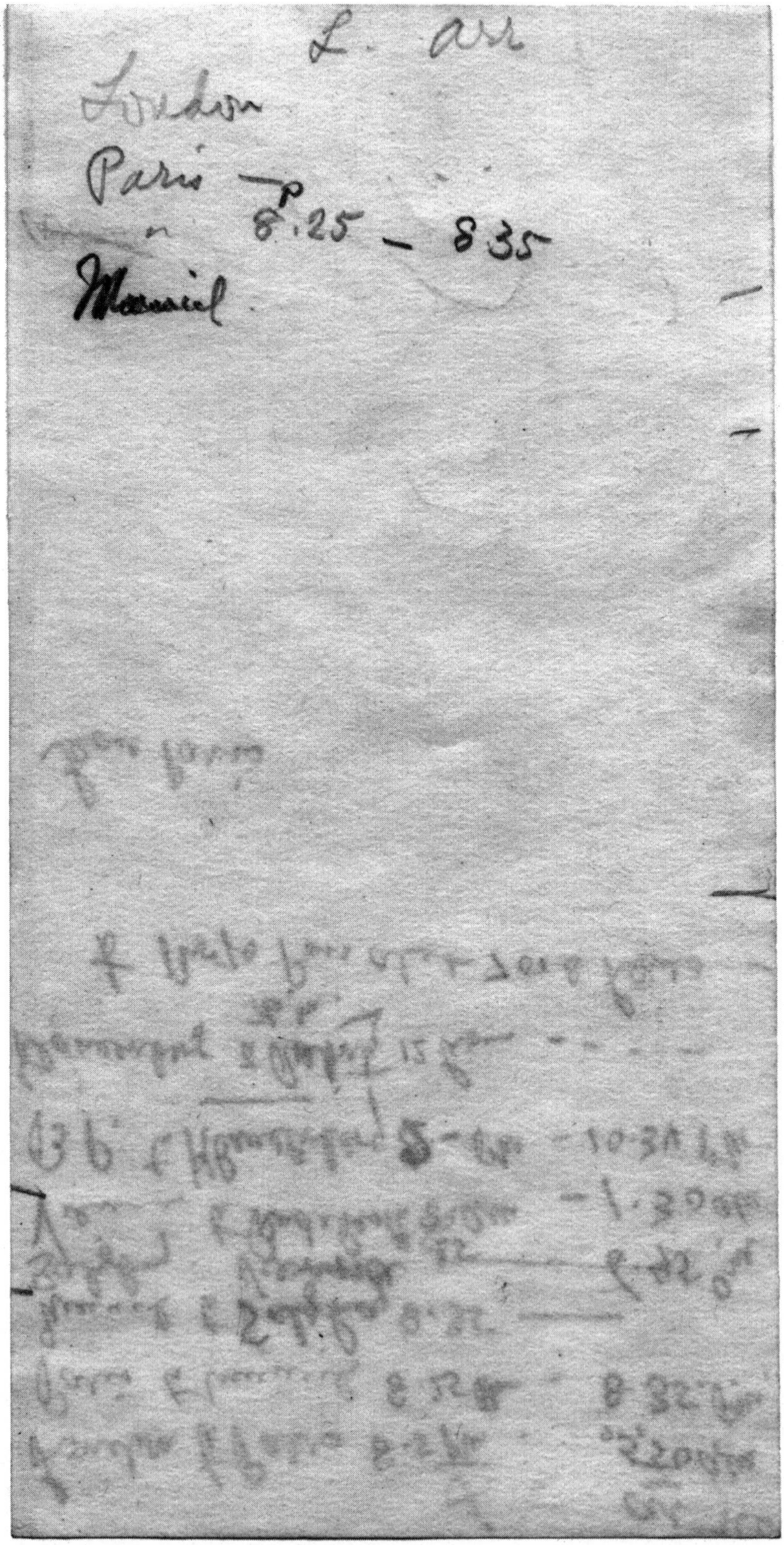
London
Paris
8.25 – 8.35
Munich

Page 37. Rosenbach #36b verso. Size: 6 × 3.

L. Arr
London

Paris 8.25 — 8.35[191]
Munich

191. I.e., leave Paris at 8.25 A.M. and arrive in Munich at 8:35 P.M.

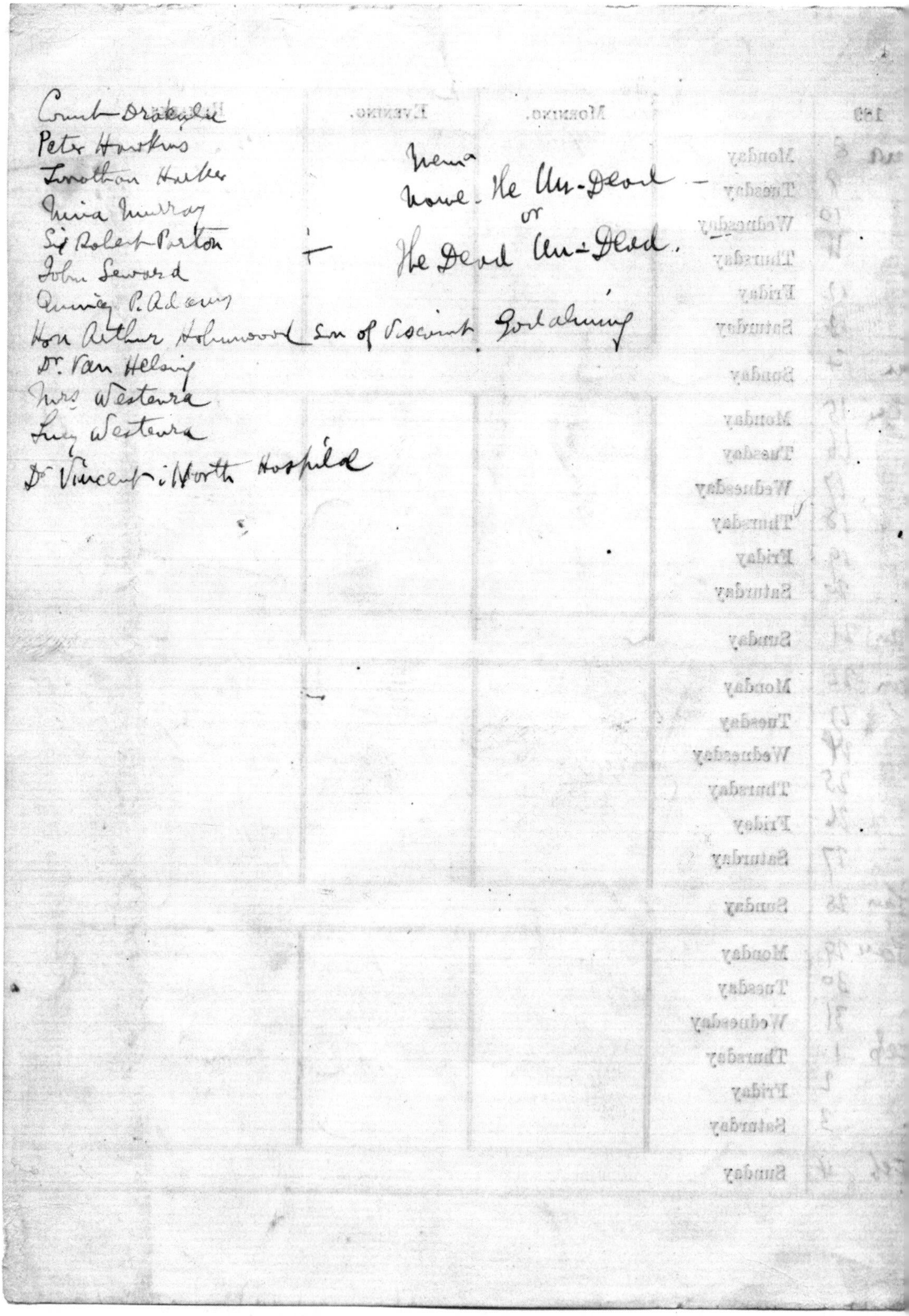

Count Dracula
Peter Hawkins
Jonathan Harker
Mina Murray
Sir Robert Parton
John Seward
Quincey P. Adams
Hon Arthur Holmwood son of Viscount Godalming
Dr. Van Helsing
Mrs Westenra
Lucy Westenra
Dr Vincent, North Hospital

Name
novel — The Un-Dead —
or
The Dead Un-Dead.

Page 38. Rosenbach #31b verso. Size: 8½ × 6.

Count Dracula
Peter Hawkins
Jonathan Harker
Mina Murray
Sir Robert Parton[192]
John Seward[193]
Quincey P. Adams[194]
Hon. Arthur Holmwood — son of Viscount Godalming[195]
Dr. Van Helsing
Mrs. Westenra
Lucy Westenra
Dr. Vincent — North Hospital[196]
Memo: Name — *The Un-Dead* or *The Dead Un-Dead*[197]

192. In the book, Parton becomes Paxton. A John Paxton is buried in Whitby (6:68) while "a gentleman representing Sir John Paxton, the President of the Incorporated Law Society" (13:175) attends Lucy Westenra's funeral.

193. In *Dracula*, John is often addressed by his nickname, "Jack."

194. Quincey was surnamed "Adams" before being called "Morris." The presence of this name suggests that this page predates the calendar of events, which always uses "Morris." Leatherdale remarks that this name comes "rather too close to John Quincy Adams, the sixth president of the United States" (*Novel & Legend* 235 n.31).

195. This is the first appearance of the suitor who will become Lucy's fiancé. The novel refers to him as the "Hon. Arthur Holmwood" and later, as "Lord Godalming," but does not mention that he is a "Viscount."

196. Dr. Vincent, who examines one of the children Lucy attacked, plays a marginal part in the novel.

197. Two possible titles for the novel grace the right-hand side of the page: *The Un-Dead* and *The Dead Un-Dead*. The former title appears on the final typescript and in the contract for *Dracula*, which was signed on 20 May 1897.

26a

189		Morning.	Evening.	Remarks.
March 6	Monday			
7	Tuesday			
8	Wednesday			
9	Thursday			
10	Friday			
11	Saturday			
Mar 12	Sunday			
Mar 13	Monday			
14	Tuesday			
15	Wednesday			
16	Thursday	Dracula's letter to Hawkins (dated 4 March old style)		
17	Friday			
18	Saturday			
Mar 19	Sunday			
20	Monday			
21	Tuesday	Sir Robert Purvis' letter to Hawkins		
22	Wednesday			
23	Thursday	Hawkins letter to Dracula		
24	Friday			
25	Saturday			
Mar 26	Sunday			
27	Monday			
28	Tuesday			
29	Wednesday			
30	Thursday	Dracula's letter to Hawkins (18 old style)		
31	Friday			
April 1	Saturday			
Apr 2	Sunday			

Page 39. Rosenbach #26a. Size: 8½ × 6.[198]

MARCH[199]

6
7
8
9
10
11
12
13
14
15
16 TH Dracula's letter to Hawkins (dated 4 March old style)[200]
17
18
19
20
21 TU Sir Robert Parton's letter to Hawkins
22
23 TH Hawkins' letter to Dracula
24
25
26
27
28
29
30 TH Dracula's letter to Hawkins (18 old style)
31

APRIL

1
2

198. Pages 39 to 47 are entered in a commercial, all-purpose calendar that lists the days of the week. It is printed on pale yellow paper with pink lines and pink lettering.

199. Stoker entered each month and date by hand.

200. The most common method of keeping track of dates in the Western world is the Gregorian calendar. By decree of Pope Gregory XIII, it replaced the "old style" Julian calendar in 1582.

26b

189		Morning.	Evening.	Remarks.
Apl 3	Monday			
4	Tuesday			
5	Wednesday			
6	Thursday			
7	Friday			
8	Saturday			
Apl 9	Sunday			
10	Monday			
11	Tuesday			
12	Wednesday	Harker goes to Purfleet	Letter 12 or 13 Harker to Hawkins	
13	Thursday	Continues search	Dracula writes to Maître d'Hotel Quatre Saisons	
14	Friday			
15	Saturday	Harkers letter to Hawkins		
Apl 16	Sunday	Harker visits Mina at school		
17	Monday			
18	Tuesday	Kate's Letter to Lucy		
19	Wednesday	Harker's letter to Hawkins		
20	Thursday	Hawkins letter to Dracula		
21	Friday			
22	Saturday			
Apl 23	Sunday			
Apl 24	Monday	Telegram from Dracula		
25	Tuesday	Leave London 8.5 P.M.		
26	Wednesday	5.0 P.M. Leave Paris 8.25 P.M.	arrive Munich 8.35 P.M.	
27	Thursday	[illegible] Snow storm and wolf		
28	Friday	arrive early morning at Hotel		
29	Saturday	Home all day		
Apl 30	Sunday	Opera Flying Dutchman		

Page 40. Rosenbach #26b. Size: 8½ × 6.

3		
4		
5		
6		
7		
8		
9		
10		
11		
12	W	Harker goes to Purfleet
		Letters 12 & 13 ° Harker to Hawkins
		Dracula writes to Maitre d'Hotel Quatre Saisons[201]
13	TH	Continues search
14		
15	SA	Harker's letter to Hawkins
16	SU	Harker visits Mina at school
17	M	Katie's Letter to Lucy
18	TU	Harker's letter to Hawkins
19	W	Hawkins' letter to Dracula[202]
20		
21		
22		
23		
24	M	Telegram from Dracula
25	TU	Leave London 8.5 PM.
26	W	arr. Paris 5.50 AM—Leave Paris 8.25 PM—Arrive Munich 8.35 PM
27	TH	adventure snow storm and wolf[203]
28	F	arrive early morning at Hotel
29	SA	home all day
30	SU	opera Flying Dutchman[204]

201. In "Dracula's Guest," a letter from the Count states, "Be careful of my guest—his safety is most precious to me. Should aught happen to him, or if he be missed, spare nothing to find him and ensure his safety. He is English and therefore adventurous. There are often dangers from snow and wolves and night. Lose not a moment if you suspect harm to him. I answer your zeal with my fortune" (17).

202. In the novel, Dracula welcomes Jonathan Harker by name—"I am Dracula; and I bid you welcome, Mr. Harker, to my house" (2:17)—but, since he had not yet read the letter on pages 17 and 18, he would have been expecting Mr. Hawkins. The abridged edition of *Dracula* corrects this oversight with "Welcome to my house!" (15).

203. The episode of the "snow storm and wolf" is part of "Dracula's Guest."

204. W. G. Wills' adaptation of the legend of the Flying Dutchman, *Vanderdecker*, debuted at the Lyceum in 1878. Stoker recalls that "[Henry Irving] gave one a wonderful impression of a dead man fictitiously alive" and "[his] eyes seemed to shine like cinders of glowing red from out the marble face" (*Personal Reminiscences* v1.56).

270

Walpurgis-Nacht

189		Morning.	Evening.	Remarks.
May 1	Monday	Dead House Harker leaves Munich 8.35 P.M.		
2	Tuesday	arrive Vienna 6.45 am	Leave Vienna 8.25 am	Arrive Buda Pesth 1.30 P.M. Leave 2 P.M. arrive Klausenburg 10.34 P.M.
3	Wednesday Seward's Diary	~~Arrive Buda Pesth 1.30 P.M.~~	Leave Klausenburg 8 a.m.	arrive Bistritz 8 P.M.
4	Thursday	~~Leave Buda Pesth 2 P.M.~~	Leave Bistritz 2 P.M.	arrive Borgo Pass at 9 P.M. (an hour early)
5	Friday JH	drive to Castle		
6	Saturday Seward Diary	Castle		
May 7	Sunday	Castle	Razor	
May 8	Monday	Castle	a prisoner	
9	Tuesday	Castle	Letters home	
10	Wednesday	Castle ~~sees Count go out of window~~	Jonathan Diary	
11	Thursday	~~Castle the warning~~		
12	Friday	~~Castle tried to write letters~~		Sees Count go out of window
13	Saturday	~~Gives letter to gypsies – Count draws up~~		
May 14	Sunday			
May 15	Monday	Women Kissing		
16	Tuesday			
17	Wednesday	Lucy's letter to Mina ~~proposals~~		
18	Thursday	~~Seward's Diary spiders~~		
19	Friday	Jonathan told to write letters		
20	Saturday			
May 21	Sunday			
May 22	Monday	~~[illegible]~~		
23	Tuesday			
24	Wednesday Seward's Diary	~~Sees women again Count returns – mother wolves~~		Lucy's letter to Mina 3 proposals
25	Thursday	Quincey Morris to Arthur		
26	Friday	Telegram Arthur to Quincey		
27	Saturday	~~Arrival of boxes~~		
May 28	Sunday	Letter to Gypsies – Count discovers it		

Page 41. Rosenbach #27a. Size: 8½ × 6.

MAY

1	M	Walpurgis-Nacht ° Dead House ° Harker leaves Munich 8.35 PM
2	TU	arrive Vienna 6.45 AM[205]—leave Vienna 8.25 AM. Arrive Buda-Pesth 1.30 PM leave 2 PM arrive Klausenberg 10.34 PM
3	W	Seward's Diary—<arrive Buda-Pesth 1.30 PM> leave Klausenberg 8 AM arrive Bistritz 8 PM
4	TH	<leave Buda-Pesth 2 PM> leave Bistritz 2 PM arrive Borgo Pass at 9 PM (an hour early)
5	F	JH drive to Castle
6	SA	Seward's diary ° Castle
7	SU	Castle—<prison>
8	M	Castle—a prison
9	TU	Castle—letters home
10	W	Castle <sees Count go out by window>[206]Jonathan's Diary
11	TH	<Castle—the women—kissing>
12	F	<Castle told to write letters> sees Count go out of window[207]
13	SA	<Gives letter to gypsies—Count discovers it>[208]
14		
15	M	women ° kissing
16		
17	W	Lucy's letter to Mina <proposals>
18	TH	<Seward's Diary—spiders>
19	F	Jonathan told to write letters
20		
21		
22	M	<note paper all gone>
23		
24	W	Seward's Diary—<see women again[209]—Count returns. Mother & wolves> Lucy's letter to Mina ° 3 proposals
25	TH	Quincey Morris to Arthur[210]
26	F	Telegram Arthur to Quincey
27	SA	<arrival of boxes>
28	SU	letter to gypsies—Count discovers it

205. Over time, this becomes "Left Munich at 8.35 P.M., on 1st May, arriving at Vienna early next morning; should have arrived at 6.46, but train was an hour late" (1:1).

206. The first mention of one of the most memorable scenes in the novel testifies to the advancement of the plot.

207. "What I saw was the Count's head coming out from the window. I did not see the face, but I knew the man by the neck and the movement of his back and arms. In any case I could not mistake the hands which I had had so many opportunities of studying. I was at first interested and somewhat amused, for it is wonderful how small a matter will interest and amuse a man when he is a prisoner. But my very feelings changed to repulsion and terror when I saw the whole man slowly emerge from the window and begin to crawl down the castle wall over that dreadful abyss, *face down*, with his cloak spreading out around him like great wings. At first I could not believe my eyes. I thought it was some trick of the moonlight, some weird effect of shadow; but I kept looking, and it could be no delusion. I saw the fingers and toes grasp the corners of the stones, worn clear of the mortar by the stress of years, and by thus using every projection and inequality move downwards with considerable speed, just as a lizard moves along a wall.

footnotes continue on page 99

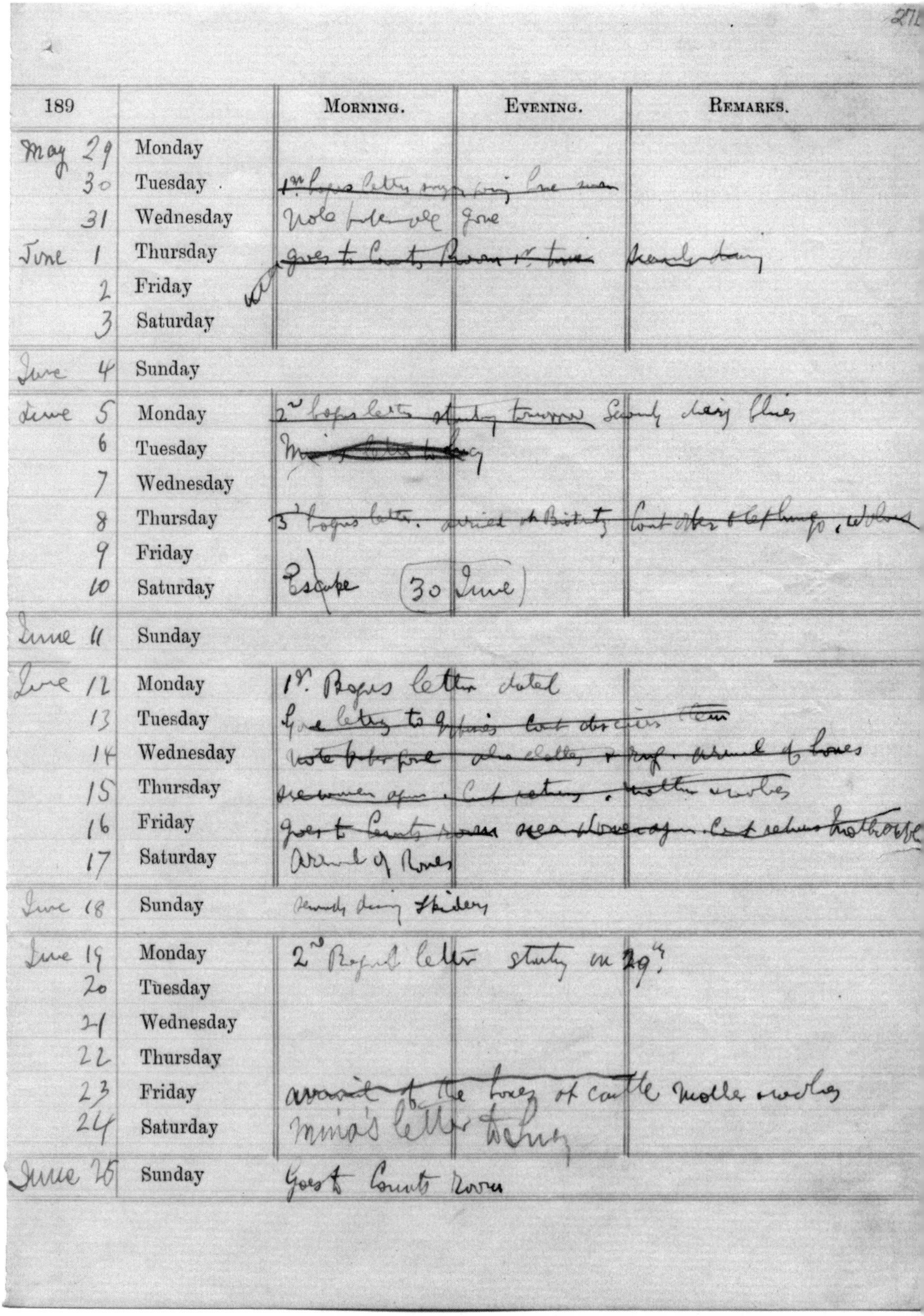

27

189		Morning.	Evening.	Remarks.
May 29	Monday			
30	Tuesday	~~1st bogus letter saying going home~~		
31	Wednesday	Note following	gone	
June 1	Thursday	~~goes to Count's Room 1st time~~		~~search for diary~~
2	Friday			
3	Saturday			
June 4	Sunday			
June 5	Monday	~~2nd bogus letter starting tomorrow~~		Seward's diary flies
6	Tuesday	~~Mina's letter to Lucy~~		
7	Wednesday			
8	Thursday	~~3rd bogus letter. arrived at Bistritz~~		~~Count takes off clothes, wolves~~
9	Friday			
10	Saturday	Escape	(30 June)	
June 11	Sunday			
June 12	Monday	1st. Bogus letter dated		
13	Tuesday	~~Gives letters to Szgany Count discovers them~~		
14	Wednesday	~~Note before ... also clothes, & bag. Arrival of boxes~~		
15	Thursday	~~Sees women again. Count returns. mother wolves~~		
16	Friday	~~Goes to Count's room sees box again. Count returns to the house~~		
17	Saturday	Arrival of Boxes		
June 18	Sunday	Seward's diary Spiders		
June 19	Monday	2nd Bogus letter starting on 29th		
20	Tuesday			
21	Wednesday			
22	Thursday			
23	Friday	~~arrival of the~~ boxes at castle mother wolves		
24	Saturday	Mina's letter to Lucy		
June 25	Sunday	Goes to Count's Room		

Page 42. Rosenbach #27b. Size: 8½ × 6.

MAY

29		
30	TU	<1st bogus letter saying going home soon>
31	W	note paper all gone[211]

JUNE

1	TH	<goes to Count's room 1st time>[212] <Seward's diary>
2		
3		
4		
5	M	<2nd bogus letter — starting tomorrow> Seward's diary ° flies[213]
6	TU	<Mina's letter to Lucy>
7		
8	TH	<3rd bogus letter — arrived at Bistritz — Count offers to let him go. Wolves>
9		
10	SA	Escape (30 June)
11		
12	M	1st bogus letter dated
13	TU	<Give letters to Gypsies — Count discovers them>
14	W	<note paper gone — also clothes & rug — arrival of boxes>
15	TH	<see women again — Count returns — mother & wolves>
16	F	<goes to Count's room — sees women again — Count returns — mother & wolves>
17	S	Arrival of boxes
18	SU	Seward's diary — Spiders
19	M	2nd bogus letter — starting on 29th
20		
21		
22		
23	F	<arrival of the boxes at castle> — Mother & wolves[214]
24	SA	Mina's letter to Lucy
25	SU	Goes to Count's room

"What manner of man is this, or what manner of creature is it in the semblance of man?" (3:35).

208. An arrow indicates that events which were to have taken place on 13 May now occur on 20 May.

209. "The phantom shapes, which were becoming gradually materialised from the moonbeams, were those of the three ghostly women to whom I was doomed" (4:46).

210. This is the first occurrence of the surname "Morris." As Leatherdale points out, "several film versions fuse Morris and Holmwood into a single personality" (*Novel & Legend* 126).

211. "Every scrap of paper was gone, and with it all my notes, my memoranda relating to railways and travel, my letter of credit, in fact all that might be useful to me were I once outside the castle" (4:44).

212. "There, in one of the great boxes, of which there were fifty in all, on a pile of newly dug earth, lay the Count! He was either dead or asleep, I could not say which — for the eyes were open and stony, but without the glassiness of death — and the cheeks had the warmth of life through all their pallor, and the lips were as red as ever. But there was no sign of movement, no pulse, no breath, no beating of the heart" (4:49).

213. On 5 June, Dr. Seward muses: "His [Renfield's] redeeming quality is a love of animals, though,

footnotes continue on page 101

28a

189		Morning.	Evening.	Remarks.
June 26	Monday	~~3rd Bistritz letter~~	Count goes [illegible]	to wolves.
27	Tuesday			
28	Wednesday		date of 3rd Bistritz	letter
29	Thursday		~~3rd Bistritz letter~~	~~dated~~
30	Friday	Escape	~~3rd [illegible]~~	
July 1	Saturday	Seward diary	notebook	
July 2	Sunday			
July 3	Monday			
4	Tuesday	Jonathan at hospice		
5	Wednesday			
6	Thursday	Off from Varna		
7	Friday			
8	Saturday	Seward diary	sparrows	
July 9	Sunday			
July 10	Monday			
11	Tuesday	Bosphorus		
12	Wednesday			
13	Thursday	Off Matapan		
14	Friday	uneasiness on ship		
15	Saturday			
July 16	Sunday	Man missing		
July 17	Monday	[illegible] to skipper		
18	Tuesday	& searched ship		
19	Wednesday	Seward diary wants a	Cat	
20	Thursday	Seward diary eats	birds	
21	Friday			
22	Saturday	Passed Gibraltar		
July 23	Sunday	man missing		

Page 43. Rosenbach #28a. Size: 8½ × 6.

JUNE

26	M	<3rd bogus letter> Count offers to let go — wolves
27		
28	W	date of 3rd bogus letter
29	TH	<3rd bogus letter dated>
30	F	escape — <Budapest>

JULY

1	SA	Seward's diary ° notebook
2		
3		
4	TU	Jonathan at hospice[215]
5		
6	TH	off from Varna[216]
7		
8	SA	Seward's diary ° sparrows
9		
10		
11	TU	Bosphorus
12		
13	TH	off Matapan
14	F	uneasiness on ship
15		
16	SU	man missing
17	M	<Mina's journal — Whitby>
18	TU	searched ship
19	W	Seward's diary ° wants a cat[217]
20	TH	Seward's diary ° eats birds[218]
21		
22	SA	passed Gibraltar
23	SU	man missing

indeed, he has such curious turns in it that I sometimes imagine he is only abnormally cruel. His pets are of odd sorts. Just now his hobby is catching flies" (6:70).

214. "As I sat I heard a sound in the courtyard without — the agonised cry of a woman. I rushed to the window, and throwing it up, peered out between the bars. There, indeed, was a woman with dishevelled hair, holding her hands over her heart as one distressed with running. She was leaning against a corner of the gateway. When she saw my face at the window she threw herself forward, and shouted in a voice laden with menace, 'Monster, give me my child!' …

"Somewhere high overhead, probably on the tower, I heard the voice of the Count calling in his harsh, metallic whisper. His call seemed to be answered from far and wide by the howling of wolves. Before many minutes had passed a pack of them poured, like a pent-up dam when liberated, through the wide entrance into the courtyard.

"There was no cry from the woman, and the howling of the wolves was but short. Before long they streamed away singly, licking their lips" (4:46–47).

215. Mina receives news of Jonathan in a letter from Sister Agatha at the Hospital of St. Joseph and

footnotes continue on page 103

286

189		Morning.	Evening.	Remarks.
July 24	Monday	Library Bay of Biscay	[illegible] Whitby	
25	Tuesday			
26	Wednesday			
27	Thursday			
28	Friday	Still storm but clearing		
29	Saturday	Storm warning		
July 30	Sunday	2 men missing		
July 31	Monday	~~Mina's [illegible] Whitby~~		
Augt 1	Tuesday	Fog		
2	Wednesday	one man overboard		
3	Thursday	mate overboard		
4	Friday	Captain ties himself to wheel		
5	Saturday			
Augt 6	Sunday			
Augt 7	Monday	Wreck		
8	Tuesday			
9	Wednesday	~~Sister Agatha letter to Mina [illegible]~~		~~Sleepwalking~~
10	Thursday	Lucy tries to get out. See Captain buried. Sleepwalking		
11	Friday	bat outside Lucy's window		
12	Saturday	Sister Agatha writes Mina		~~Lucy [illegible]~~
Augt 13	Sunday			
Augt 14	Monday	Lucy at window — bat		
15	Tuesday	~~[illegible]~~		
16	Wednesday			
17	Thursday	Boxes to London. Carter Paterson advised		
18	Friday	Mina's Diary Lucy well but night		Boxes arrive. [illegible]
19	Saturday	Mina's diary Sister Agatha's letter		arrives. Seward's Diary
Augt 20	Sunday	Dr Seward's Diary		

Page 44. Rosenbach #28b. Size: 8½ × 6.

JULY

24 M entering Bay of Biscay ° Mina's journal Whitby
25
26
27
28 F Still storm but clearing
29 SA man missing
30 SU 2 men missing
31 M <Mina's Journal ° Whitby>

AUGUST

1 TU Log
2 W one more overboard
3 TH Mate overboard
4 F Captain ties himself to wheel
5
6
7 M Wreck
8
9 W <Sister Agatha's letter to Mina Murray. Sleepwalking>
10 TH Lucy tries to get out. Sea captain buried.[219] Sleepwalking
11 F bat outside Lucy's window[220]
12 SA Sister Agatha writes Mina <Lucy leans out window — bat>
13
14 M Lucy at window — bat
15 TU <Mina's Diary — Sister Agatha's letter arrives in Exeter>
16
17 TH Boxes to London. Carter Paterson advised[221]
18 F Mina's Diary ° Lucy well last night. Boxes arrive. Flyman excited[222]
19 SA Mina's Diary ° Sister Agatha's letter arrives. Seward's Diary
20 SU Dr. Seward's Diary

Ste. Mary in Buda-Pesth: "I write by desire of Mr. Jonathan Harker, who is himself not strong enough to write, though progressing well, thanks to God and St. Joseph and Ste. Mary. He has been under our care for nearly six weeks, suffering from a violent brain fever. He wishes me to convey his love....

"He has had some fearful shock — so says our doctor — and in his delirium his ravings have been dreadful; of wolves and poison and blood; of ghosts and demons; and I fear to say of what" (8:101–102).

216. This entry will initiate the "Log of the Demeter" in chapter 7.

217. "When I came in he [Renfield] ran to me and said he wanted to ask me a great favour — a very, very great favour; and as he spoke he fawned on me like a dog. I asked him what it was, and he said, with a sort of rapture in his voice and bearing, 'A kitten, a nice, little, sleek playful kitten, that I can play with, and teach, and feed — and feed — and feed!'" (6:71).

218. "I looked around for his birds, and not seeing them, asked him where they were. He replied, without turning round, that they had all flown away. There were a few feathers about the room and on his pillow a drop of blood....

"The attendant has just been to me to say that Renfield has been very sick and has disgorged a whole

footnotes continue on page 105

29a

189		Morning.	Evening.	Remarks.
Augt 21	Monday	Carter Paterson	write close	
22	Tuesday			
23	Wednesday	~~Mina's letter~~ Seward's Diary		
24	Thursday	Lucy's diary dreaming again.		
25	Friday	do		
26	Saturday	Mina's letter to Lucy	married to Jonathan	
Augt 27	Sunday			
Augt 28	Monday			
29	Tuesday			
30	Wednesday	Lucy letter to Mina		
31	Thursday	Arthur letter to Seward / Seward to Lucy [illegible]		
Sept. 1	Friday	Arthur's wire to Seward		
2	Saturday	Seward's letter to Arthur / Van Helsing's letter to Seward		
Sept 3	Sunday	telegram Seward to Arthur / Van Helsing visits ~~Lucy~~ / letter Seward to Arthur		
Sept 4	Monday Seward's wire to Van Helsing	Seward's diary Flyman violent at sunset / Trollope's visit for Count)		
5	Tuesday	Seward's wire to Van Helsing / Lucy's words to Mina		
6	Wednesday	Count's letter to Pickford Seward's wire to Van Helsing. worse		
7	Thursday	Seward's diary. Van Helsing visits Lucy – transfusion of blood Arthur		
8	Friday	Seward's diary		
9	Saturday	do stays with Lucy. / Lucy's diary		
Sept 10	Sunday	Van Helsing arrives Lucy worse ~~transfusion~~ Seward		
Sept 11	Monday			
12	Tuesday Lucy's diary	Seward's visit Lucy – garlic arrives. mother opens window removes flo[wers]		
13	Wednesday	Seward's diary. Flyman waiting / transfusion Van Helsing		
14	Thursday			
15	Friday			
16	Saturday	~~Lucy's diary~~ + Lucy's window broken – Mina's letter to Lucy – Father		
Sept 17	Sunday	Lucy's diary / wolf escapes. / Seward's diary Flyman tries murder [illegible] wolf opens window – Lucy's memorandum to Van Helsing [illegible]		

Page 45. Rosenbach #29a. Size: 8½ × 6.

AUGUST

21	M	Carter Paterson wrote done
22		
23	W	<Mina's letter> Seward's Diary
24	TH	Lucy's diary ° dreaming again
25	F	[ditto]
26	SA	Mina's letter to Lucy ° married to Jonathan
27		
28		
29		
30	W	Lucy letter to Mina
31	TH	Arthur's letter to Seward ° Mina to Lucy ° going home tomorrow

SEPTEMBER

1	F	Arthur's wire to Seward
2	SA	Seward's letter to Arthur ° Van Helsing's letter to Seward
3	SU	telegram ° Seward to Arthur ° Van Helsing visits Lucy ° letter sent to Arthur
4	M	Seward's Diary — Flyman violent at sunset ° Trollope's[223] visit from Count
5	TU	Seward's wire to Van Helsing ° Lucy wrote to Mina
6	W	Count's letter to Pickford. Seward's wire to Van Helsing. Worse
7	TH	Seward's Diary. Van Helsing visit ° Lucy transfusion of blood[224] ° Arthur[225]
8	F	Seward's Diary
9	SA	[ditto] stays with Lucy. Lucy's diary
10	SU	Van Helsing arrives ° Lucy worse ° transfusion Seward
11		
12	TU	Lucy's diary. Seward visits Lucy — garlic arrives. Mother opens window ° removing flowers
13	W	Seward's Diary. Flyman ° waiting ° transfusion Van Helsing
14		
15		
16	SA	<Lucy's diary> L(uc)y at window xxx Mina's letter to Lucy xxx
17	SU	Lucy's diary ° Wolf escapes ° Seward's diary ° flyman tries murder Seward ° wolf opens window — Lucy's memorandum — Mrs. Westenra dies

---

lot of feathers. 'My belief is, doctor,' he said, 'that he has eaten his birds, and that he just took and ate them raw!'" (6:72).

219. According to Barbara Belford, "The Stokers watched the Grand Fete on the River Esk, an annual procession of decorated boats, and Stoker borrowed this image for the funeral of the *Demeter*'s captain" (225).

220. Mina writes, "Again I awoke in the night, and found Lucy sitting up in bed, still asleep, pointing to the window. I got up quietly, and pulling aside the blind, looked out. It was brilliant moonlight, and the soft effect of the light over the sea and sky — merged together in one great, silent mystery — was beautiful beyond words. Between me and the moonlight flitted a great bat, coming and going in great whirling circles. Once or twice it came quite close, but was, I suppose, frightened at seeing me, and flitted away across the harbour towards the Abbey" (8:96). Stoker chose to ignore the fact that the vampire bat is quite small. In contrast to many movies about "the lord of vampires," vampire bats do not fly around Dracula's castle either in the Notes or the novel.

221. "Herewith please receive invoice of goods sent by Great Northern Railway. Same are to be deliv-

footnotes continue on page 107

2 296

189		Morning.	Evening.	Remarks.
Sept 18	Monday	Mina letter & Lucy Hawkins dead. Poll well at the — silence of keeper Wolf returns		~~Seward's diary~~ Seward's diary
		4th transfusion Quincey Morris		
19	Tuesday	~~Mina's letter to Lucy~~ ~~Jonathan letter~~		Lucy dies. Crucifix stolen
		Mina letter & Lucy Hawkins dead		
20	Wednesday	Hawkins funeral — [illegible] attacks [illegible]		[illegible]
21	Thursday	~~Mina's letter to Lucy~~ Lucy Buried		Harker sees Dracula
22	Friday	Mina reads Jonathan's diary		
23	Saturday	Mina's diary Van Helsing writes to Mina		
Sept 24	Sunday			
Sept 25	Monday	Westminster Gazette children injured —		[illegible]
		Mina's diary Van Helsing's visit. Van H. gets the two diaries		
26	Tuesday	Jonathan's diary / Van Helsing sees Jonathan / Dr Seward's diary / Night visit to the tomb		
27	Wednesday	Dr. Seward's diary / Visit the tomb daylight —		
28	Thursday	fixed for Lucy's wedding day / night watching [illegible] tomb.		
29	Friday	Lucy's head cut off. [illegible] at Seward's		
30	Saturday	Jonathan arrives Seward's do Godalming & Morris. do Van Helsing		
Oct 1	Sunday	Explore Count's house		
Oct 2	Monday			
3	Tuesday			
4	Wednesday	Count leaves		
5	Thursday	~~Leave for Varna~~		
6	Friday			
7	Saturday			
Oct 8	Sunday	~~Arrive Varna 3.48 P.m~~		
Oct 9	Monday			
10	Tuesday			
11	Wednesday			
12	Thursday	Leave for Varna.		
13	Friday			
14	Saturday			
Oct 15	Sunday	Arrive Varna 3.48 P.m.		

Page 46. Rosenbach #29b. Size: 8½ × 6.

SEPTEMBER

18 M Mina's letter to Lucy ° Hawkins dead — Seward's diary — Pall Mall article — interview of keeper ° wolf returns ° <Seward's diary> Seward's diary
4th transfusion Quincey Morris
19 TU <Mina's letter to Lucy. Settled Jonathan returns> Lucy dies ° Crucifix stolen
<Mina's letter to Lucy Hawkins death>
20 W report Hennessey to Seward — Flyman attacks carriers ° Arthur xxx
21 TH <Mina's letter to Lucy> Lucy Buried — Harker sees Dracula — Hawkins Burial
22 F Mina reads Jonathan's Diary
23 S Mina's diary ° Van Helsing writes to Mina
24
25 M Westminster Gazette ° children injured — one just found ° Wire Mina to Van Helsing
Mina's decision ° Van Helsing's visit. Van H gets the two diaries
26 T Jonathan Harker's diary ° Van Helsing sees Pall Mall[226] ° Dr. Seward's Diary ° Night visit to the tomb
27 W Dr. Seward's Diary ° Visit the tomb daylight
28 TH fixed for Lucy's wedding day ° night — Lucy returns to tomb
29 F Lucy's head cut off.[227] <Lucy> Mina arrives at Seward's
30 S Jonathan arrives Seward's ditto Godalming[228] & Morris. ditto Van Helsing

OCTOBER

1 SU Explore Count's house
2
3
4 W Count leaves
5 TH <leave for Varna>
6
7
8 SU <arrive Varna 3:48 PM>
9
10
11
12 TH leave for Varna
13
14
15 SU arrive Varna 3:48 PM

---

ered at Carfax, near Purfleet, immediately on receipt at goods station King's Cross. The house is at present empty, but enclosed please find keys, all of which are labeled" (8:98–99).

222. "This time he had broken out through the window of his room, and was running down the avenue. I called to the attendants to follow me, and ran after him, for I feared he was intent on some mischief. My fear was justified when I saw the same cart which had passed before coming down the road, having on it some great wooden boxes.... The patient rushed at them, and pulling one of them off the cart, began to knock his head against the ground. If I had not seized him just at the moment I believe he would have killed the man there and then. The other fellow jumped down and struck him over the head with the butt-end of his heavy whip. It was a terrible blow; but he did not seem to mind it, but seized

footnotes continue on page 109

30a

189		Morning.	Evening.	Remarks.
Oct 16	Monday			
17	Tuesday			
18	Wednesday			
19	Thursday			
20	Friday			
21	Saturday			
Oct 22	Sunday			
Oct 23	Monday			
24	Tuesday			
25	Wednesday			
26	Thursday			
27	Friday	Telegram arrived	Galatz	
28	Saturday	telegram Czarina	Catherine arrived	Galatz
Oct 29	Sunday Leave Varna 6.30 am train through Rustchuk & Bucharest to Galatz			
Oct 30	Monday	arrive Galatz 1.20	am.	
31	Tuesday	all start up, Godalming	& Harker up	Sereth & Bistritza
Nov. 1	Wednesday	Seward & Morris up	river bank - Van	Helsing & Mina up rail to Veresti
2	Thursday	—		
3	Friday			
4	Saturday			
Nov 5	Sunday			
Nov 6	Monday			
7	Tuesday			
8	Wednesday			
9	Thursday			
10	Friday			
11	Saturday			
Nov 12	Sunday			

Page 47. Rosenbach #30a. Size: 8½ × 6.

16
17
18
19
20
21
22
23
24
25
26
27 F telegram ° arrived Galatz[229]
28 S telegram ° Czarina Catherine[230] arrived Galatz
29 SU leave Varna 6.30 AM—travel through xxx & Bucharest to Galatz
30 M arrive Galatz 1.20 AM
31 T all start <up> Godalming & Jonathan up Sireth and Bistritza—Seward and Morris up river Pruth—Van Helsing and Mina up land to Veresti.[231]

NOVEMBER[232]

1
2
3
4
5
6
7
8
9
10
11
12

---

him also, and struggled with the three of us.... At first he was silent in his fighting; but as we began to master him, and the attendants were putting a strait waistcoat on him, he began to shout: 'I'll frustrate them! They shan't rob me! They shan't murder me by inches! I'll fight for my Lord and Master!' and all sorts of similar incoherent ravings. It was with very considerable difficulty that they got him back to the house and put him in the padded room" (12:159).

223. Who is Trollope? (Or "Trollofe?") Like Pickford, who appears two lines later, this is the only time he is mentioned in the Notes.

224. Sage observes, "'Blood' in this novel is a grotesque pun, which brings together several different mythic associations" (52).

225. This is the first of four blood transfusions Lucy receives. Note that the existence of blood types was not discovered until the twentieth century.

226. The *Pall Mall Gazette* carried the story of the wolf that escaped from the Zoo.

227. "Arthur placed the point over the heart, and as I looked I could see its dint in the white flesh. Then he struck with all his might.

"The Thing in the coffin writhed; and a hideous, blood-curdling screech came from the opened red

footnotes continue on page 111

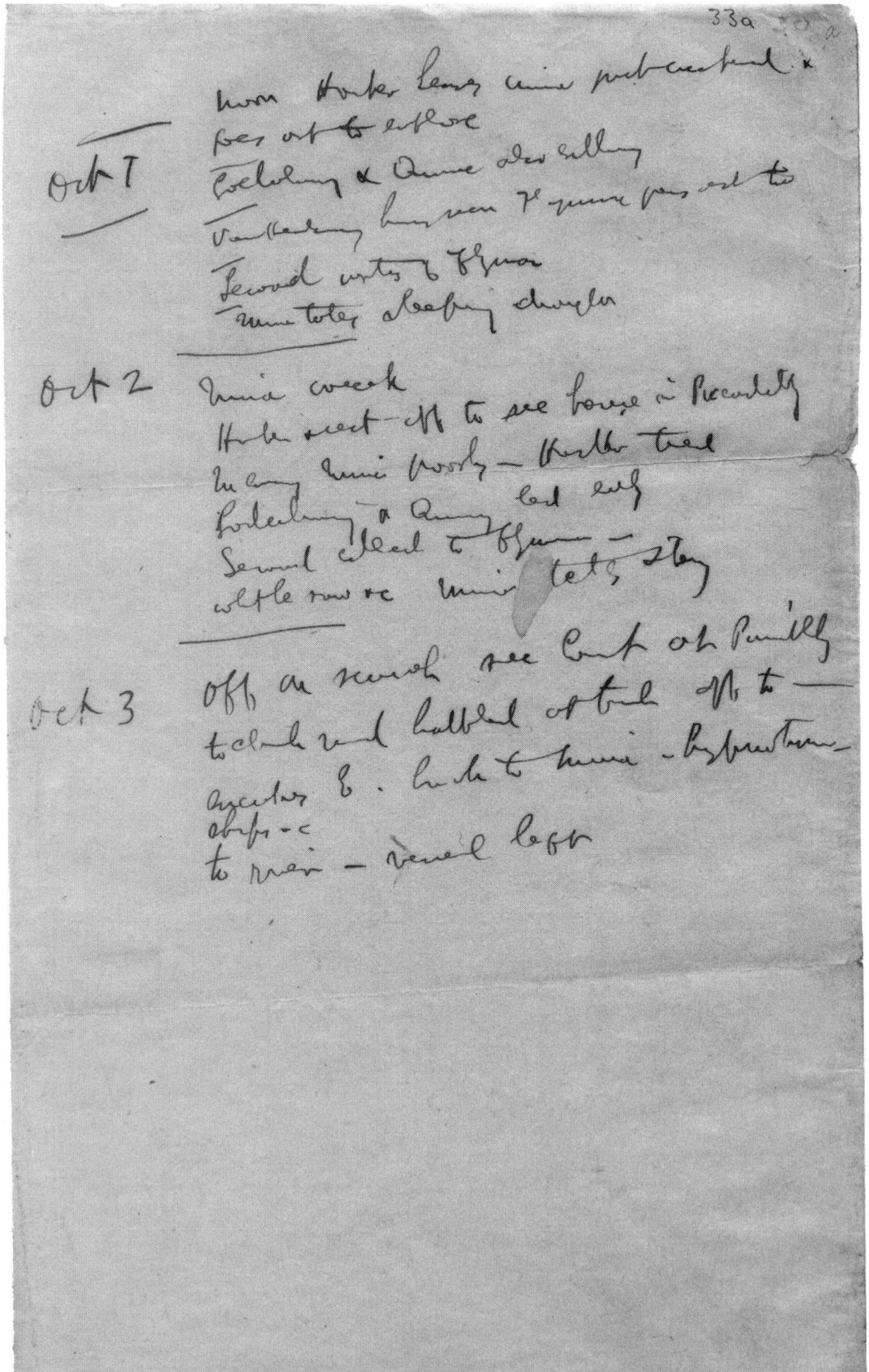
33a

Oct 1 morn Harker leaves Mina [illegible]
goes out to explore
Godalming & Quincey also sallying
Van Helsing [illegible] Quincey goes out to
Seward writes to [illegible]
Mina tells sleeping [illegible]

Oct 2 Mina [illegible]
Harker went off to see house in Piccadilly
In evening Mina poorly — Harker tired
Godalming & Quincey [illegible]
Seward called to [illegible] —
[illegible] Mina tells story

Oct 3 Off on search see Count at Piccadilly
[illegible] off to —
[illegible] to Mina — [illegible]
[illegible]
to river — [illegible] left

Page 48. Rosenbach #33a. Size: 8⅜ × 5¼.

Oct. 1

noon — Harker leaves Mina much weakened & goes out to explore
Godalming & Quincey also willing
Van Helsing has seen Flyman ° goes out too
Seward writes of flyman
Mina takes sleeping draught

Oct. 2

Mina weak
Harker & rest off to see house in Piccadilly
In evening Mina poorly — Harker tired
Godalming & Quincey bed early
Seward called to flyman
Whistle xxx — Mina tells story[233]

Oct. 3

off on search — see Count at Piccadilly
to Church yard baffled at tomb off to — xxx E. back to Mina — by xxx ships
to river — vessel left

---

lips. The body shook and quivered and twisted in wild contortions; the sharp white teeth champed together till the lips were cut, and the mouth was smeared with a crimson foam. But Arthur never faltered. He looked like a figure of Thor as his untrembling arm rose and fell, driving deeper and deeper the mercy-bearing stake, whilst the blood from the pierced heart welled and spurted up around it. His face was set, and high duty seemed to shine through it; the sight of it gave us courage so that our voices seemed to ring through the little vault.

"And then the writhing and quivering of the body became less, and the teeth seemed to champ, and the face to quiver. Finally it lay still. The terrible task was over....

"[T]he professor and I sawed the top off the stake, leaving the point of it in the body. Then we cut off the head and filled the mouth with garlic" (16:220–222).

228. As the eldest or only son of Lord Godalming, the Hon. Arthur Holmwood assumes the title after his father dies.

229. Galatz is a Romanian port on the Danube.

230. Dracula arrives in England on a ship named after a Greek fertility goddess (the "Demeter") and returns to his homeland on a vessel named after the promiscuous Russian monarch, Catherine the Great.

231. The Rosenbach page numbers 30b, 31a and 31b continue the calendar format from 13 November to 4 February; however, Stoker made no entries.

232. The calendar has no entries for the final six days of the novel (1–6 November).

233. "With a mocking smile, he [Dracula] placed one hand upon my shoulder and, holding me tight, bared my throat with the other, saying as he did so: 'First, a little refreshment to reward my exertions. You may as well be quiet; it is not the first time, or the second, that your veins have appeased my thirst!' I was bewildered, and, strangely enough, I did not want to hinder him. I suppose it is a part of the horrible curse that such is, when his touch is on the victim. And oh, my God, my God, pity me! He placed his reeking lips upon my throat!" (21:295).

Vienna Drac

28.12.95

Harker takes back [illegible] sent to Munich — (this is an experiment of travel of Drac.

visit at ship

reason out that he wants to escape —

Van H. shows that Drac [illegible] folder in time and finds that he can [illegible] now [illegible]

24/11/96

Real [illegible] of Harker [illegible] of [illegible] —

[illegible] Harker [illegible] the must go after Drac.

Look closer at end in Castle

[illegible] vessel [illegible]

[illegible] face

[illegible]

At Piccadilly [illegible]

at Piccadilly

17/3/96

[illegible] 29. telegram to Varna. [illegible]

[illegible] — [illegible] Galatz. [illegible] Time. [illegible] agent [illegible] Varna [illegible] Castle. [illegible] Vulcano [illegible]

R. Sereth

R Bistritza runs into Sereth

— at Fundu

between Strasha & Isvorol

— is 47 E Long

& 25¾ N. Lat

[illegible] at Fundu

— Deaths Head moth : Deaths Head moth

= Acherontia atropos

(of Sphinges) = Acherontia atropos of Sphinges

5/4/96

Mem. Prof. on operation of Brain [illegible]

Page 49. Rosenbach #33b.[234] Size: 5 × 8. Landscape.

Memo Drac

28.12.95

Harker takes back his report to xxx This is an experiment of travel of Drac
mist at ship
reason out that he wants to escape
Van H. shows that Drac gets bolder in time and finds out he can shift his own earth etc.

24/11/95

Red mark of Host on forehead of Mina
Mina tells Harker at sunset
Must go after Drac.
Look down at end on Castle & see figures vanish in river
Sunset glows on Mina's face & shows red mark gone
<at Piccadilly> at Piccadilly[235] xxx xxx xxx to

17/3/96 Chap 29[236]

Telegram to Varna. Ship at Bosphorus — delay — wire arrived Galatz, hurry there ° box out taken on shore <at night> & given to agent (sent up Pruth by Slovaks on return) ° Mina tells hurry & xxx. Still on water running against them — some follow in steam launch — Count can't leave over running water — make apparent earlier in story. Others control Sereth and others go to Bistritz as certain from telegram. xxx xxx xxx go to Dracula's Castle. All arrive near sunset, wolves. Snow ° Tzgany fight ° volcano, red light — no scar

R Sereth
R Bistritza runs into Sereth at Fundu between Straska & Isvorol
Is 47 E Long
25 ¾ N Lat

Deaths Head Moth
Acherontia atropos of sphinges[237]

Memo[238]

Prof in speaking of Drac's brain growth speaks of the heart-brain and the sense-brain — forever he is as a baby and has to learn all from the outside[239] — 5/4/96[240]

---

234. Rosenbach #33b consists of three columns.

235. This reference to Piccadilly in the context of Dracula's castle is a mystery.

236. At this point, the novel was to have 29 chapters; later, it had at least 31.

237. Renfield tells of Dracula's promises: "'[J]ust as he used to send in the flies when the sun was shining. Great big fat ones with steel and sapphire on their wings; and big moths, in the night, with skull and cross-bones on their backs.' Van Helsing nodded to him as he whispered to me unconsciously,

"'The Acherontia Atropos of the Sphinges — what you call the 'Death's-head moth!'" (21:286).

238. The segment that begins with "Memo / Prof in speaking of Drac's brain..." is part of the third column; it was entered in pencil, then rewritten upside-down in pen.

239. Van Helsing observes, "This criminal has not full man-brain. He is clever and cunning and resourceful; but he be not of man-stature as to brain. He be of child-brain in much...."

Mina adds, "The Count is a criminal and of criminal type. Nordau and Lombroso would so classify him, and *quâ* criminal he is of an imperfectly formed mind. Thus, in a difficulty he has to seek resource in habit....

"Then, as he is criminal he is selfish; and as his intellect is small and his action is based on selfishness, he confines himself to one purpose. That purpose is remorseless" (25:351–353).

240. 5 April 1896 is the latest date in the Notes.

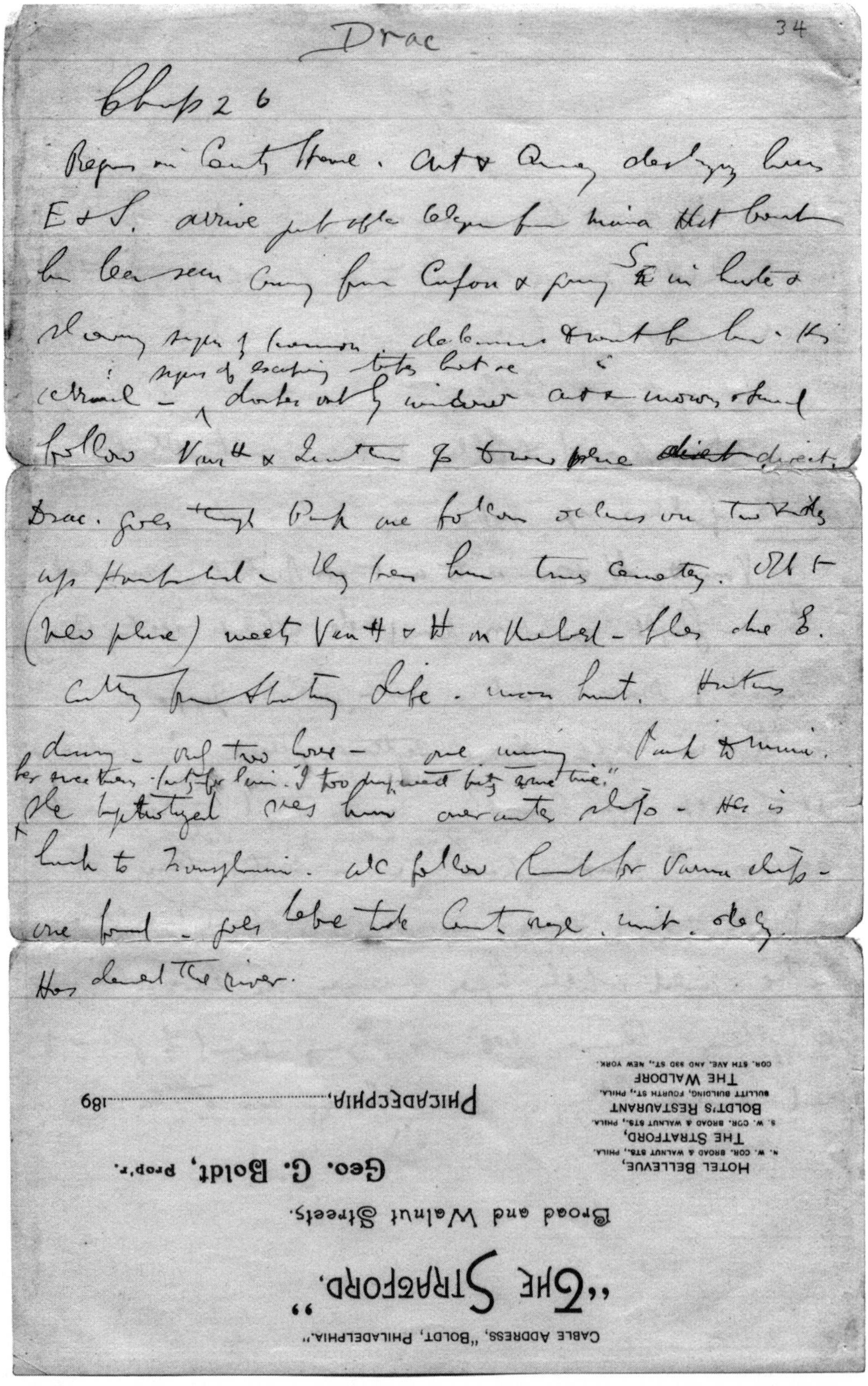

Drac 34

Chap 26

Reports in County House. Art & Quincey destroying boxes

E & S. arrive just after. Telegram from Mina that Count

has been seen coming from Carfax & going S in haste &

showing signs of humour, [illegible] & want of [illegible].

signs of escaping [illegible]

[illegible] — doctor out of window. Art & Morris & [illegible]

follow VanH & [illegible] to new place direct.

Drac. goes through Park one follows others on two [illegible]

up [illegible] they trace him [illegible] Cemetery. [illegible]

(new place) meets VanH & H on [illegible] — [illegible]

Cutting for Shooting [illegible] — man hurt. Harkers

dinner — only two boxes — one missing. Back to Mina.

her sweetness — faith for him. "I too prepared [illegible] some time."

She hypnotised says him aboard ship — He is

back to Transylvania. We follow. Look for Varna ship —

one found — goes [illegible] take Count [illegible]

Has dared the river.

CABLE ADDRESS, "BOLDT, PHILADELPHIA."

"THE STRATFORD."

Broad and Walnut Streets.

Geo. C. Boldt, Prop'r.

PHILADELPHIA, ...189

HOTEL BELLEVUE, N. W. COR. BROAD & WALNUT STS., PHILA.

THE STRATFORD, S. W. COR. BROAD & WALNUT STS., PHILA.

BOLDT'S RESTAURANT, BULLITT BUILDING, FOURTH ST., PHILA.

THE WALDORF, COR. 5TH AVE. AND 33D ST., NEW YORK.

Page 50. Rosenbach #34. Size: 9 × 5½.[241]

Drac.

Chap. 26

Begins in Count's house. Art & Quincey destroying lairs E. & S. ° arrive just after telegram from Mina that Count has been seen coming from Carfax[242] & going <E> S in haste & showing signs of passion. Determined to wait for him. His arrival — signs of escaping ° takes xxx doctor out by window — Art Morris & Seward follow Van H. & Jonathan go to the place <direct> direct — Drac goes through park ° we follow others on two sides up Hampstead — they follow him through cemetery.[243]

Oct. 5. (new place) meet Van H. & H. on threshold — flees due E. — cutting from Sporting Life[244] — man hurt. Harker's diary — only two boxes ° one missing. Back to Mina. Her sweetness pity for him.[245] "I too may need pity some time."[246] She hypnotized[247] ° sees him over water ship — He is back to Transylvania. We follow Count for Varna ship — one found[248] — goes before tide ° Count's rage, mist, delay. Has cleared the river.

---

241. Pages 50 and 51 are written on blue-lined stationery from the Stratford Hotel on Broad and Walnut Streets in Philadelphia. Stoker visited this city with the Lyceum Theatre Company in the winters of 1894 and 1896. The Bellevue-Stratford Hotel, which occupied the same site, was notorious for the first outbreak of Legionnaire's disease in 1976.

242. After noting that Carfax ("Quatre Face") means "the place where four roads meet," Leatherdale continues, "It is under such sites that suicides were traditionally buried, since should they come back to life they would get lost, not knowing which direction to take" (*Dracula Unearthed* 50 n.109).

243. Many people assume that Lucy's tomb is in Highgate Cemetery, but we are never told where she is interred.

244. *Sporting Life* was a popular magazine that often carried items about Henry Irving and the Lyceum Theatre.

245. Mina expresses pity for the Count: "Jonathan dear, and you all my true, true friends, I want you to bear something in mind through all this dreadful time. I know that you must fight — that you must destroy even as you destroyed the false Lucy so that the true Lucy might live hereafter; but it is not a work of hate. That poor soul who has wrought all this misery is the saddest case of all. Just think what will be his joy when he too is destroyed in his worser part that his better part may have spiritual immortality. You must be pitiful to him too, though it may not hold your hands from his destruction" (23:317).

246. "Oh, hush! oh, hush! in the name of the good God. Don't say such things, Jonathan, my husband; or you will crush me with fear and horror. Just think, my dear — I have been thinking all this long, long day of it — that ... perhaps ... some day ... I too may need such pity; and that some other like you — and with equal cause for anger — may deny it to me!" (23:318).

247. "'I want you to hypnotise me!' she said. 'Do it before the dawn, for I feel that then I can speak, and speak freely. Be quick, for the time is short!' Without a word he motioned her to sit up in bed.

"Looking fixedly at her, he commenced to make passes in front of her, from over the top of her head downward, with each hand in turn. Mina gazed at him fixedly for a few minutes, during which my own heart beat like a trip hammer, for I felt that some crisis was at hand. Gradually her eyes closed, and she sat, stock still; only by the gentle heaving of her bosom could one know that she was alive. The Professor made a few more passes and then stopped, and I could see that his forehead was covered with great beads of perspiration. Mina opened her eyes; but she did not seem the same woman. There was a far-away look in her eyes, and her voice had a sad dreaminess which was new to me. Raising his hand to impose silence, the Professor motioned to me to bring the others in. They came on tip-toe, closing the door behind them, and stood at the foot of the bed, looking on. Mina appeared not to see them. The stillness was broken by Van Helsing's voice speaking in a low level tone which would not break the current of her thoughts" (23:320–321).

248. Presumably, a ship.

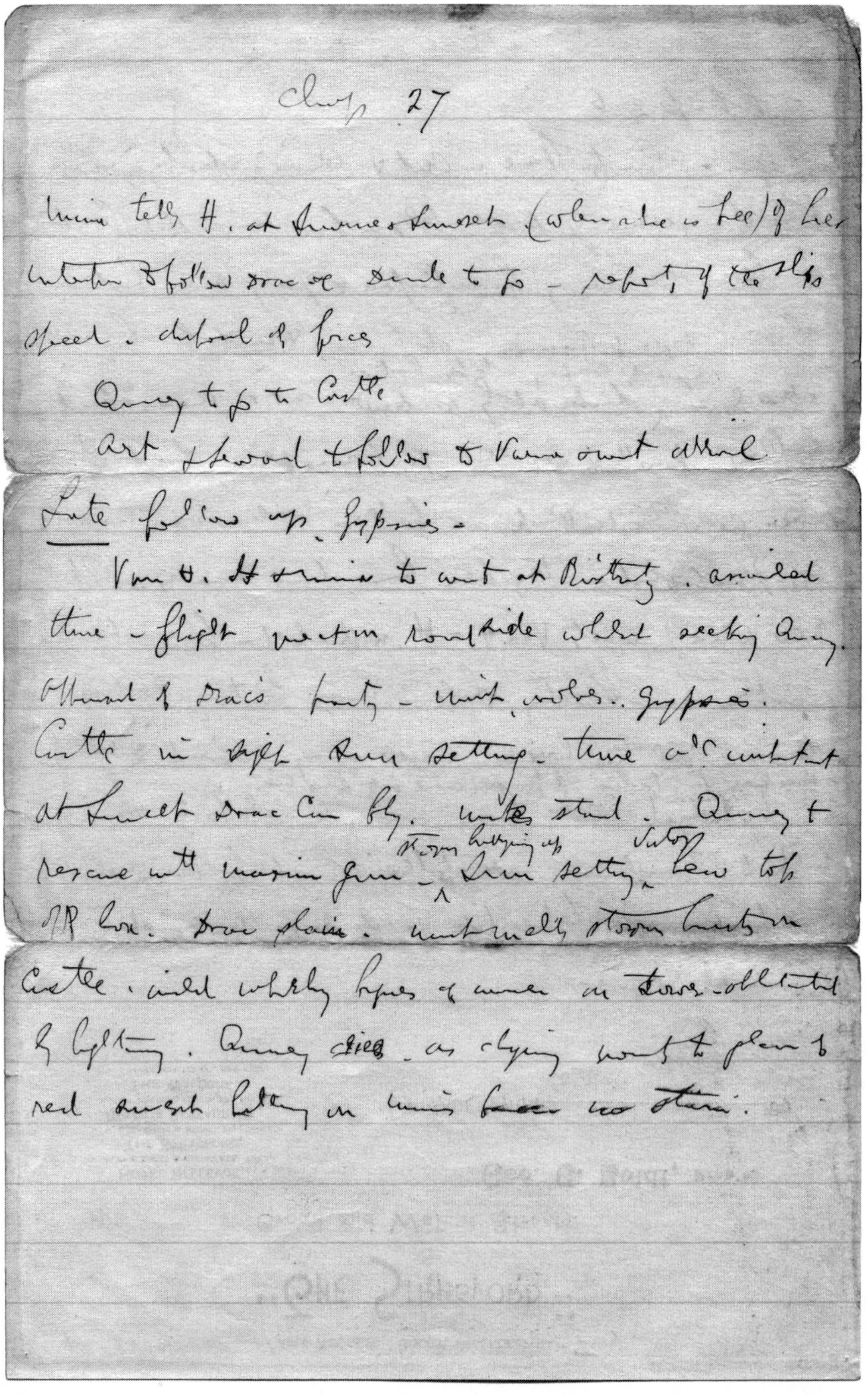

Chap 27

Mina tells H. at sunrise & sunset (when she is free) of her intention to follow Drac & decide to go — report of the ship's speed. disposal of forces

Quincey to go to Castle

Art & Seward to follow to Varna & await arrival

Later follow up Gypsies —

Van H. & Mina to wait at Bistritz. arrived there — flight met in roadside whilst seeking Quincey. Attack of Drac's party — mist, wolves. Gypsies. Castle in sight sun setting — time all important at sunset Drac can fly. wolves stand. Quincey to rescue with maxim gun — storm brewing up sun setting victory saw top off box. Drac plain. wind suddenly storm bursts on Castle. wild whirling figures of women in storm — obliterated by lightning. Quincey killed — as dying points to place of red sunlight lighting on Mina's ~~face~~ no stain.

Page 51. Rosenbach #34 verso. Size: 9 × 5½.

Chap 27

Mina tells H. at sunrise & sunset (when she is free) of her intention to follow Drac & Dracula to go — report of the ship's speed — dispersal of forces

Quincey to go to Castle.

Art & Seward to follow to Varna & wait arrival — Late follow up — gypsies

Van H. & Mina to wait at Bistritz — assembled there — flight meet in roadside whilst seeking Quincey — arrival of Drac's party — mist — wolves — gypsies

Castle in sight — sun setting — time all important ° at sunset Drac can fly. Makes stand. Quincey to rescue with maxim gun[249] — storm building up — sun setting ° victors hew top off box. Drac slain — mist melts — storm bursts on castle. Wild whirling figures of women on tower — obliterated by lightning.[250] Quincey dies[251] — as dying points to glow of red sunset hitting on Mina's face ° no stain

249. A maxim gun is a primitive type of machine gun. In the novel, the vampire hunters are armed with Winchester rifles.

250. In the final chapter of the novel, Professor Van Helsing will slay the vampire women in their graves, but a passage that was deleted from the typescript follows the Notes: "storm bursts on castle. Wild whirling figures of women on tower — obliterated by lightning" (538).

251. According to Warren, "[Change] the name of Buffalo Bill to Quincey Morris, and you have the novel's climax" (330).

Part II

Handwritten Research Notes ("'Dracula' Notes, etc.")

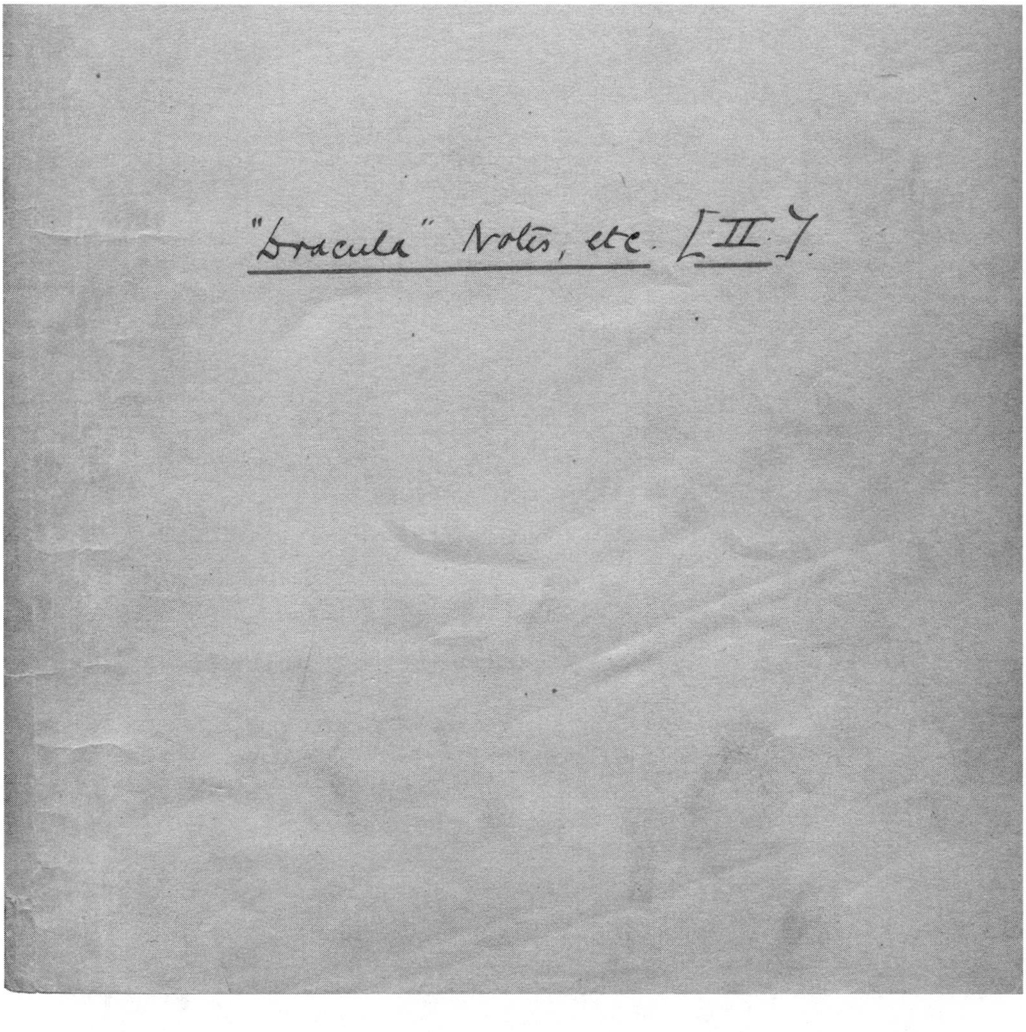

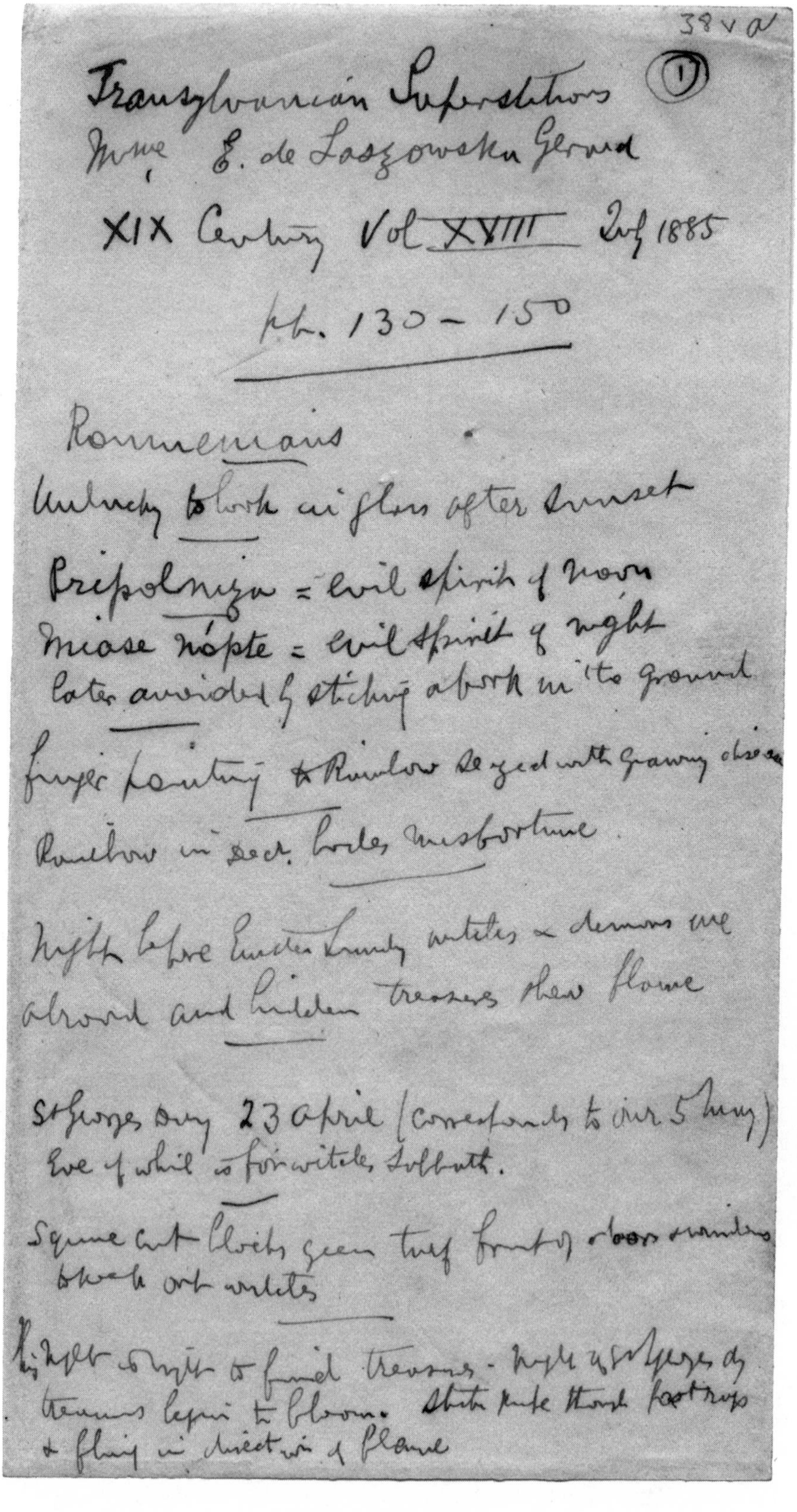

38 v a

(1)

Transylvanian Superstitions
Mme E. de Laszowska Gerard

XIX Century Vol XVIII July 1885

pp. 130–150

Roumenians
Unlucky to work in glass after sunset

Pripolnitza = evil spirit of noon
Miase nópte = evil spirit of night
latter avoided by sticking a fork in the ground

finger pointing to Rainbow seized with gnawing disease

Rainbow in sect. bodes misfortune.

Night before Easter Sunday witches & demons are abroad and hidden treasures show flame

St George's Day 23 April (corresponds to our 5 May)
Eve of which is for witches Sabbath.

Square cut clods green turf front of doors windows
block out witches

Night sought to find treasures – Night of St George's day
treasures begin to bloom. Stick knife through footsteps
& fling in direction of flame

Page 52. Rosenbach #38 verso a. Size: 6 × 3.

Mme. E. de Laszowska Gerard[252]
"Transylvanian Superstitions"[253]
Nineteenth Century XVIII (July 1885) 130–150

Roumenians[254]

Unlucky to look in glass after sunset

Pripolniza = evil spirit of noon

Miase nopte = evil spirit of night
latter avoided by sticking a fork in the ground

Finger pointing to rainbow seized with gnawing disease

Rainbow in Dec. bodes misfortune

Night before Easter Sunday witches & demons are abroad and hidden treasures then flame

St George's Day 23 April (corresponds to our 5 May) eve of which is for witches Sabbath

Square cut blocks green turf front of doors & windows to keep out witches

This night is right to find treasures — night of St George's Day treasures begin to bloom. Stick knife through foot rags & fling in direction of flames

Emily Gerard (courtesy Lokke Heiss).

252. Emily Gerard revised "Transylvanian Superstitions" in *The Land Beyond the Forest* (1888), but there is no evidence that Stoker consulted this book.
253. "Transylvanian Superstitions" was one of Stoker's most important sources of information about folklore. References to this article in his early Notes (p. 6, 8 and 11) prove that he read it before or shortly after he began writing the novel.
254. Other spellings of "Romanian" include "Rumanian" and "Roumanian."

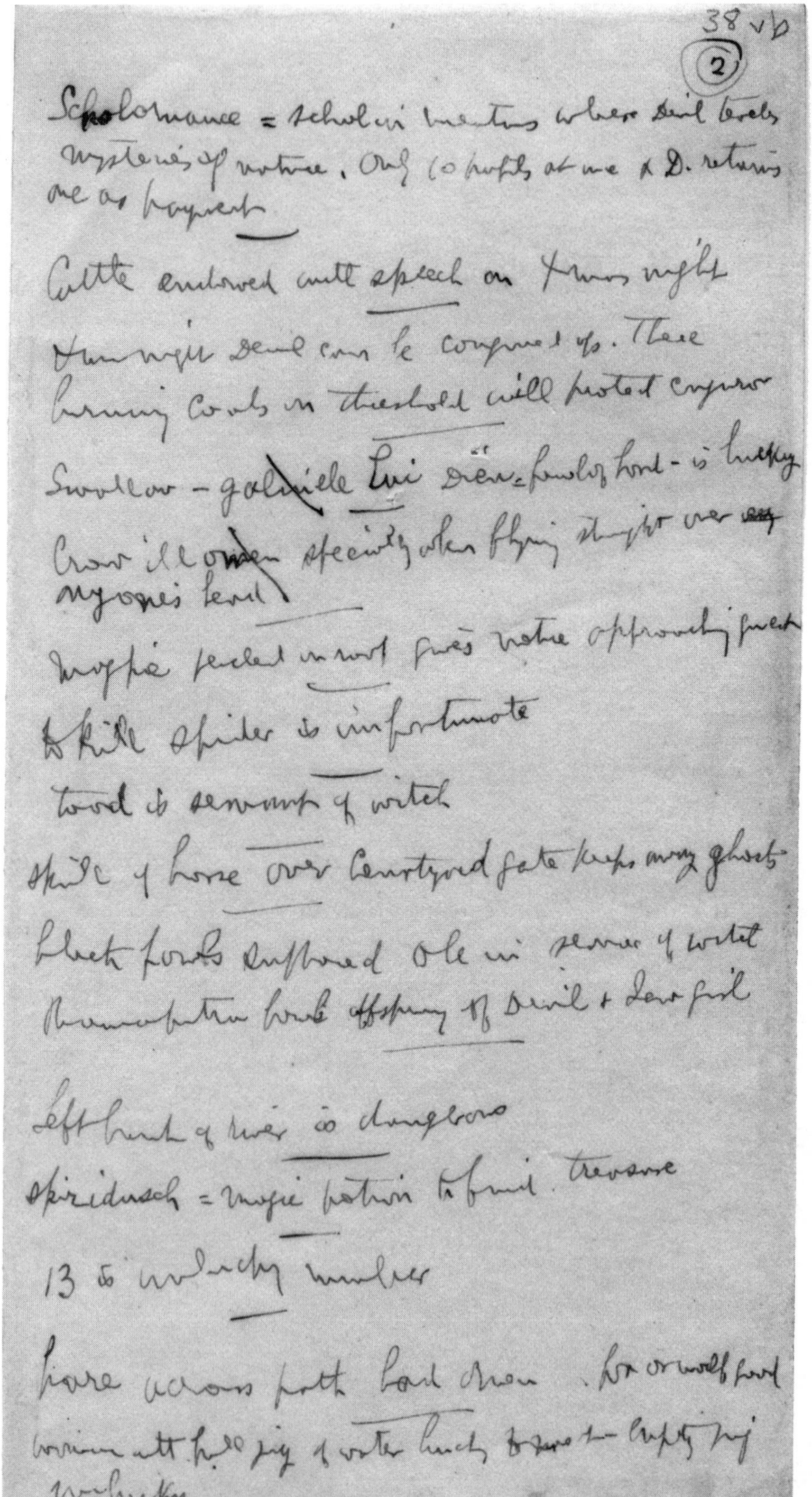

38 vb

(2)

Scholomance = school in mountains where Devil teaches mysteries of nature. Only 10 pupils at once & D. retains one as payment

Cattle endowed with speech on Xmas night

Xmas night devil can be conjured up. Three burning coals on threshold will protect against

Swallow – galuscele lui Dieu = fowl of Lord – is lucky

Crow ill omen specially when flying straight over anyone's head

Magpie perched on roof gives notice approaching guest

To kill spider is unfortunate

Toad is servant of witch

Skull of horse over courtyard gate keeps away ghosts

Black fowls supposed ole in service of witch

Brancapatura black offspring of Devil & Dear girl

Left bank of river is dangerous

Spiridusch = magic potion to find treasure

13 is unlucky number

Hare across path bad omen. Fox or wolf good

Woman with full jug of water lucky to meet – empty jug unlucky

Page 53. Rosenbach #38 verso b. Size: 6 × 3.

Scholomance = school in mountains where Devil teaches mysteries of nature. Only 10 pupils a time and D. retains one as payment[255]

Cattle endowed with speech on Xmas night

This night devil can be conjured up. Three burning coals on threshold will protect conjuror

Swallow — galinele lui dieu — fowl of Lord — is lucky

Crow ill omen specifically when flying straight over anyone's head·

Magpie perched on roof gives notice of approaching guest

To kill spider is unfortunate

Toad is servant of witch

Skull of horse over courtyard gate keeps away ghosts

Black fowls supposed to be in service of witch
Brahmapootra fowl offspring of devil & Jew girl

Left bank of river is dangerous

Spiridusch = magic potion to find treasure

13 is unlucky number

Hare across path bad omen — fox or wolf— good woman with full jug of water lucky ° to have empty jug unlucky

255. Van Helsing claims that "The Draculas … had dealings with the Evil One. They learned his secrets in the Scholomance, amongst the mountains over Lake Hermanstadt, where the devil claims the tenth scholar as his due" (18:246). Romanian folklorist Silvia Chitimia suggests that Gerard had heard of the Solomonari, who, according to local legend, had a school "located at the centre of the world" where students were instructed in the magic arts (143).

(3) 39a

wodna Zena = water spirit of spring
women won't draw water of spirit current or would
anger the spirit.

balaur or wodna muz = Cruel water spirit of
deep pools.

Mama padura = forest spirit. is good fairy

panusch — (Pan) is wood spirit lies in wait for maidens

Dschuma = spirit of plague — appears
as girl or hag

Roumanian must not die without lighted
Candle

Roumanians take it that death is only sleep
requiring waking.

Sometimes holes are cut in coffin opposite ears
of corpse so that can hear.

Vampire or nosferatu

To kill vampire drive stake through corpse or fire
pistol shot into coffin. or cut off head & place
in coffin with mouth full of garlic. or extract heart &
burn it & strew ashes over grave

Page 54. Rosenbach #39a. Size: 6 × 3¼.

wodna zena = water spirit of spring
women can't draw water against current or will anger the spirit

balaur or wodna muz = cruel water sprite — deep pools

mama padura = forest spirit is good fairy

panusch (Pan) is wood spirit lies wait for maidens

dschuma = spirit of plague — appears as girl or hag

Roumenian must not die without lighted candles

Roumenians take it that death is only sleep requiring cooking

sometimes holes are cut in coffin opposite ears of corpse so that can hear

vampire or nosferatu[256]: To kill vampire drive stake through corpse or fire pistol shot into coffin[257] or cut off head & replace in coffin with mouth full of garlic, or extract heart & burn it & strew ashes over grave

256. The description of the "nosferatu," which Gerard uses erroneously as a synonym for "vampire," is the only part of this page that worked its way into the novel.

257. The idea that a vampire can be slain by firing a pistol into a coffin seems odd today, for it is not part of what everybody-knows-about-vampires. Most societies have stories about creatures that rise from their graves to prey upon the living, but few of these revenants have had any effect on modern literature and cinema.

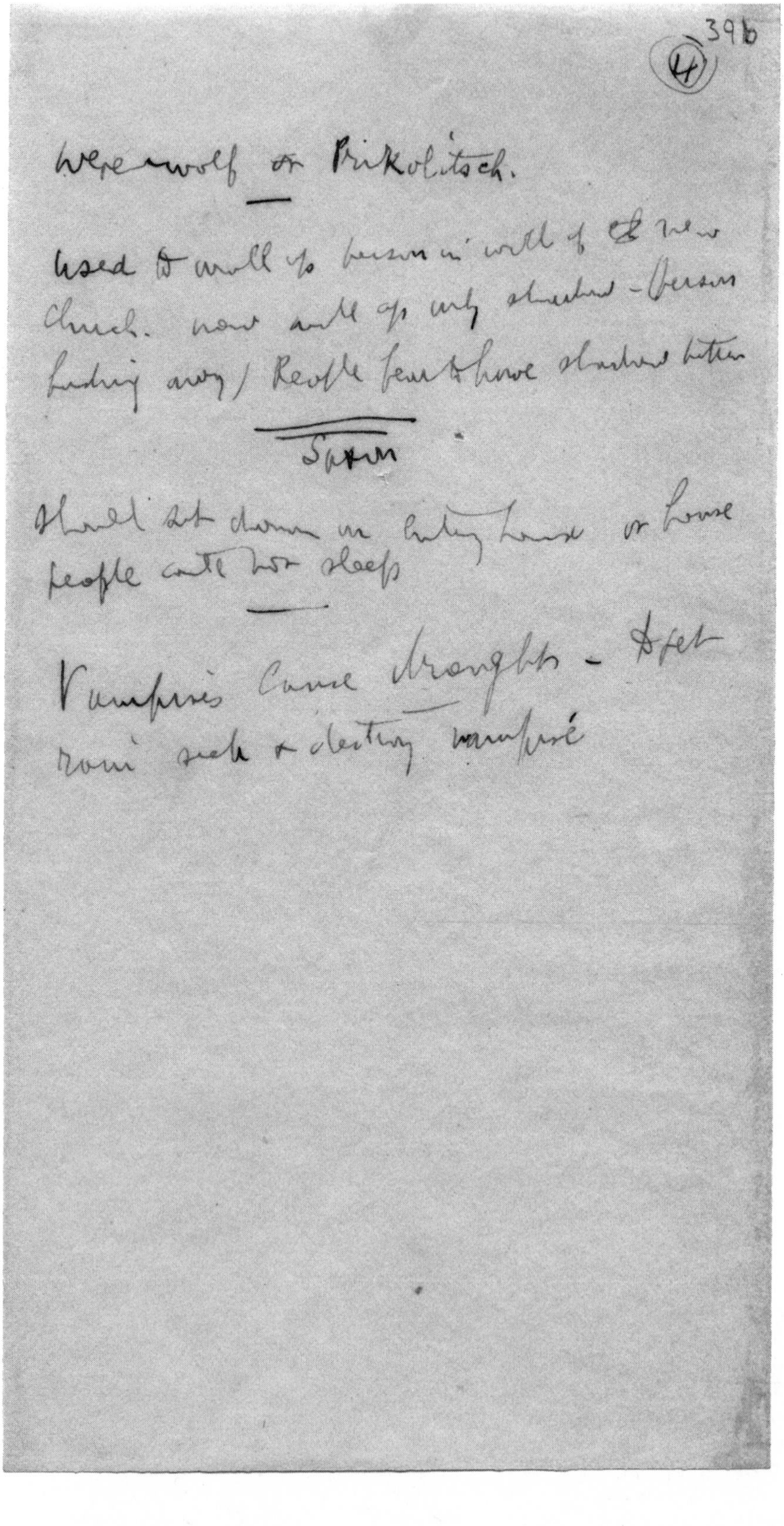

(4) 39b

Were-wolf or Prikolitsch.

Used to wall up person in wall of the new Church. now wall up only shadow — person fading away / People fear to have shadows taken

Saxon

Should sit down in entering house or house people cannot sleep

Vampires cause droughts — [illegible] room sick & destroy vampire

Page 55. Rosenbach #39b. Size: 6 × 3¼.

werewolf or prikolitsch

Used to wall up person in wall of new church. Now wall up only shadow — person hiding away. People fear to have shadow taken

Saxon[258]

Should sit down on entering house or house people will not sleep

Vampire cause droughts — to get rain seek and destroy vampire[259]

258. Although Gerard's article includes a long section on Saxon superstitions, Stoker took only two notes from it.

259. Stoker wisely chose not to burden his monster with certain folkloric traits. As Paul Barber points out, "If a typical vampire of folklore, not fiction, were to come to your house this Halloween, you might open the door to encounter a plump Slavic fellow with long fingernails and a stubbly beard, his mouth and left eye open, his face ruddy and swollen. He wears informal attire — in fact, a linen shroud — and he looks for all the world like a disheveled peasant" (*Vampires, Burial, and Death* 2).

43va

Book of Were Wolves — (Baring Gould)

werewolf or berserker had period of exhaustion after berserker fury P 45

were wolves meet night of Nativity of Christ P. 53

green taper with blue flame in Count's house P. 71

Canine teeth protruding ~~over~~ lower lip when mouth closed, pointed nails P 87 (F)

{told not to bite thumb nail of left hand which was longer than the other

{than others. & not to lose sight of the whilst werewolf (Jean Grenier) P. 94

Lycanthropy — men jump into water {spring / fountain} & come out wolves P. 105 & do to return to human shape

werewolf. has ~~broad~~ hands short fingers & has some hairs in hollow of hand P. 107 (F)

To free werewolf from bondage three times stabbing forehead with knife — or 3 drops of blood with needle P. 107

rising from tomb howls P. 107

eyebrows meeting over nose — ~~telling~~ or reproaching with fault of being w.w. sets free P 110 (F)

Page 56. Rosenbach #43 verso a. Size: 3 × 6. Landscape.

Rev. Sabine Baring-Gould[260]
The Book of Were-Wolves[261]
London: Smith, Elder, 1865

werewolf[262] or berserkir had period of exhaustion after berserkr [sic] fury p. 45

were wolves met night of Nativity of Christ p. 53

mem. Green taper with blue flame in Count's house p. 71[263]

canine teeth protruding over lower lip when mouth closed pointed nails p. 87[264]

told not to bite thumb nail of left hand which was longer xxx thicker than others & not to lose sight of it whilst werewolf (Jean Grenier) p. 94[265]

Lycanthropy—men jump into spring water fountain & come out wolves p. 105 & [ditto] to return to human shape

werewolf has broad hands, short fingers & has some hairs in hollow of hand p. 107

to liberate werewolf from bondage three times stabbing forehead with knife or 3 drops of blood into needle p. 107

rising from tomb howls p. 107

eyebrows meeting over nose telling or reproaching with fact of being w.w. set free p. 110

---

260. Rev. Sabine Baring-Gould (1834–1924) is best remembered today for his hymn "Onward Christian Soldiers." His many accomplishments include the story "Margery of Quether" (*Cornhill Magazine*, April and May 1884) in which a simple farmer's life is slowly taken over by an ancient vampire that inhabits the ruined tower of an old church. A review of *Dracula* in the *Daily Mail* (1 June 1897) likened it to "Marjery [sic] of Quether."

261. Brian J. Frost notes that "Scholarly interest in werewolfery declined during the seventeenth and eighteenth centuries and wasn't rekindled until the middle of the nineteenth century, when Wilhelm Hertz's *Der Werwolf* (1862) and Sabine Baring-Gould's *The Book of Werewolves* ... brought the subject to the public's attention once more" (31–32).

262. Baring-Gould uses "were-wolf," but Stoker transcribes this word as "wehr wolf," "were wolf" or "werewolf" or with the abbreviation "ww."

263. "In a wood near Chastel Charnon we met with many others whom I did not recognize; we danced, and each [Satanist] had in his or her hand a green taper with a blue flame ... after I [Pierre Bourgot] had stripped myself, he [Michael Verdung] smeared me with a salve, and I believed myself then to be turned into a wolf" (Baring-Gould 71).

264. Stoker inserted the letter "F" in the margin next to the end of this line. Similar groups of letters appear throughout the Notes, especially in the typewritten section. They appear to be part of a haphazard system of organization.

265. Jean Grenier was a nineteenth-century French serial killer who claimed to be a werewolf.

43vb

Baring – Gould Were-wolf –

W.W. – no power ~~in~~ rage ~~field~~ P.112 (E)

Cast hat at w.w. no harm happen P.112

Girdle human skin changes man to w.w. P113

East Friesland of 7 girls running in family one is w.w. P 113

Among Bulgarians & Slovakians w w ~~is~~ called vrkolak like modern Greek Βρύκολακας – Greek w.w. is
(E) closely related to vampire – after death ~~of~~ werewolf spirit becomes vampire – Serbs connect vampire & w.w. together
& call them same name vlkoslak – rage is in winter – meet annually & hang wolfskins on trees –
power to become w.w. by drinking water settled in footprint in clay by wolf. Russian wawkalak is forbidden
w.w. – ~~about~~ among relations – must keep moving. Polish W.W. rage twice a year & midsummer P. 114-6

Golden horned moon P117

The dog serpent – the night mare P.119

Page 57. Rosenbach #43 verso b. Size: 3 × 6. Landscape.

Baring-Gould Were-wolf[266]

Ww.—no power in rye field—p. 112

Cast hat at ww. no harm happen p. 112

Girdle human skin changes man to ww. p. 113

East Friesland—if 7 girls succeeding in family, one is ww. p. 113

Among Bulgarians & Slovakians ww. is called vrkolak like modern [GREEK][267] Greek ww. is closely related to vampire—after death lycanthropist becomes vampire—Serbs connect vampire & ww. together & call them same name vlkoslak—rage is in winter, meet annually & hang wolfskins in trees

Power to become ww. by drinking water settled in footprint in clay by wolf

White Russian wawkalak is fatherless ww. sent among relations—must keep moving. Polish ww. rage twice Xmas & midsummer p. 114–6

golden horned moon p. 117

by day serpent—by night man p. 119[268]

---

266. As Douglas and Olshaker remark, "stories and legends about witches, werewolves and vampires ... may have been a way of explaining outrages so hideous that no one in the small and close-knit towns of Europe and early America could comprehend such perversities" (29–30).

267. Greek: "brykolakas" (or "brukolakas"); a werewolf or vampire.

268. *The Book of Were-Wolves* contains information about the Hungarian Countess Elizabeth Bathory (1560–1614): "Elizabeth ___ was wont to dress well in order to please her husband, and she spent half the day over her toilet. On one occasion, a lady's-maid saw something wrong in her head-dress, and as a recompense for observing it, received such a severe box on the ears that the blood gushed from her nose, and spirted [sic] on to her mistress's face. When the blood drops were washed off her face, her skin appeared much more beautiful—whiter and more transparent on the spots where the blood had been.

"Elizabeth formed the resolution to bathe her face and her whole body in human blood so as to enhance her beauty ..." (139–140).

Although Elizabeth Bathory is often portrayed as a "human vampire" today—and has been referred to as "Countess Dracula"—there is no proof that her story influenced the creation of *Dracula*.

39va

1 ⓪

Fishery Barometer Manual
Robt. H. Scott. M.A.; F.R.S
1887

P26
Buys Ballot's Law (of Utrecht)

Stand with your back to the wind and the barometer will be lower on your Left than on your Right.—This is for the Northern Hemisphere & the opposite being for Southern Hemisphere.

Thus the Wind may be expected to be:—

Easterly when pressure is highest	N & lowest	S
Southerly " " "	E " "	W
Westerly " " "	S " "	N
Northerly " " "	W. " "	E

[illegible]
P.27 "When the wind shifts against the sun" "Trust it not for back it doth run."

P.27 The Wind usually shifts "with the watch hands" i.e. from L to R in front of you. A change in this direction is called "Veering"

P.27 The West wind shifts to E through N.W.—N & N.E.—
If wind shifts in opposite way—by from W. to SW. S. & S.E. it is called "Backing" & generally indicates that a new storm is approaching [illegible]

Page 58. Rosenbach #39 verso a.[269] Size: 6 × 3¼.

Robert H. Scott[270]
Fishery Barometer Manual
London, HMSO, 1887

p. 26. Buys Ballot's Law (of Utrecht)

Stand with your back to the wind and the barometer will be lower on your left than on your right.—This is for the Northern Hemisphere—the opposite being for Southern Hemisphere.

Thus the wind may be expected to be[271]:

Easterly when pressure is highest N.—lowest S.
Southerly [ditto] E [ditto] W
Westerly [ditto] S [ditto] N
Northerly [ditto] W [ditto] E

p. 27. "When the wind shifts against the sun"
"Trust it not for back it doth run"

p. 27. The wind usually shifts "with the watch hands" i.e. from L to R in front of you. A change in this direction is called "veering"

p. 27. The west wind shifts to E through NW—N & NE. If wind shifts in opposite way, viz. from W to SW. S to SE it is called "Backing" & generally indicates that a new storm is approaching (mem. this is what we want)

269. Rosenbach #39 verso a and 39 verso b are pasted onto the same page.
270. Page 58 (Rosenbach #39 verso a) is one of several pages that Stoker wrote in Whitby.
271. Many of the following notes find their way into reports of the storm that marked Dracula's arrival in England.

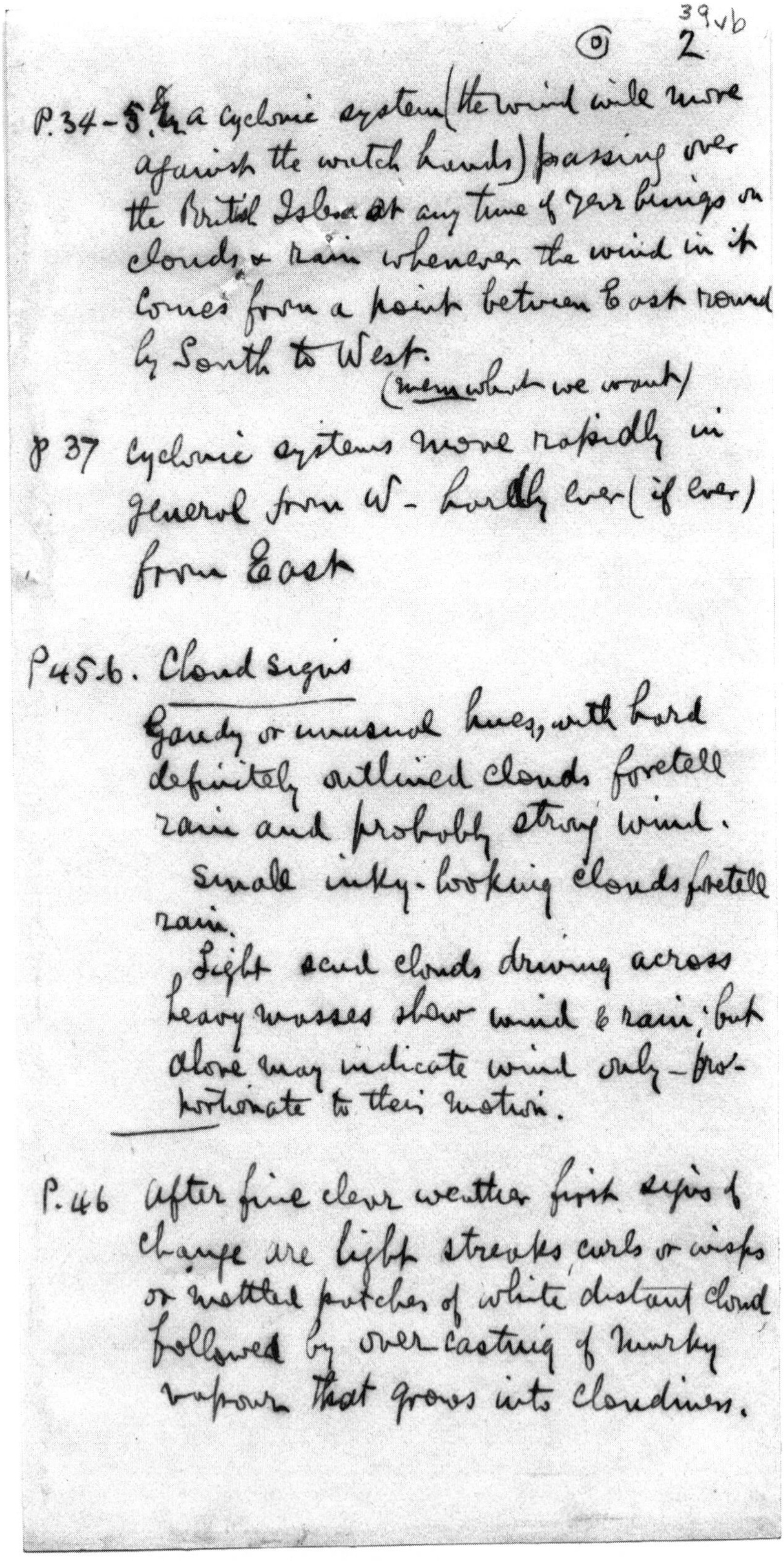

39vb

⊙ 2

P.34-5. In a cyclonic system (the wind will move against the watch hands) passing over the British Isles at any time of year brings on clouds & rain whenever the wind in it comes from a point between East round by South to West.

(mem what we want)

P 37 Cyclonic systems move rapidly in general from W – hardly ever (if ever) from East

P45-6. Cloud signs

Gaudy or unusual hues, with hard definitely outlined clouds foretell rain and probably strong wind.

Small inky-looking clouds foretell rain.

Light scud clouds driving across heavy masses show wind & rain; but alone may indicate wind only – proportionate to their motion.

P.46 After fine clear weather first signs of change are light streaks, curls or wisps or mottled patches of white distant cloud followed by over-casting of murky vapour that grows into cloudiness.

Page 59. Rosenbach #39 verso b. Size: 6 × 3¼.

p. 34–5. A cyclonic system (the wind will move against the watch hands) passing over the British Isles at any time of year brings on clouds & rain whenever the wind in it comes from a point between East round by South to West. (mem. what we want)

p. 37. cyclonic systems move rapidly in general from W — hardly ever (if ever) from East

p. 45–6. Cloud signs

Gaudy or unusual hues, with hard definitely outlined clouds foretell rain and probably strong wind.
Small inky-looking clouds foretell rain
Light scud clouds driving across heavy masses show wind & rain; but alone may indicate wind only — proportionate to their motion

p. 46. After fine clear weather first signs of change are light streaks, curls or wisps or mottled patches of white distant cloud followed by overcasting of murky vapour that grows into cloudiness

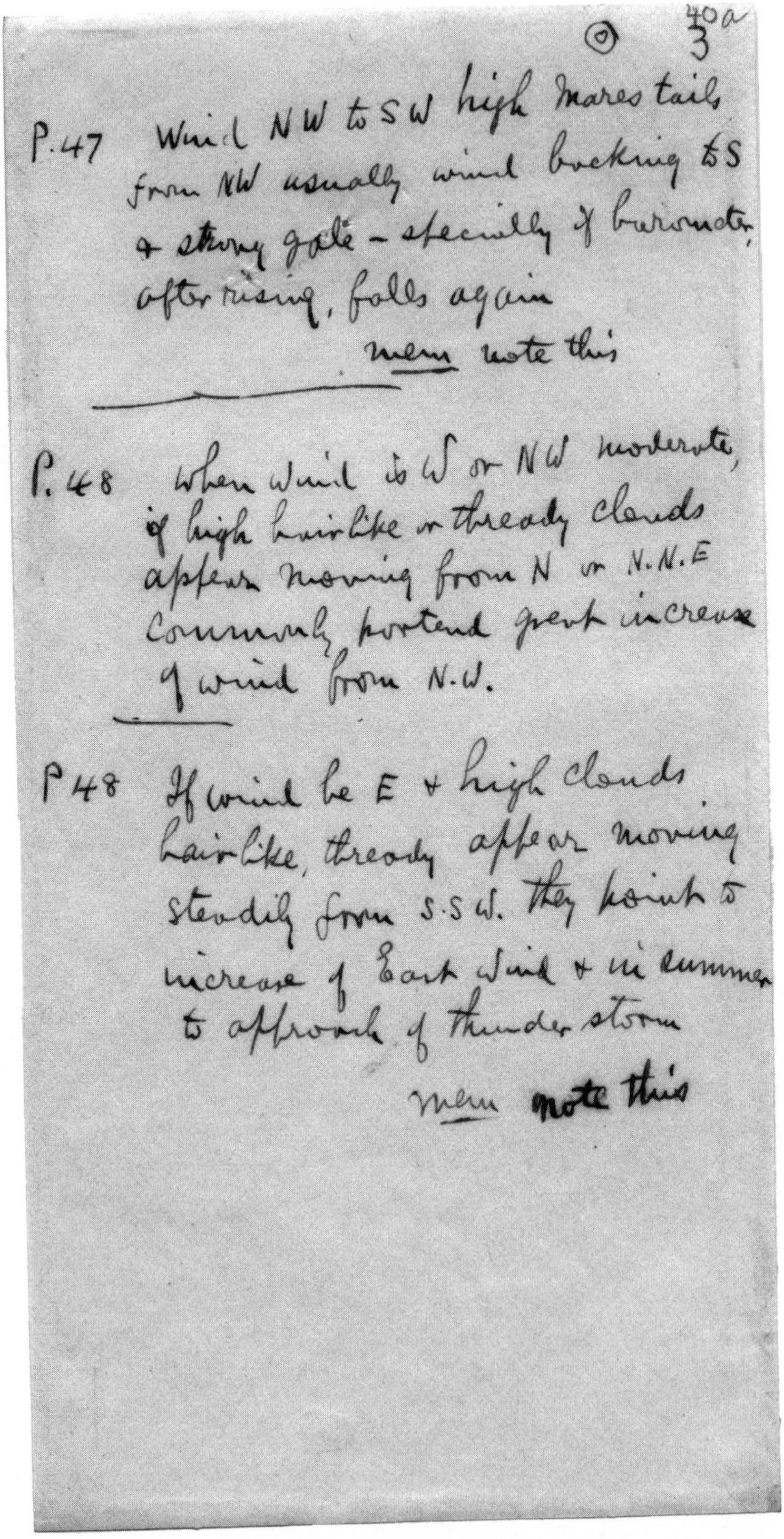

40a
3

P.47 Wind NW to SW high mares tails
from NW usually wind backing to S
& strong gale — specially if barometer,
after rising, falls again

mem note this

P.48 when wind is W or NW moderate,
if high hairlike or thready clouds
appear moving from N or N.N.E
commonly portend great increase
of wind from N.W.

P48 If wind be E & high clouds
hairlike, thready appear moving
steadily from S.S.W. they point to
increase of East Wind & in summer
to approach of thunder storm

mem note this

Page 60. Rosenbach #40a. Size: 6 × 3¼.

p. 47. Wind NW to SW high mares tails from NW usually wind backing to S & strong gale — specially if barometer, after rising, falls again
mem. note this[272]

p. 48. When wind is W or NW moderate, if high hairlike or thready clouds appear moving from N or NNE commonly portend great increase of wind from NW

p. 48. If wind be E. & high clouds hairlike thready appear moving steadily from SSW they point to increase of East wind & in summer to approach of thunderstorm
Mem. note this

Whitby, ocean view (courtesy Barbara Zapffe Vielma).

272. Memos appear throughout the Notes, while Stoker inserts reminders such as "(*Mem.*, get recipe for Mina)" (1:1) in the novel.

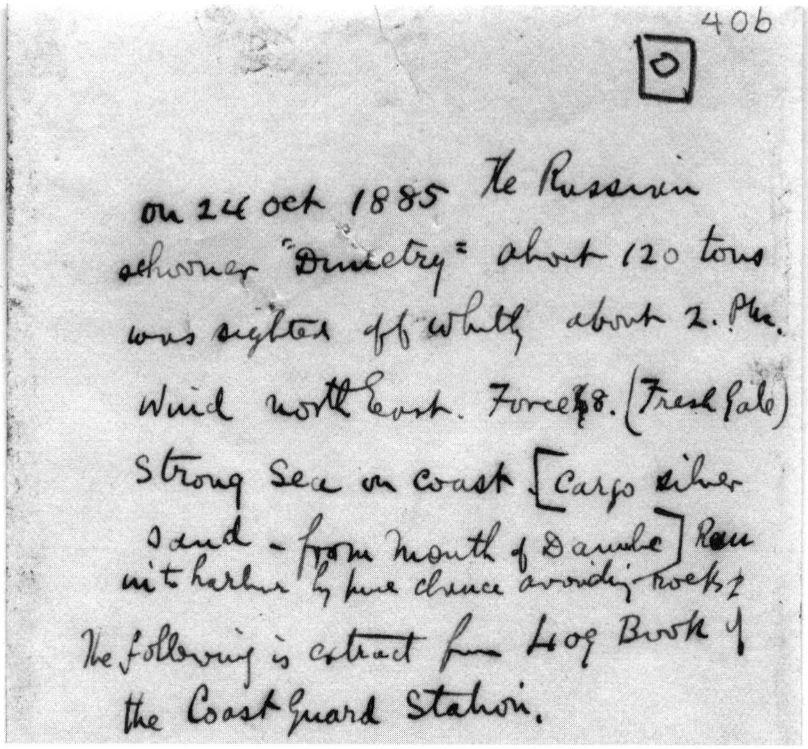

40b

O

On 24 Oct 1885 the Russian
schooner "Dmitry" about 120 tons
was sighted off Whitby about 2. P.m.
Wind north East. Force 8. (Fresh Gale)
Strong Sea on coast [Cargo silver
sand — from month of Danube] Ran
into harbour by pure chance avoiding rocks &
The following is extract from Log Book of
the Coast Guard Station.

Whitby, beach where the *Dmitry* came ashore in 1885 (courtesy Barbara Zapffe Vielma).

Page 61. Rosenbach #40b. Size: 6 × 3¼.

On 24 Oct. 1885 the Russian schooner "Dimetry" [sic][273] about 120 tons was sighted off Whitby about 2 PM. Wind north east. Force 8 (Fresh gale)—strong sea on coast (cargo silver sand—from mouth of Danube) ran into harbour by pure chance avoiding rocks. The following is extract from Log Book of the Coast Guard Station.

273. In the Coast Guard's report on the next page, the ship is called the "Dimitry." Stoker renames it the "Demeter" and makes it the vessel that carries Dracula to England. *The Dailygraph* reports that the derelict which arrived in the storm "is a Russian from Varna and is called the 'Demeter.' She is almost entirely in ballast of silver sand, with only a small amount of cargo—a number of great wooden boxes filled with mould" (7:82). In *Dracula*, the events on the "Demeter" are recorded in the ship's log, as the following excerpts illustrate:

"On 6 July we finished taking in cargo, silver sand and boxes of earth. At noon set sail. East wind, fresh. Crew, five hands, ... two mates, cook, and myself (captain)" (7:83–84).

"On 13 July passed Cape Matapan. Crew dissatisfied about something. Seemed scared, but would not speak out" (7:84).

"On 14 July was somewhat anxious about crew. Men all steady fellows, who sailed with me before. Mate could not make out what was wrong; they only told him there was *something*, and crossed themselves. Mate lost temper with one of them that day and struck him. Expected fierce quarrel, but all was quiet" (7:84).

"On 16 July mate reported in the morning that one of the crew, Petrovsky, was missing. Could not account for it" (7:84).

"On 17 July, yesterday, one of the men, Olgaren, came to my cabin, and in an awestruck way confided to me that he thought there was a strange man aboard the ship. He said that ... he saw a tall, thin man, who was not like any of the crew, come up the companion-way, and go along the deck forward, and disappear" (7:84).

"24 July.—There seems some doom over this ship. Already a hand short, and entering on the Bay of Biscay with wild weather ahead, and yet last night another man lost—disappeared. Like the first, he came off his watch and was not seen again" (7:85).

"30 July.—Last night. Rejoiced we are nearing England. Weather fine, all sails set. Retired worn out; slept soundly; awakened by mate telling me that both man of watch and steersman missing. Only self and mate and two hands left to work ship" (7:85).

"2 August, midnight.—Woke up from few minutes' sleep by hearing a cry, seemingly outside my port. Could see nothing in fog. Rushed on deck, and ran against mate. Tells me heard cry and ran, but no sign of man on watch. One more gone. Lord, help us" (7:86).

"3 August.—At midnight I went to relieve the man at the wheel, and when I got to it found no one there.... After a few wild seconds he rushed up on deck in his flannels. He looked wild-eyed and haggard, and I greatly fear his reason has given way. He came close to me and whispered hoarsely, with his mouth to my ear, as though fearing the very air might hear: '*It* is here; I know it, now. On the watch last night I saw It, like a man, tall and thin, and ghastly pale.' ... Before I could say a word, or move forward to seize him, he sprang on the bulwark and deliberately threw himself into the sea" (7:87).

"4 August.—... [I]n the dimness of the night I saw It—Him! God forgive me, but the mate was right to jump overboard. It is better to die like a man; to die like a sailor in blue water no man can object. But I am captain, and I must not leave my ship. But I shall baffle this fiend or monster, for I shall tie my hands to the wheel when my strength begins to fail, and along with them I shall tie that which He—It!—dare not touch" (7:87).

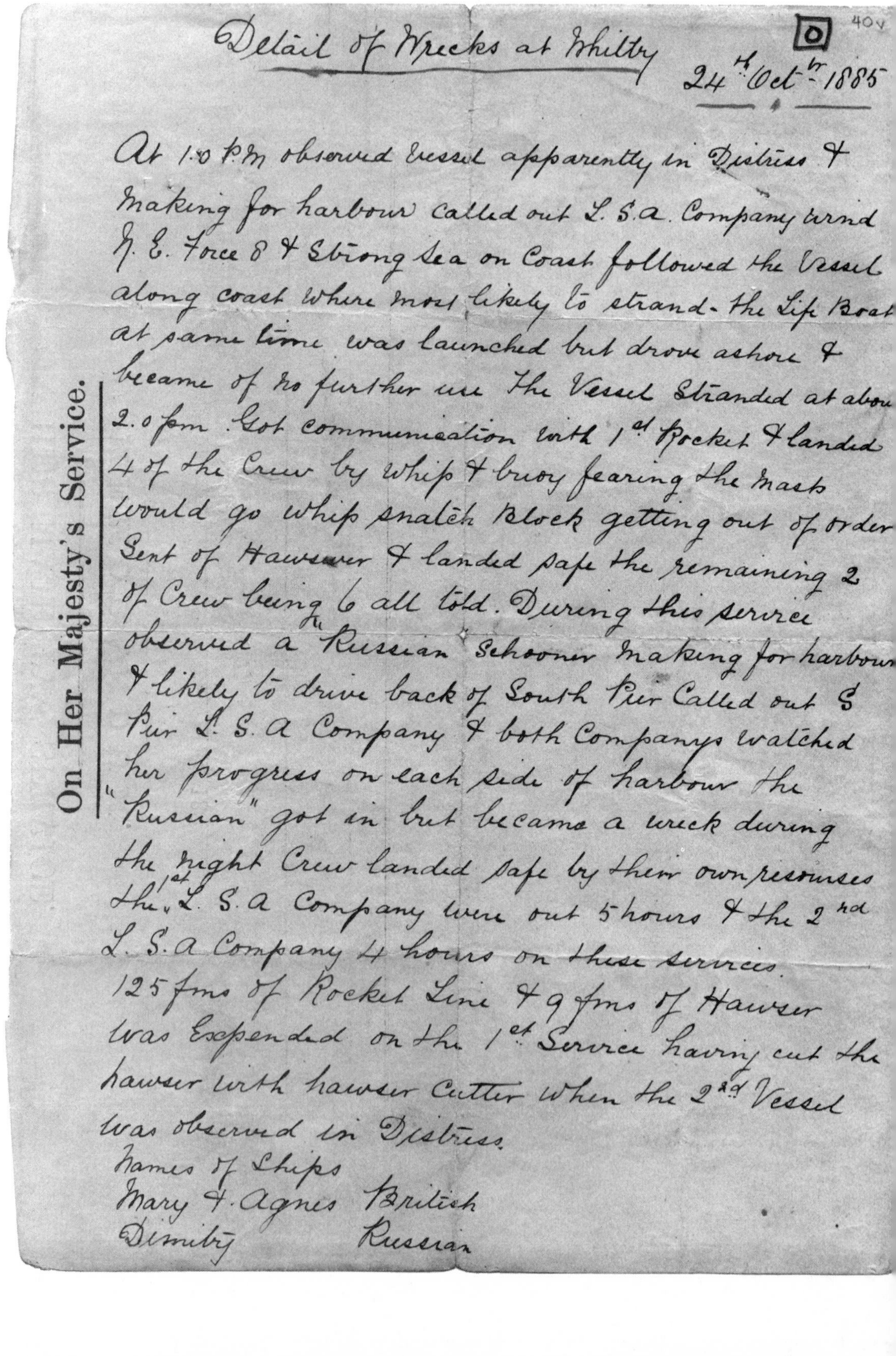

On Her Majesty's Service.

O

404

Detail of Wrecks at Whitby

24th Octr 1885

At 1.0 P.M observed Vessel apparently in Distress & Making for harbour called out L.S.A. Company wind N.E. Force 8 & Strong Sea on Coast followed the Vessel along coast where most likely to strand - the Life Boat at same time was launched but drove ashore & became of no further use The Vessel Stranded at abou 2.0 pm. Got communication with 1st Rocket & landed 4 of the Crew by Whip & buoy fearing the mast would go whip snatch block getting out of order Sent of Hawser & landed safe the remaining 2 of Crew being 6 all told. During this service observed a "Russian" Schooner making for harbour & likely to drive back of South Pier Called out S Pier L.S.A Company & both Companys watched her progress on each side of harbour the "Russian" got in but became a wreck during the night Crew landed safe by their own resources the 1st L.S.A Company were out 5 hours & the 2nd L.S.A Company 4 hours on these services. 125 fms of Rocket Line & 9 fms of Hawser was Expended on the 1st Service having cut the hawser with hawser Cutter when the 2nd Vessel was observed in Distress.

Names of Ships

Mary & Agnes British

Dimitry Russian

Page 62. Rosenbach #40 verso.[274] **Size: 8 × 5.**

Detail of Wrecks at Whitby / 24th Oct. 1885[275]

At 1.0 PM observed vessel apparently in distress & making for harbour called out L.S.A. Company wind N.E. Force 8 & strong sea on coast followed the vessel along coast where most likely to strand. The Life Boat at same time was launched but drove ashore & became of no further use. The vessel stranded at about 2.0 PM. Got communication with 1st Rocket & landed 4 of the crew by whip and buoy fearing the masts would go whip snatch block getting out of order. Sent of hawser & landed safe the remaining 2 of crew being 6 all told. During this service observed a Russian schooner making for harbour & likely to drive back of South Pier. Called out S Pier L.S.A. Company & both companies watched her progress on each side of harbour the "Russian" got in but became a wreck during the night. Crew landed safe by their own resources The L.S.A. Company were out 5 hours & the 2nd L.S.A. Company 4 hours on these services. 125 fms[276] of Rocket Line & 9 fms of Hawser was expended on the 1st service having cut the hawser with hawser cutter when the 2nd vessel was observed in distress.

Names of ships

Mary & Agnes British

Dimitry Russian

274. This report, which is written on grey stationery, appears on the back of a form that begins "On Her Majesty's Service." The left edge of this page is torn off.

275. This page appears to have been written by someone at the coastguard station in Whitby, possibly Mr. Petherick, who is referred to on page 69.

276. "Fms." a fathom is a unit of measurement equal to six feet and used, principally, to measure depths at sea.

Glossary — Whitby Trubner 1876 F.K. Robinson

abaft = behind
abune = above
acant = leaning on one side
acrow or acrewk'd twisted, crooked
addle = live
afore = before
aftermost = hindmost
ageeanwards = towards
ahint = behind
ails = evils
airt = quarter or direction
airth = afraid
air-blebs = bubbles
agee = crooked
ale-draper = publican
anenst = near
anent = concerning

angerly = fiercely
autherums = doubts
arr = a scar
arvill = funeral
ass-neuk = ash-nook
aud = old
aund = ordained, warned
auf = elf
awsome = awful
bad lad = the devil
bairn = a child
bolin-bowl = a [illegible]
ban = to curse
bar-guest = or Page 11
boh-ghosts = terrifying [illegible]

beild = a shed
beldering = blubbering
bell-hooling = funeral bell
bed-happings = bed clothes
belly-timber = food
beuk-body = learned person
bier-bank = churchyard path
bink = a bench
blate = modest
blee = a tear
blush'd = red
boggle or boggle =
boggle-bo = place of ghost
bolt = narrow passage between houses
brig = bridge
bruff = halo round moon storm
by-gang = by path

Page 63. Rosenbach #41a. Size: 3½ × 6. Landscape.

F. K. Robinson
A Glossary of Words Used in the Neighbourhood of Whitby
London, Trubner, 1876

aback = behind*[277]
aboon = above*[278]
acant = leaning on one side*
acow or acrewk'd = twisted, crotchety*
addle = live*
afore = before
aftest = hindmost
ageeanwards = towards*
ahint = behind
ails = evils
airt = quarter or direction*
airth = afraid
air-bleb = bubble
ajee = crooked
ale-draper = publican
anenst = near
anent = concerning*
angerly = fiercely
antherums = doubts*
arr = a scar
averill = funeral
ass-neuk = ash-nook
aud = old*
aund = ordained, warned
auf = elf
awsome = awful
bad lad = the devil
bairn = a child
balm-bowl = a chamberpot*
ban = curse
bar-guests or boh-ghosts = terrifying apparitions*
beild = a shed
beldering = blubbering
bell-knolling = funeral toll
bed-happings = bed clothes
belly-timber = food*
beuk-body = learned person*
bier-bank = churchyard path*
bink = a bench
blate = modest
blee = a tear
blush'd = red
bogle or boggle =
boggle-glour = glare of ghost
bolt = narrow passage between houses
brig = bridge
bruff = halo round moon (storm)
by-gang = bypath

277. The words that are marked with an asterisk (*) appear in the novel in chapter 6.

278. In *Dracula* "aboon" means "down" rather than "up" or "above." When Mr. Swales excuses himself with "I must gang ageeanwards home now, miss. My grand-daughter doesn't like to be kept waitin' when the tea is ready, for it takes me time to crammle aboon the grees, for there be a many of 'em" (6:66), he intends to *descend* the 199 steps that lead from the churchyard to the town below.

2
41b

Caff = to chaff 'chaff
Caff-riddling = dreamily chaff on St Mark's eve at dark.

Calit = a quarrelsome person
Canty = brisk
Carroty-scawpd = red headed
Chaffs or chafts = jaws
Clampers = claws
Clegs = horseflies
Clicker = bodysnatcher
Claggy = damp, foggy (weather)
Cluthering = assembling close
Cobs = sea gulls
Coffin lead rings = for cramp
Coitle = to tickle
Comers = visitors
Consate = to imagine
Corpse-yat = lichgate

Cramble = to hobble as with corns
Creed = to believe
Crowp = to grumble

Daff = to chat- loiter
Daffle = to become weakminded from age
Death-sark = a shroud
Death-strike = denoting death
Dither = tremulous over (cold or fear)
Dizzy = half-witted
Dool = grief - to lament
Dowp = carrion crow
Dozzened = shrivelled
Drucken = drunken
Dwam = a slight swoon
Faal-talk = nonsense
Feeat-folks = foot passengers
Flite = to scold
Flumpy = short in person
Flyte = to laugh

Garth = a yard - kirk-garth
Gang = to go - walk
Gaum = to understand
Geck = to sneer
Gladsome = joyful
Gleg = glance
Gloore = glare
Gradely = moderately
Grees = stairs
Greet = weep
Grim = a ghost
Kirke-grim
Haffin = a half wit
Hap = to bury
Hoster = mist
Hutter = to stammer
Ill gane = evil disposed
Inclin = desire
Irefull = angry
Jowl & joggle = jolt

Page 64. Rosenbach #41b. Size: 3½ × 6. Landscape.

caff = to chaff*
caff-riddling = divination by chaff on St Marks Eve as to death
callit = a quarrelsome person
canty = brisk
carroty-scaup'd = red-headed
chaffs or chafts = jaws*
clampers = claws
clegs = horseflies*
clicker = body snatcher
cloggy = damp, foggy (weather)
cluthering = assembling close
cobs = sea gulls
coffin lead rings = for cramp
coitle = to tickle
comers = visitors*
consate = to imagine
corpse-yat = lichgate
crammle = to hobble as with corns*
creed = to believe
crowp = to grumble
daff = to chat, loiter
daffle = to become weak-minded by age*
deeath-sark = shroud*[279]
deeath-skrike = denoting death
dither = tremulousness (cold or fear)
dizzy = half-witted
dooal = grief, to lament*
dowp = carrion crow*
dozzen'd = shriveled
drucken = drunken
dwam = a slight swoon
faal-talk = nonsense
feeat-folks = foot passengers*
flite = to scold
flumpy = short in person
flyre = to laugh
garth = a yard — kirk-garth[280]
gang = to go — walk
gawm = to understand
geck = to sneer
gladsome = joyful
gleg = glance
gloore = glare
gradely = moderately
grees = stairs*
greet = weep*
grim = a ghost
kirke-grim
hafflin = a half wit*
hap = to bury
hoast = mist*
hutter = to stammer
illsome = evil disposed
inclin = desire
irefull = angry
jowl & joggle = jolt

279. I.e., "burial-shroud."
280. I.e., "church-yard."

3

41va

jowps = to pimble together
keckle = to chuckle
keeker = official onlooker
kipper = nimble
kirk-garth = church yard
kirk-hooal = a grave
knag = to gnaw
knurl = to twist
lamiter = a deformed person
lay-bed = a grave
laze = to idle
leath-wick = flexible III
(corpse)
lift = at a funeral
lig = lie down
ligger-out = layer out of the dead
lonnin = cloudy

lowze = letting out of particulars
lichwake = corpse wake
mule = between a coble & fishing boat
nanpie = magpie
nar = near
oot = out
ower leuk'd = overlooked
pads = frogs
pairage = equality
parlous = perilous
powrich few = small number
raggil = a vagrant
raw-gobb'd = coarse of speech
reetlings = by rights
III Rowantree = [illegible] ash keeps off witches
witchwood day = 13 may)
ruddock = the robin
sark = a shirt
sauf = yellow

skime = to squint
scowderment = confusion
scud = vapour
scunner = to scare
sithee = look you
seeing-glass = mirror
sel = self
shoor = to scare
spew-gobb'd = wry mouthed
slape = a kiss
smock-turning - for fair winds [illegible]
snod & snog = safe & sound
smooth & compact
soul-bell = passing bell
thirl = to shudder
thowt-seear = thought sure - almost certain
thropple = windpipe
thruff steean (through stone) = a table tomb
tide-ratch = high-water mark
toom = empty
trimmle = tremble

Page 65. Rosenbach #41 verso a. Size: 3½ × 6. Landscape.

joup = to jumble together
keckle = to chuckle*
keeker = official onlooker
kipper = nimble
kirk-garth = churchyard
krok-hooal = a grave*
knag = to gnaw
knarl = to twist
lamiter = a deformed person*
lay-bed = a grave*
laze = to idle
leathweak = flexible (corpse)
lift = as at a funeral
lig = lie down
ligger-out = laying out of the dead
loomy = cloudy
lowze = letting out of particulars
lichwake = corpse wake
mule = between a coble & fishing boat
nanpie = magpie
nar = near
oot = out
owerleukd = overlooked
pads = frogs
pairage = equality
parlous = perilous
poorish = few, small number
raggil = a vagrant
raw-gobb'd = coarse of speech
reetings = by rights
Rowantree = mountain ash keeps off witches witchwood day = 13 May
ruddock = the robin
sark = a shirt
sauf = yellow
skime = to squint
scowderment = confusion*
scud = vapour
scunner = to scare*
sithee = look you
seeing-glass = mirror
sel = self
shoor = to scare
skew-gobb'd = wrymouthed
slake = a kiss
smock-turning = for fair winds to xxx
snod & snog = safe & sound, smooth & compact*
soul-bell = passing bell
thirl = to shudder
thowt-seear = thought sure — almost certain
thropple = windpipe
thruff steean (through stone) = a table tomb*
tide-ratch = high-water mark
toom = empty
trimmle = tremble*

4

41vb

ugsome = ugly

unlucky days - them Friday

waft = ghost

whemmle = totten - upset

whish = silent

whisk = to whirl fast

whole = tolve 'wholes up badly'

wuff = a wolf

Yabbling = possibly!

yethforst = smell of damp earth

Page 66. Rosenbach #41 verso b. Size: 3½ × 6. Landscape.

ugsome = ugly
unlucky days = mem Friday
waft = ghost
whemmle = totter — upset
whish = silent
whisk = to whirl past
whole= total wholes up badly
wuff = a wolf
yabblins = possibly!
yethfoist = smell of damp earth[281]

281. The list does not contain all of the Whitby dialect that appears in the novel.

42a

Mem

Three old fishermen on cliff tonight
30/7/90 in churchyard told me of
whaler The Esk which was lost
at (dusk?) between Redcar & Saltburn
Master (Dunbar) would go on – said
"Hell or Whitby tonight" & when begged
him to slacken sail – he knocked
them down one by one as they came
to implore him. He was a powerful
man with hands reaching below
his knees & once in the Greenland
fleet challenged the fleet &
fought on the ice three hours
and beat an American who
came out to G on purpose to fight
him – (a stone ich American) skipper
& all were lost of Esk except
three of crew all cripples. None
of bodies was in one piece of time washed up

Page 67. Rosenbach #42a. Size: 6 × 3.

Mem.

Three old fishermen on cliff tonight 30/7/90[282] in churchyard told me of whaler the Esk which was lost at (dusk?) between Redcar & Saltburn. Master (Dunbar) would go on—said "Hell or Whitby tonight" & men prayed him to slacken sail. He knocked them down one by one as they came to implore him. He was a powerful man with hands reaching below his knees & once in the Greenland fleet challenged the fleet & fought on the ice three hours and beat an American who came out <xxx> on purpose to fight him—(a storm xxx American skipper & all were lost off Esk except three of crew all cripples. Name of boat was on one piece of timber washed up

282. This is the earliest date in the Whitby notes; the latest is 18 August. These dates roughly correspond to the time Stoker spent in Whitby as well as to the time-frame of the Whitby episodes in the book.

There were said of legend of
bells at sea & white lady in
abbey windows — Them things is
all wore out — 8

Page 68. Rosenbach #42a verso. Size: 6 × 3.

These men said if legend of bells at sea[283] & white lady in Abbey window.[284] Then things is all wore out

Whitby Abbey windows (courtesy Barbara Zapffe Vielma).

283. "They have a legend here that when a ship is lost bells are heard out at sea" (6:65).

284. "It is a most noble ruin, of immense size, and full of beautiful and romantic bits; there is a legend that a white lady is seen in one of the windows" (6:64). Note: "This is the ghost of St. Hilda, founder of the original monastery" (Leatherdale, *Dracula Unearthed* 98 n.13).

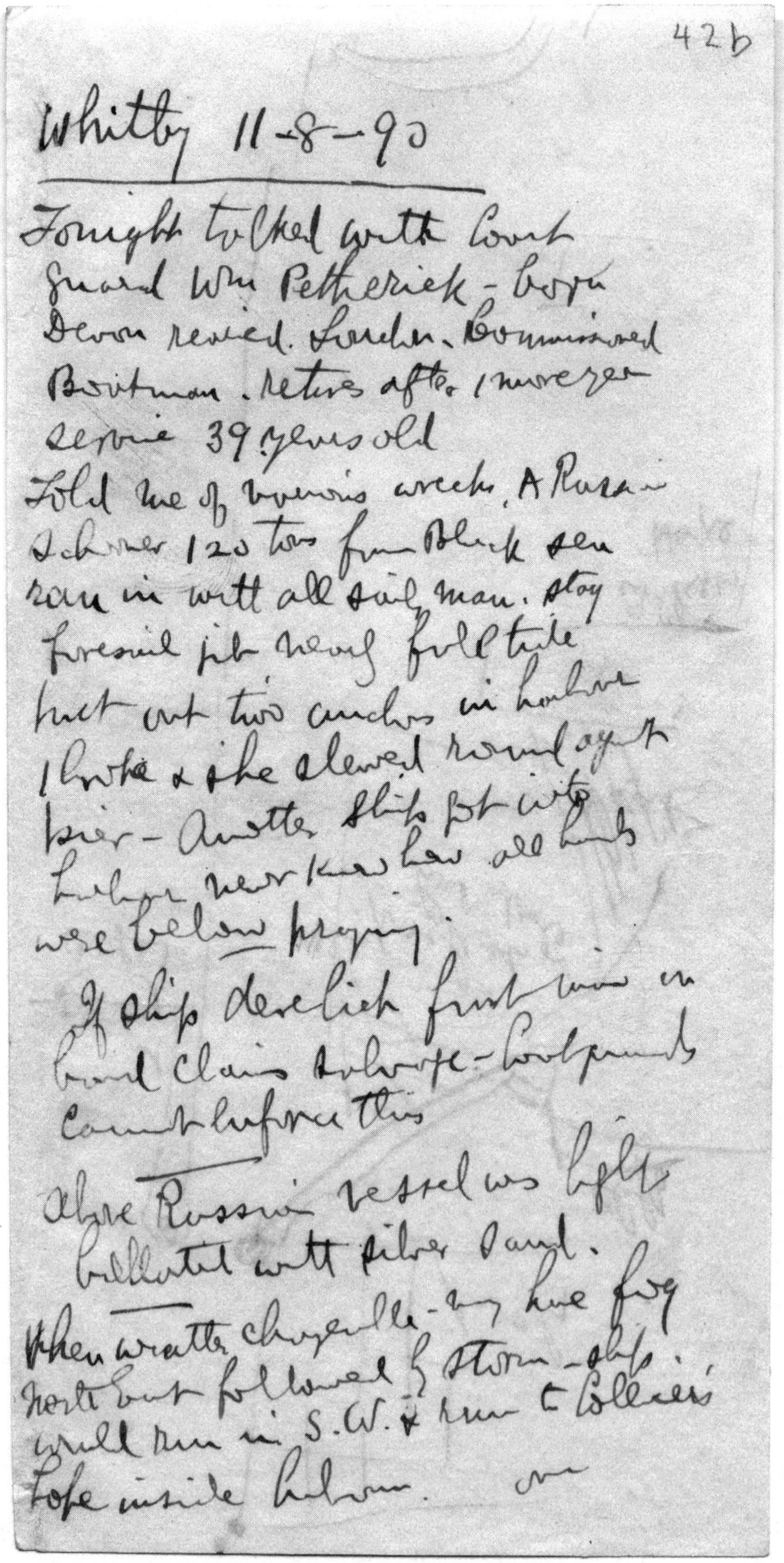

42b

Whitby 11-8-90

Tonight talked with Coast Guard Wm Petherick — born Devon resid. London. Commissioned Boatman. Retires after 1 more year service 39 years old

Told me of various wrecks. A Russian Schooner 120 tons from Black sea ran in with all sail on. Stay foresail jib nearly full tide put out two anchors in harbour 1 broke & she slewed round agst pier — Another ship got into harbour never knew how all hands were below praying.

If ship derelict first man on board claims salvage — Coastguards count before this

Above Russian vessel was light ballasted with silver sand.

When weather changeable — may have fog North East followed by storm — ships would run in S.W. & run to Colliers' Hope inside harbour. over

Page 69. Rosenbach #42b. Size: 6 × 3.

Whitby 11-8-90

Tonight talked with Coast Guard Wm. Petherick — born Devon raised London. Commissioned Boatman. Retires after 1 more year service 39 years old

Told me of various wrecks. A Russian schooner 120 tons from Black Sea ran in with all sails main-stay foresail jib nearly full tide put out two anchors in harbour broke & she slewed round against pier[285] — Another ship got into harbour never knew how all hands were below praying

If ship derelict first man on board claims salvage — coastguards cannot enforce this

Above Russian vessel was light ballasted with silver sand

When weather changeable, may have fog north east followed by storm — ship will run in S.W. & run to Collier's Hope inside harbour

285. "Stoker was fascinated by the tale and incorporated it into *Dracula*. What more dramatic entrance for the Count than to arrive in England on a ship that strikes the Yorkshire coast?" (*Bram Stoker's Dracula* 24).

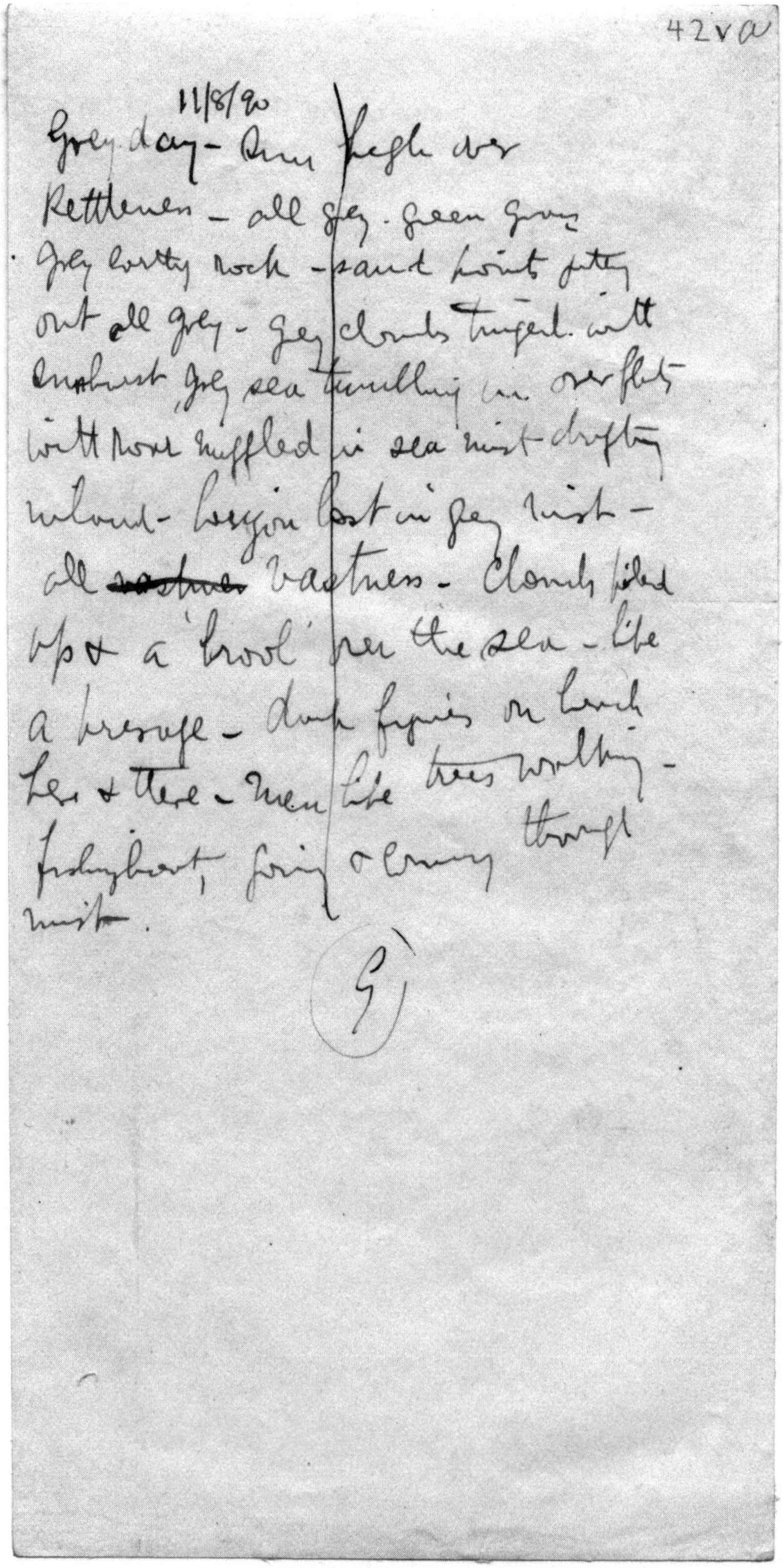
42va

11/8/90
Grey day — Sun high over
Kettleness — all grey. green grass
grey earthy rock — sand points jutting
out all grey — grey clouds tinged with
sunburst grey sea tumbling in over flats
with roar muffled in sea mist — drifting
inland — horizon lost in grey mist —
all ~~vastness~~ vastness — Clouds piled
up & a 'brool' over the sea — like
a presage — dark figures on beach
here & there — men like trees walking —
fishing boats going & coming through
mist.

9

Page 70. Rosenbach #42 verso a. Size: 6 × 3.

11/8/90

Grey day — sun high over Kettleness — all grey-green grass — grey earthy rock — sand points jutting out all grey — grey clouds tinged with sunburst grey sea tumbling in over flats with roar muffled in sea mist drifting inland — horizon lost in grey mist — all vastness — clouds piled up & a 'brool' over the sea — like a presage — dark figures on beach here & there — men like trees walking —fishingboat, going & coming through mist[286]

286. These brief notes become the mainstay of an entry in Mina Murray's journal: "To-day is a grey day, and the sun as I write is hidden in thick clouds, high over Kettleness. Everything is grey — except the green grass, which seems like emerald amongst it; grey earthy rock; grey clouds, tinged with the sunburst at the far edge, hang over the grey sea, into which the sand-points stretch like grey fingers. The sea is tumbling in over the shallows and the sandy flats with a roar, muffled in the sea-mists drifting inland. The horizon is lost in a grey mist. All is vastness; the clouds are piled up like giant rocks, and there is a 'brool' over the sea that sounds like some presage of doom. Dark figures are on the beach here and there, sometimes half shrouded in the mist, and seem 'men like tress walking.' The fishing-boats are racing for home, and rise and dip in the ground swell as they sweep into the harbour, bending to the scuppers" (6:75).

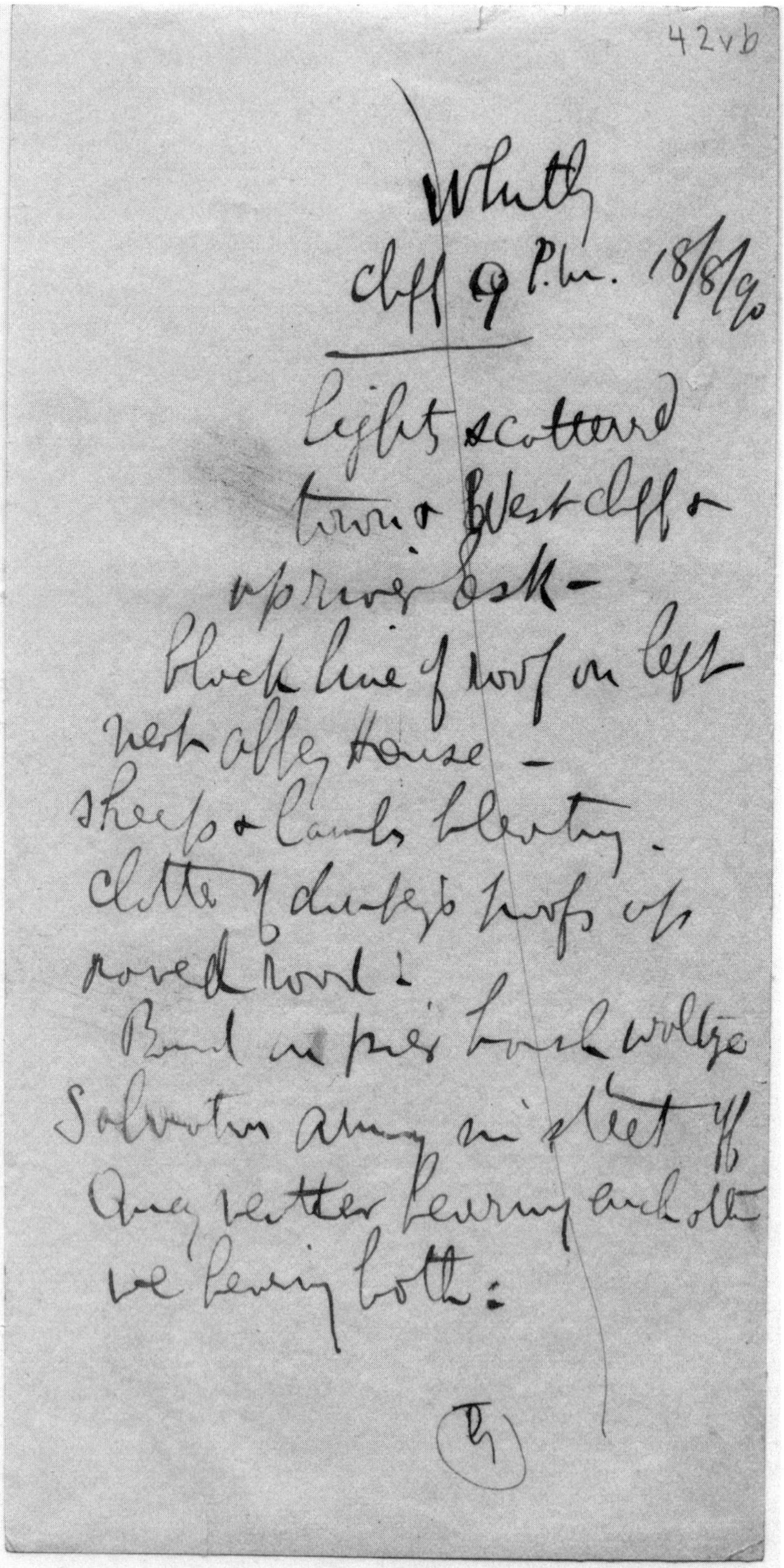
42vb

Whitby

Cliff 9 P.M. 18/8/90

lights scattered
town & West Cliff &
up river Esk—
black line of roofs on left
next Abbey House—
sheeps & lambs bleating.
clatter of donkeys hoofs up
paved road:
Band on pier playing waltz
Salvation Army in street off
Quay neither hearing each other
we hearing both:

Page 71. Rosenbach #42 verso b. Size: 6 × 3.

18/8/90.

Whitby cliff 9 P.M.

Lights scattered town & West Cliff & up river Esk — black line of roof on left — near Abbey House — sheep & lambs bleating — clatter of donkey's hoofs up paved road: Band in pier harsh waltz. Salvation Army[287] in street off Quay neither hearing each other we hearing both.[288]

287. William Booth founded the Christian-based Salvation Army in 1865. This organization is known for its quasi-military uniforms, street bands and charity work.

288. Mina describes the view from East Cliff: "I see the lights scattered all over the town, sometimes in rows where the streets are, and sometimes singly; they run right up the Esk and die away in the curve of the valley. To my left the view is cut off by a black line of roof of the old house next the Abbey. The sheep and lambs are bleating in the fields away behind me, and there is a clatter of a donkey's hoofs up the paved road below. The band on the pier is playing a harsh waltz in good time, and further along the quay there is a Salvation Army meeting in a back street. Neither of the bands hears the other, but up here I hear and see them both" (6:69–70).

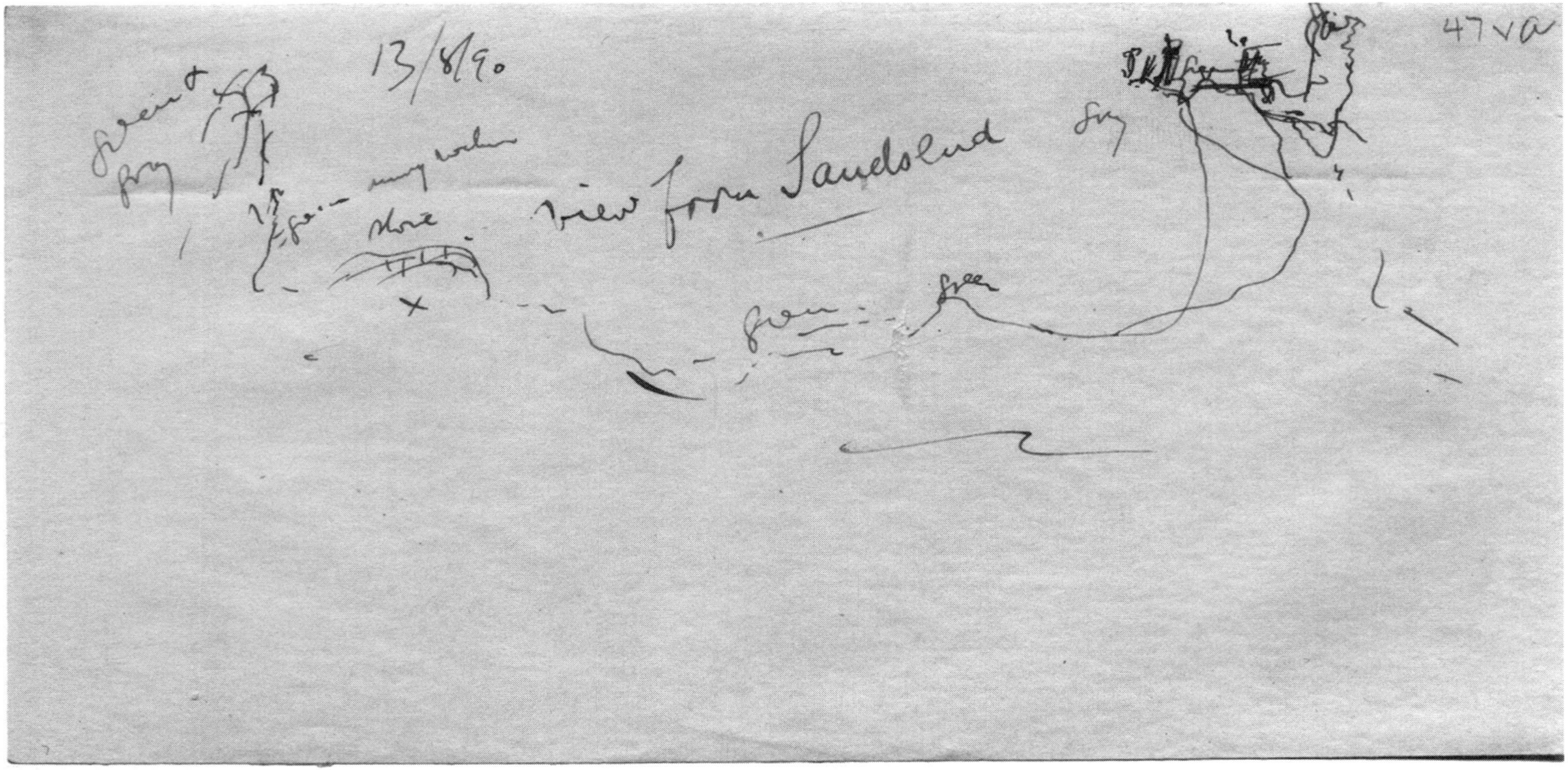

47va
13/8/90
view from Sandsend

Page 72. Rosenbach #47 verso a. Size: 3 × 6. Landscape.

Map

13/8/90

View from Sandsend[289]

289. This is the first of four sketches that Stoker made of Whitby. Some annotations are indecipherable.

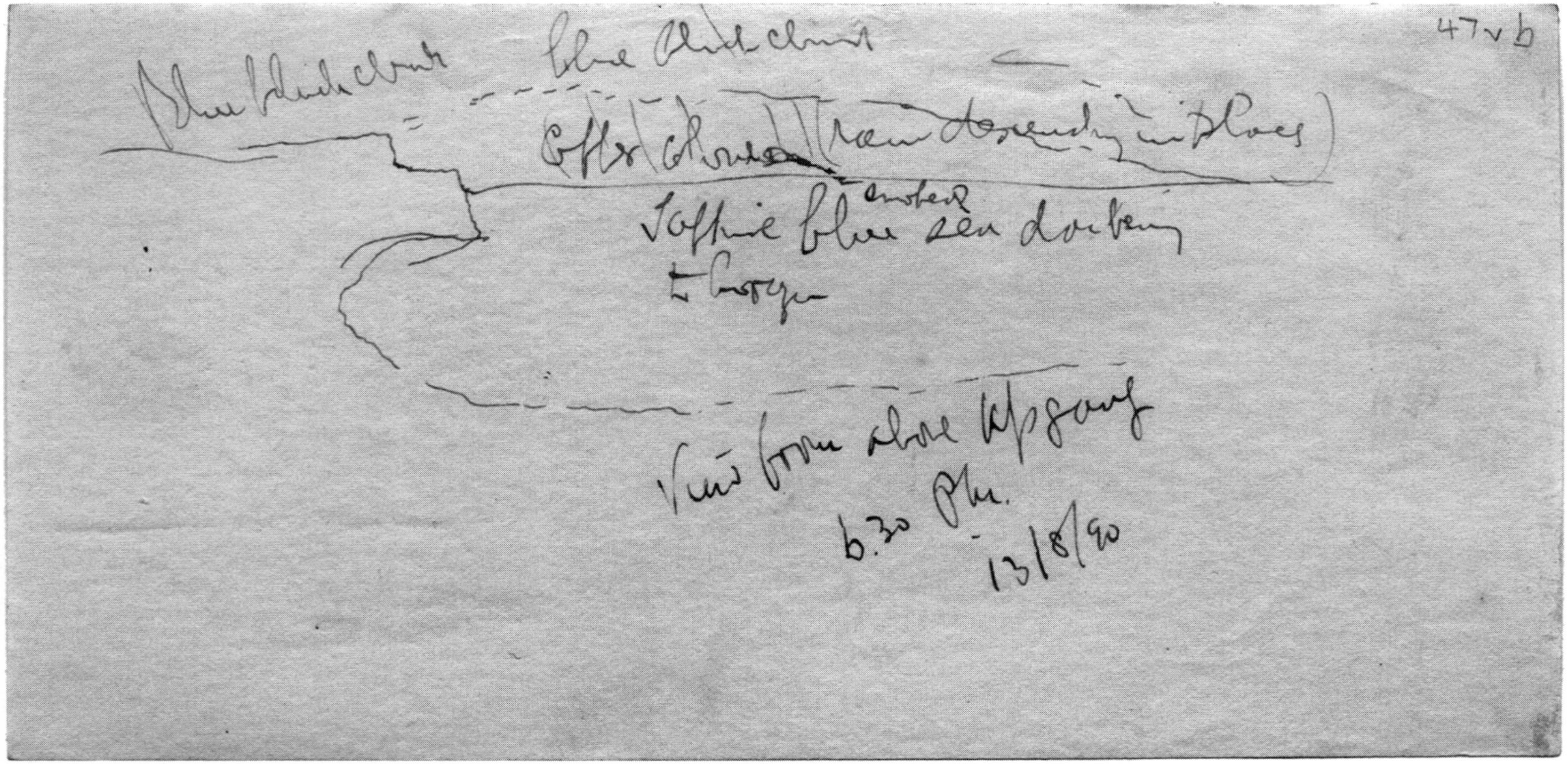
47 v b
Blue black cloud
blue black cloud
rain descending in places
blue sea
View from above
6.30 pm.
13/8/90

Page 73. Rosenbach #47 verso b. Size: 3 × 6. Landscape.

Map

Blue black clouds

cliffs cloud rain descending in places

saffire [sic] blue sea darkening to turquoise

View from above Upgang

6.30 PM

13/8/90

47a

21/8/90

~~View down the Esk~~

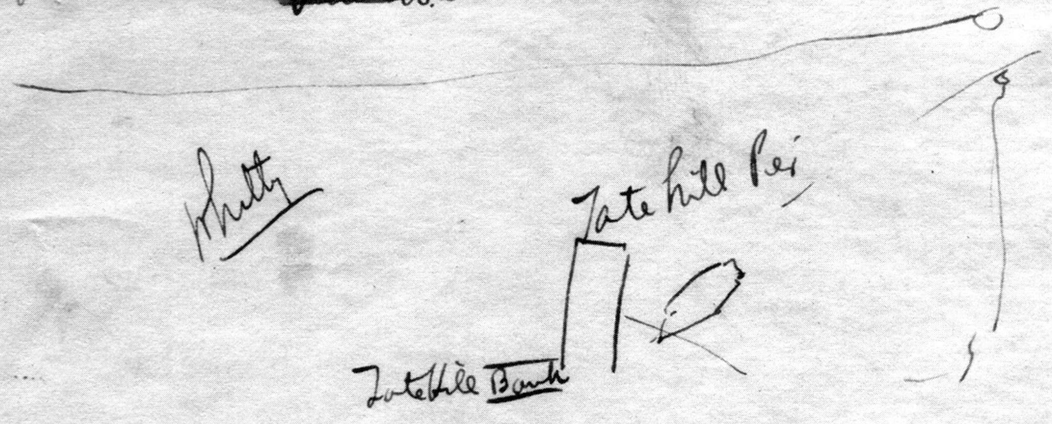

Page 74. Rosenbach #47a. Size: 3 × 6. Landscape.

Map

21/8/90
<View down the Esk>
Whitby
Tate Hill Pier[290]
Tate Hill Bank

290. This sketch includes a ship that is about to run aground near Tate Hill Pier: "The schooner paused not, but rushing across the harbour, pitched herself on that accumulation of sand and gravel washed by many tides and many storms into the south-east corner of the pier jutting under the East Cliff, known locally as Tate Hill Pier" (7:80).

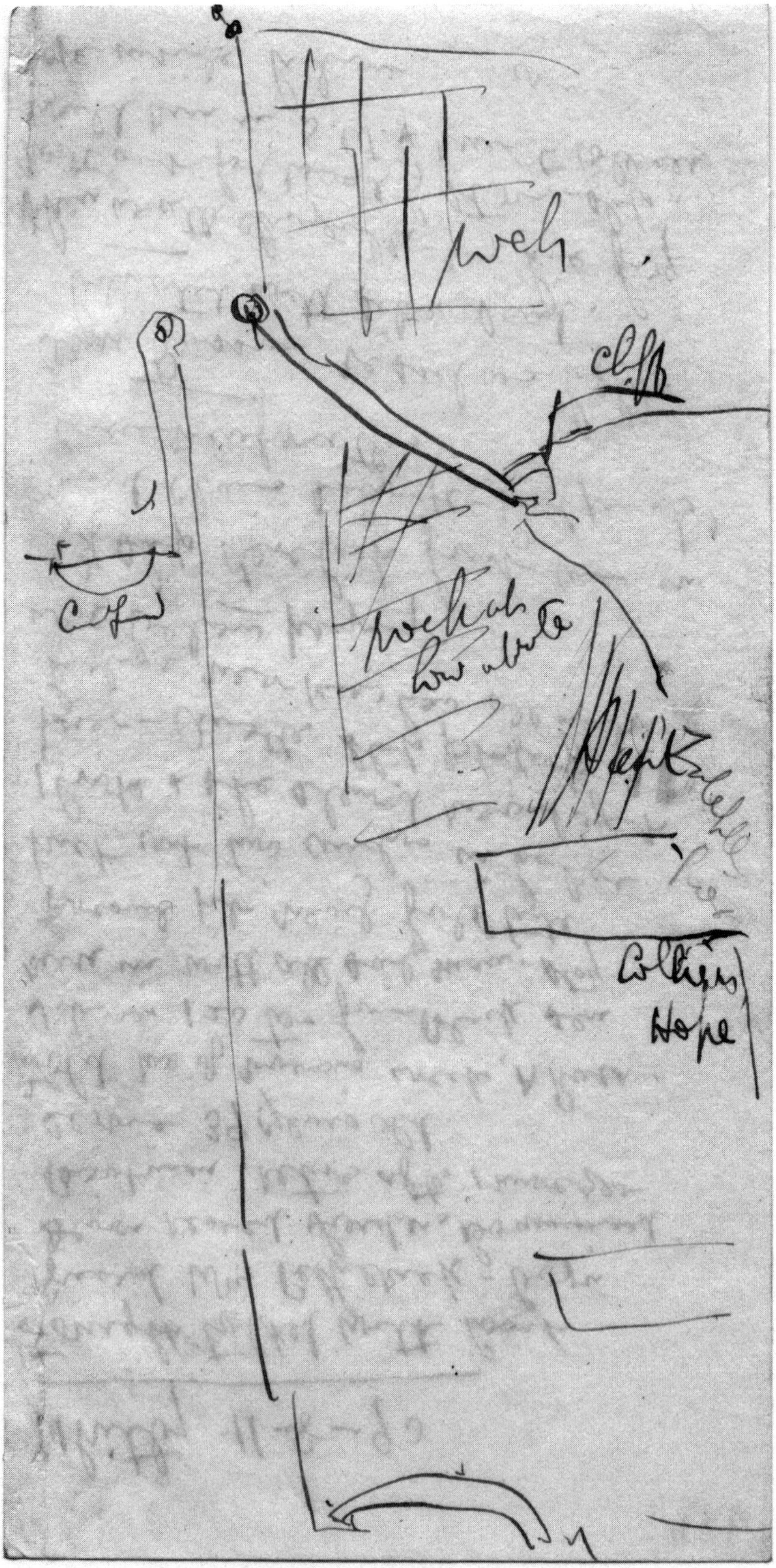

Rocks
Cliffs
Rocks low water
Deep
Collins Hope

Page 75. Rosenbach #42b verso. Size: 6 × 3.

Map

[Sketch of Whitby noting Collier's Hope and other local landmarks.]

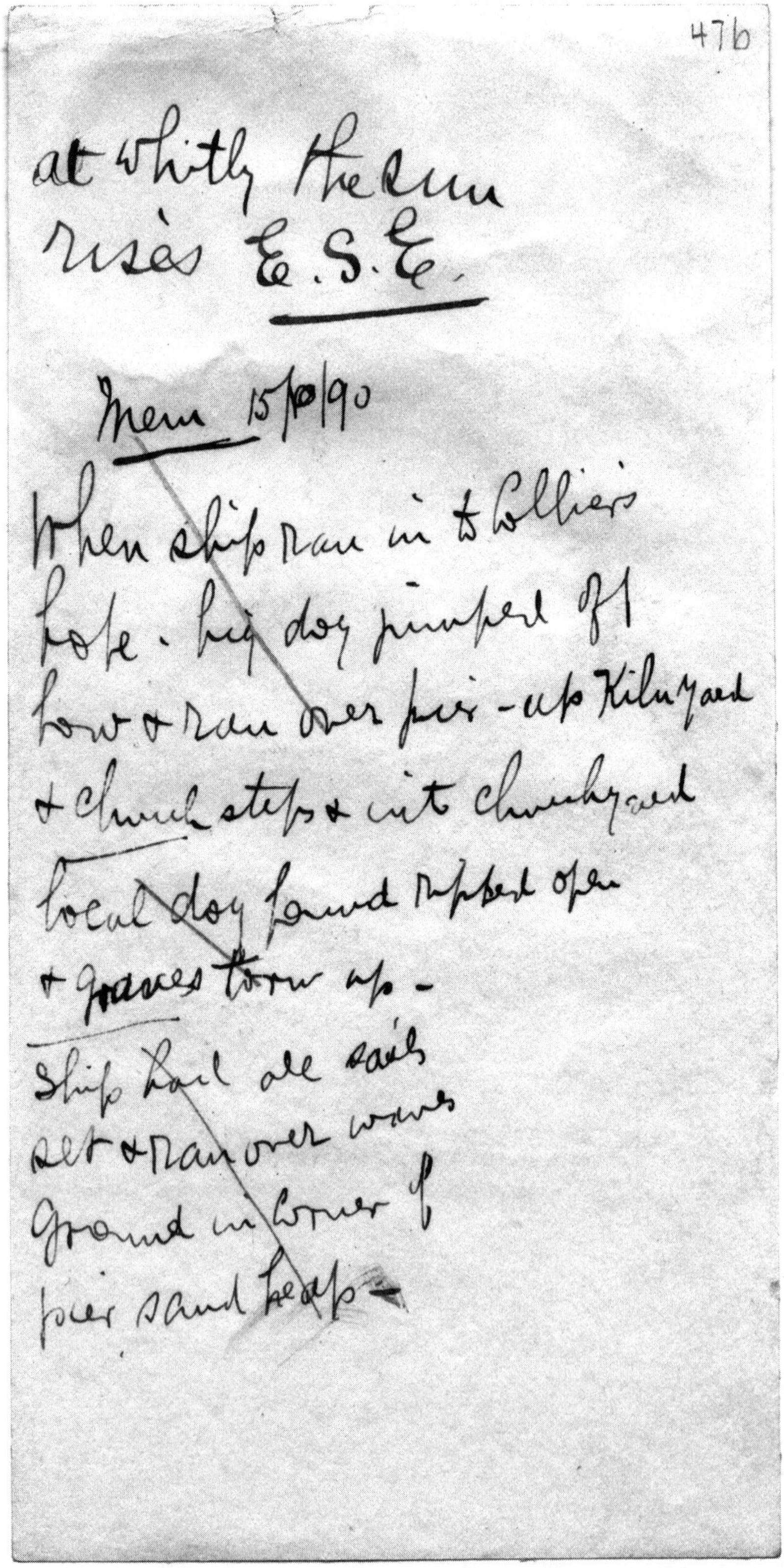
47b

at Whitby the sun
rises E.S.E.

Mem 15/10/90

When ship ran in to Colliers
hope. big dog jumped off
bow & ran over pier - up Kiln yard
& church steps & into churchyard

local dog found ripped open
& graves torn up -

Ship had all sails
set & ran over waves
Ground in corner of
pier sand heaps -

Page 76. Rosenbach #47b. Size: 6 × 3.

at Whitby the sun rises E.S.E.

mem. 15/10/90[291]

When ship ran in to Collier's Hope, big dog jumped off bow & ran over pier
— up Kiln Yard & church steps & into churchyard.

Local dog found ripped open & graves torn up

Ship had all sails set & ran over waves
Ground in corner of pier sand heap

291. This memo was not written in Whitby, for Stoker had returned to London by 15 October. The wreck at Collier's Hope inspired the scene in which Dracula leaps from the wreckage of the "Demeter" in the form of a large dog (or wolf): "There was of course a considerable concussion as the vessel drove up on the sand heap. Every spar, rope, and stay was strained, and some of the 'top-hammer' came crashing down. But, strangest of all, the very instant the shore was touched, an immense dog sprang up on deck from below, as if shot up by the concussion, and running forward, jumped from the bow on the sand. Making straight for the steep cliff … it disappeared in the darkness, which seemed intensified just beyond the focus of the searchlight" (7:80–81).

The next day the report continues, "Early this morning a large dog, a half-bred mastiff belonging to a coal merchant close to Tate Hill Pier, was found dead in the roadway opposite its master's yard. It had been fighting, and manifestly had had a savage opponent, for its throat was torn away, and its belly was slit open as if with a savage claw" (7:83).

Wallachs descendant of Dacians & Saxons

Century

1

2 (376–433 431–451 Attila) 444 Huns ravage East

3 Huns came under Attila - Szeckelys claim to be their descendants

4 Magyars were called Ugrogs - 376 AD Huns drove out Goths

5 — Avars - Northern race

~~Magyars came under Arpad~~

6 - 543 Huns ... of Gepidae (Goths)

7 - Bulgars got ascendancy of Avars 678

8

Magyars came under Arpad - Szeckelys were their descendants

9 Honfoglalas = Conquest of Hungarian fatherland under Arpad

10 Szekelys then in possession

11 1008. Hungarians annexed Transylvania under Stephen. Governed by voivods

12

13

14

15 Wallachians joined Hungarians & made war on Turkey - defeated at battle of Cassova (Bulgaria)

16 150 After abdication of Sigismund Transylvania revolted but defeated by Austrians 1600

17 1695 - Turks against Wallachians, after battle of Mohacs which extinguished Hungarian nationhood Transylvania Turkish

18 Protectorate, Turkey withdrew 1699

19

Transylvania part of Hungary

Page 77. Rosenbach #3. Size: 8 × 5.

Wallachs descendants of Dacians & Saxons[292]

Century

1
2 376–433 — 431–451 Attila 441 Huns ravage East[293]
3 Huns came under Attila — Szekelys claim to be their descendants
4 Magyars were called Ugrogs — 376 AD — Huns drove out Goths
5 Avars — Northern race — <Magyars came under Arpad>
6 543 — Huns defeated by Gepidae (Goths)
7 Bulgars got ascendancy of Dacia — 678
8 Magyars came under Arpad — Rusnicks were their descendants
9 Honfoglalas = Conquest of Hungarian fatherland under Arpad
10 Szekelys then in possession
11 1008. Hungarians arrived Transylvania under Stephen — afterwards ruled by voivodes
12
13
14
15 Wallachians joined Hungarians & made war on Turkey — defeated at battle of Cassova[294] (Bulgaria)
16 after abdication of Sigismund Transylvanians revolted but defeated by Austrians 1600
17 1695 — Turks against Wallachians. — after battle of Mohacs which extinguished Hungarian independence Transylvania Turkish — Protection of Turkey withdrawn 1699
18
19

Transylvania part of Hungary[295]

292. The following information is from various sources. Chapters 2 and 3 of the novel weave much of it into a fictional biography of Count Dracula.

293. These notes are inserted between items three and four.

294. In 1389, the first battle of Cassova (or Kosovo) marked Serbia's loss of independence to the Turks. This is a reference to the second skirmish, which took place in 1448.

295. These four words are written obliquely in the margin between numbers 16 and 11. When Stoker wrote *Dracula*, Transylvania was still under Hungarian control; it did not join Romania until after World War I.

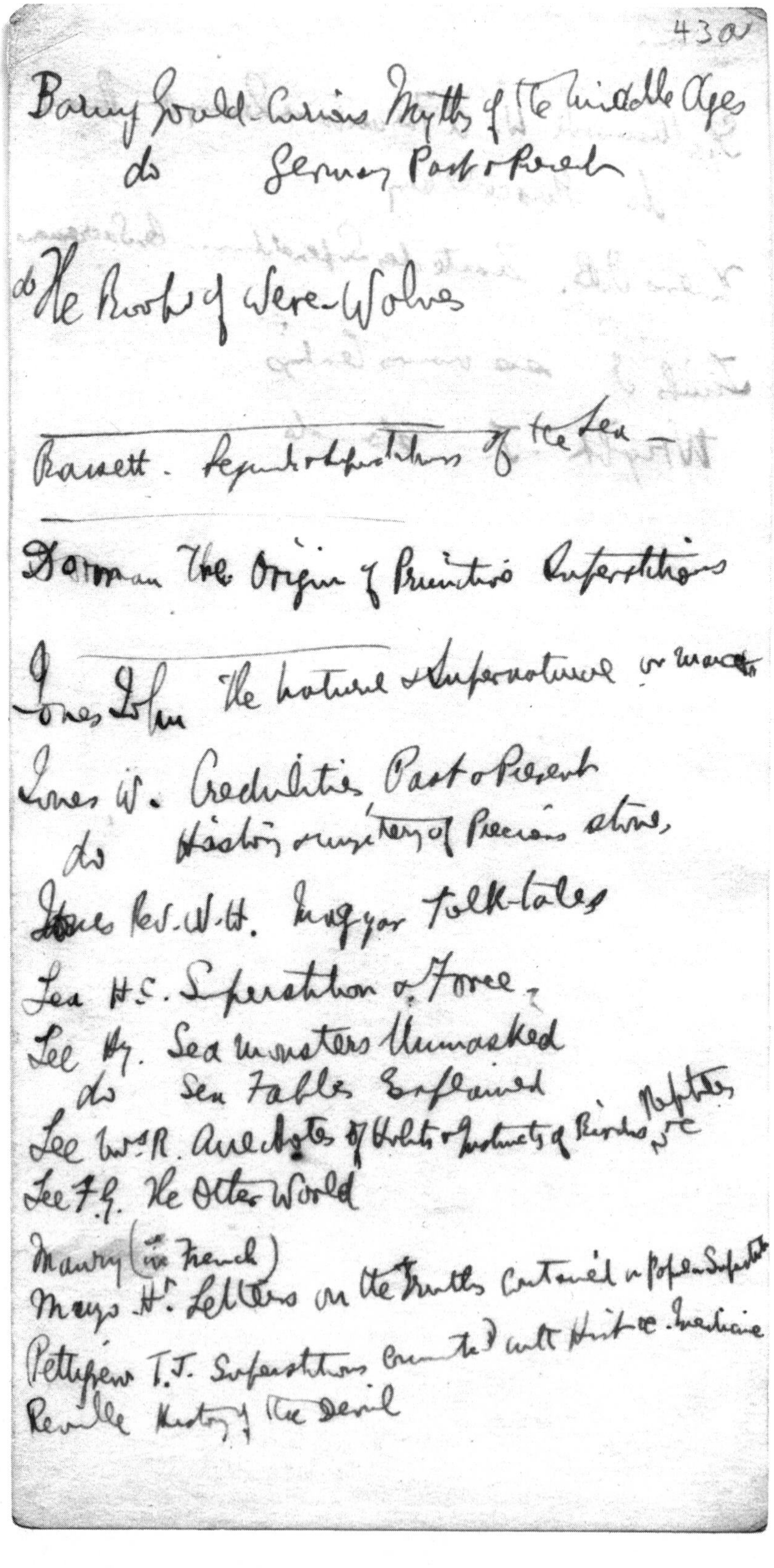

43a

Baring Gould—Curious Myths of the Middle Ages
do Germany Past & Present

do The Book of Were-Wolves

Bassett. Legends & Superstitions of the Sea

Dorman The Origin of Primitive Superstitions

Jones John The Natural & Supernatural or man...

Jones W. Credulities Past & Present
do History & mystery of Precious stones

Jones Rev. W. H. Magyar Folk-tales

Lea H. C. Superstition & Force

Lee Hy. Sea Monsters Unmasked
do Sea Fables Explained

Lee Mrs R. Anecdotes of Habits & Instincts of Birds, Reptiles &c

Lee F. G. The Other World

Maury (in French)

Mayo Hr. Letters on the Truths Contained in Popular Superstitions

Pettigrew T. J. Superstitions Connected with Hist. & Medicine

Reville History of the Devil

Page 78. Rosenbach #43a. Size: 6 × 3.

Baring-Gould. Curious Myths of the Middle Ages[296]
[ditto] Germany Past & Present
[ditto] The Book of Were-Wolves
Bassett. Legends & Superstitions of the Sea
Dorman. The Origin of Primitive Superstitions
Jones John. The Natural & Supernatural or Man
Jones, W. Credulities Past & Present
[ditto] History & Mystery of Precious Stones
Jones Rev W. H. Magyar Folk-Tales
Lea, H. C. Superstition & Force
Lee, Hy [Henry] Sea Monsters Unmasked
[ditto] Sea Fables Explained
Lee, Mrs R [Sarah] Anecdotes of Habits & Instincts of Birds, Reptiles
Lee, F. G. The Other World
Maury (in French)
Mayo, H. Letters on the Truths Contained in Popular Superstitions
Pettigrew, T. J. Superstition Connected with Hist. & Medicine
Reville. History of the Devil.

296. We do not know how many of the books in this list Stoker read.

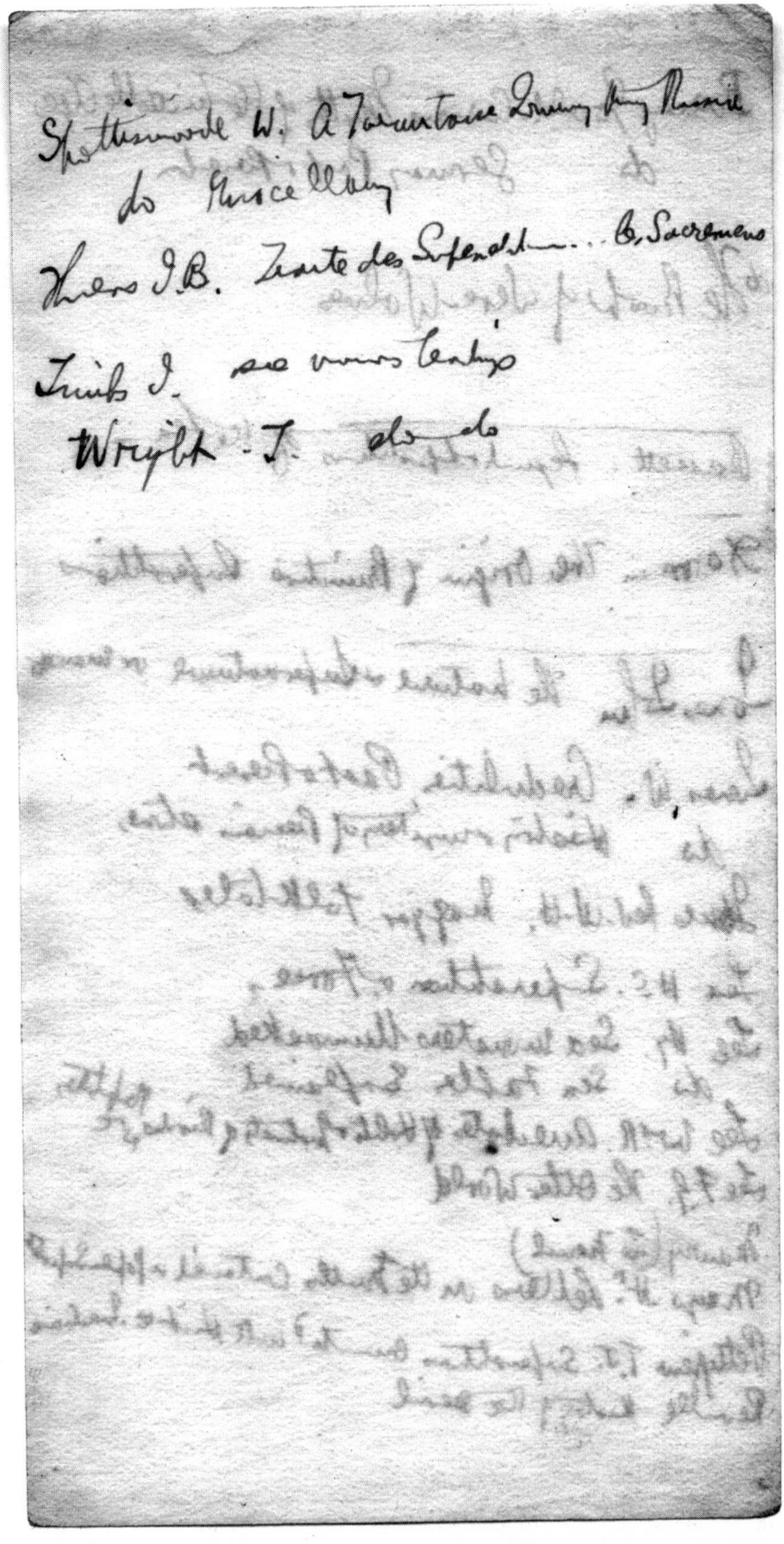
Spottiswoode W. A Tarantasse Journey thro' Russia
do Miscellany
Thiers J.B. Traité des Superstitions... Ce Sacremens
Trinks J. see various Cantys
Wright T. do do

Page 79. Rosenbach #43a verso. Size: 6 × 3.

Spottiswoode, W. A Tarantasse Journey through Russia[297]
[ditto] Miscellany

Thiers, J.B. Traite des superstitions...les sacraments[298]
Truibs, J. See various headings
Wright, T. [ditto][299]

297. William Spottiswoode's *A Tarantasse Journey through Eastern Russia in the Autumn of 1856* was published in London in 1857. We do not know if Stoker used any information from this hitherto unidentified source, but it does contain a map that shows three rivers — the Bistritza, the Sereth and the Pruth — which are mentioned in the final chapters of *Dracula.*

298. Jean Baptiste Thiers' study, *Traite des superstitions qui regardent les sacraments*, was published in Paris between 1700 and 1704.

299. This could be Thomas Wright, which is a pseudonym for J. Ewing Ritchie, a reporter who wrote articles about London.

Necromancy — divination by the dead 43b

Sir T. Browne Book 1 Cap 10

"For many things secret are true; sympathies and antipathies are safely authentick unto us, who ignorant of their causes may yet acknowledge their effects." P. 41

— "Many secrets there are in Nature of difficult discovery unto man, of easie knowledge unto Satan" ——

P. 42

— "Whereof having once begot in our minds an assured dependance, he makes us relie on powers which he but precariously obeys; and to desert those true and only charms which Hell cannot withstand.

P 42

? "But of such a diffused nature, and so large is the Empire of Truth, that it hath place within the walls of Hell, and the Devils themselves are daily forced to practise it ———— as well understanding that all Community is continued by Truth, and that of Hell cannot consist without it," P. 49

Page 80. Rosenbach #43b. Size: 6 × 3.

Necromancy — divination by the dead
Sir T. Browne Book 1, chap 10[300]

"For many things secret are true; sympathies and antipathies are safely authentick unto us, who ignorant of their causes may yet acknowledge their effects." p. 41

"Many secrets there are in Nature of difficult discovery unto man, of easie knowledge unto Satan." p. 42

"Whereof having once begot in our minds an assured dependence, he makes us relie on powers which he but precariously obeys, and to desert those true and only charms which Hell cannot withstand." p. 42

"But of such a diffused nature and so large is the Empire of truth, that it hath place within the walls of Hell, and the Devils themselves are daily forced to practice it ... as well understanding that all community is continued by Truth, and that of Hell cannot consist without it." p. 49

300. These quotations are from Sir Thomas Browne's *Pseudodoxia Epidemica, or Vulgar Errors* (1646), Book I: Chapters 10 and 11. This title is not mentioned anywhere in the Notes.

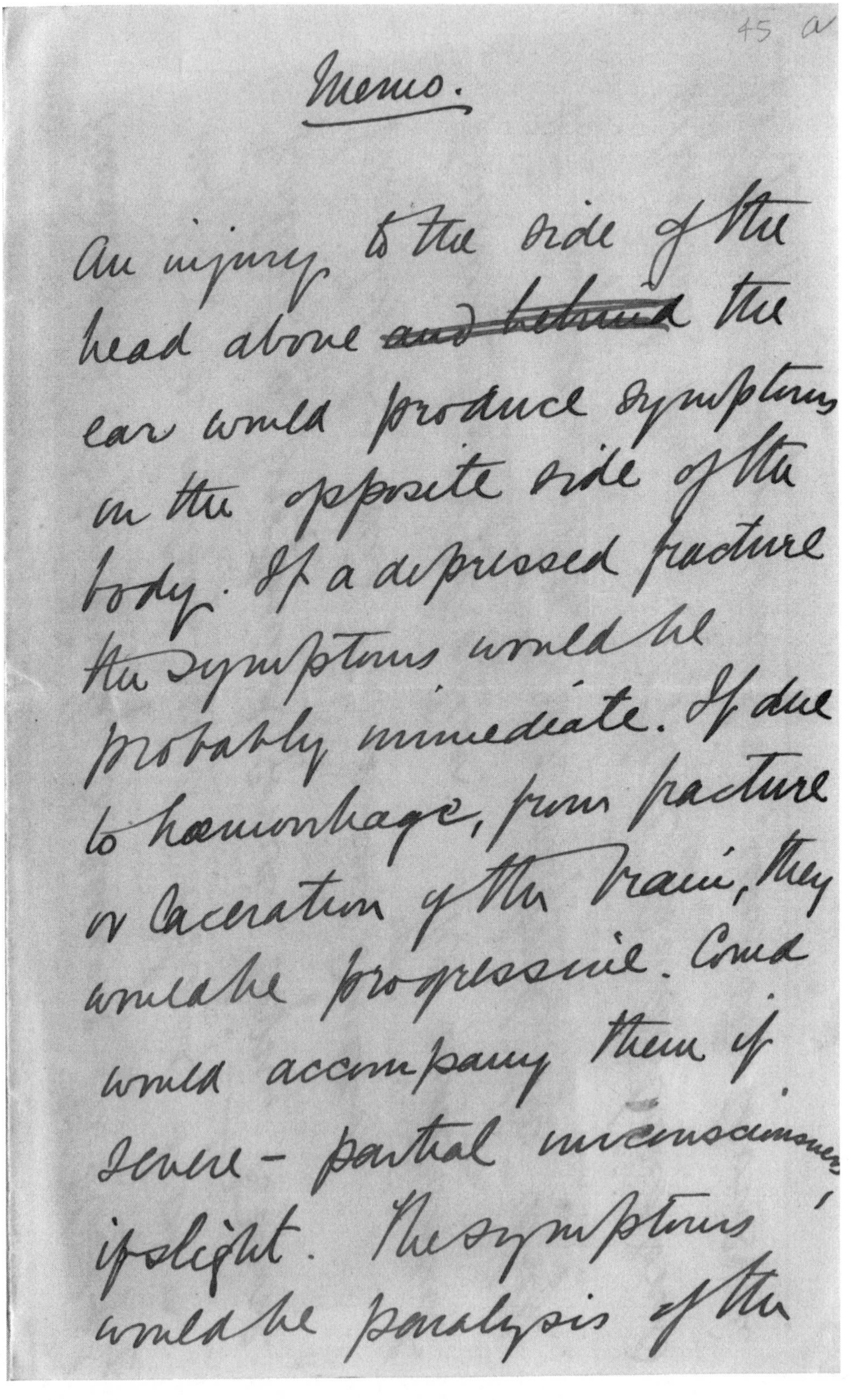

45 a

Memo.

An injury to the side of the head above ~~and behind~~ the ear would produce symptoms on the opposite side of the body. If a depressed fracture the symptoms would be probably immediate. If due to hæmorrhage, from fracture or laceration of the brain, they would be progressive. Coma would accompany them if severe—partial unconsciousness if slight. The symptoms would be paralysis of the

Page 81. Rosenbach #45a. Size: 8 × 5.

Memo.[301]

An injury to the side of the head above <and behind> the ear would produce symptoms in the opposite side of the body. If a depressed fracture the symptoms would be probably immediate. If due to haemorrhage, from fracture or laceration of the brain, they would be progressive. Coma would accompany them if severe — partial unconsciousness, if slight. The symptoms would be paralysis of the

301. This memo was written by Bram's older brother, Sir William Thornley Stoker, who was a prominent brain surgeon. We are presenting it as continuous text in contrast to the Rosenbach page order. The medical knowledge it contains was up-to-date when it was written, but it is obsolete and inaccurate today.

45b

opposite side. If the pressure

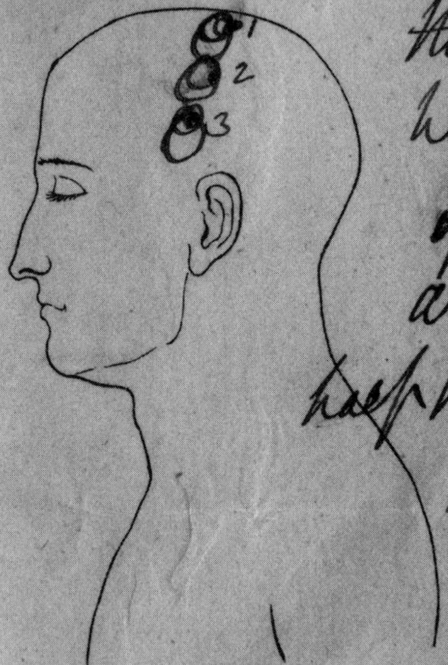

began at (1)
the leg would
be paralyzed;
if at (2) the
arm: if at (3)
half the face.
If the pressure
was due to
blood it
might extend
from one to the others, or if
the haemorrhage was large and
rapid they might all be
involved at once.
Trephining to remove the
depressed bone, or to give

Page 82. Rosenbach #45b. Size: 8 × 5.

[diagram][302]

opposite side. If the pressure began at ① the leg would be paralyzed; if at ② the arm; if at ③ half the face. If the pressure was due to blood it might extend from one to the others, or if the haemorrhage was large and rapid they might all be involved at once.
Trephining to remove the depressed bone, or to give

302. This diagram was pasted in. The text must have been added later, for it covers part of the drawing.

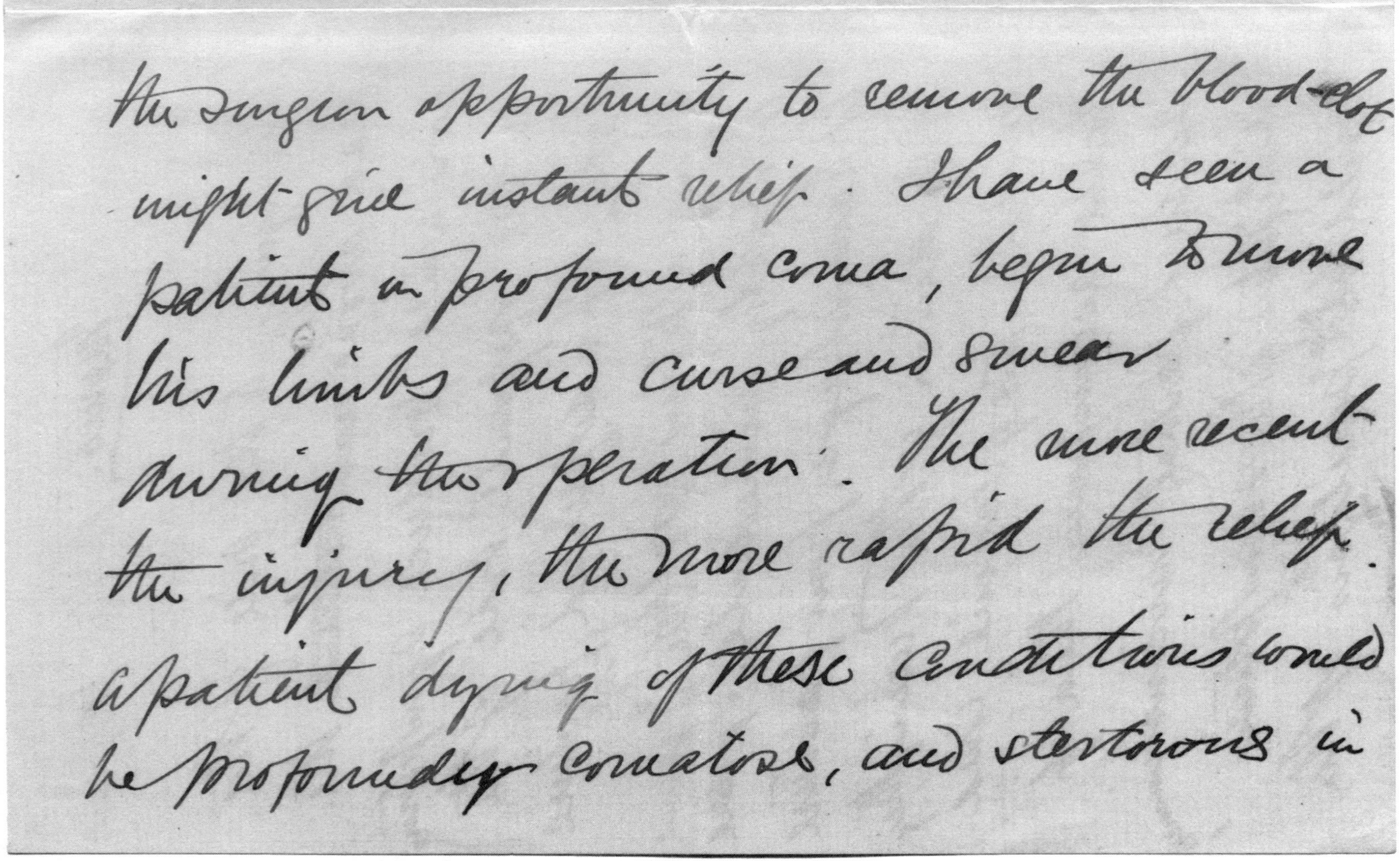
the surgeon opportunity to remove the blood-clot
might give instant relief. I have seen a
patient in profound coma, begin to move
his limbs and curse and swear
during the operation. The more recent
the injury, the more rapid the relief.
A patient dying of these conditions would
be profoundly comatose, and stertorous in

Page 83. Rosenbach #45b. Size: 5 × 8. Landscape.

the surgeon opportunity to remove the blood clot might give instant relief. I have seen a patient in profound coma, begin to move his limbs and curse and swear during the operation. The more recent the injury, the more rapid the relief. A patient dying of these conditions would be profoundly comatose and stertorous in

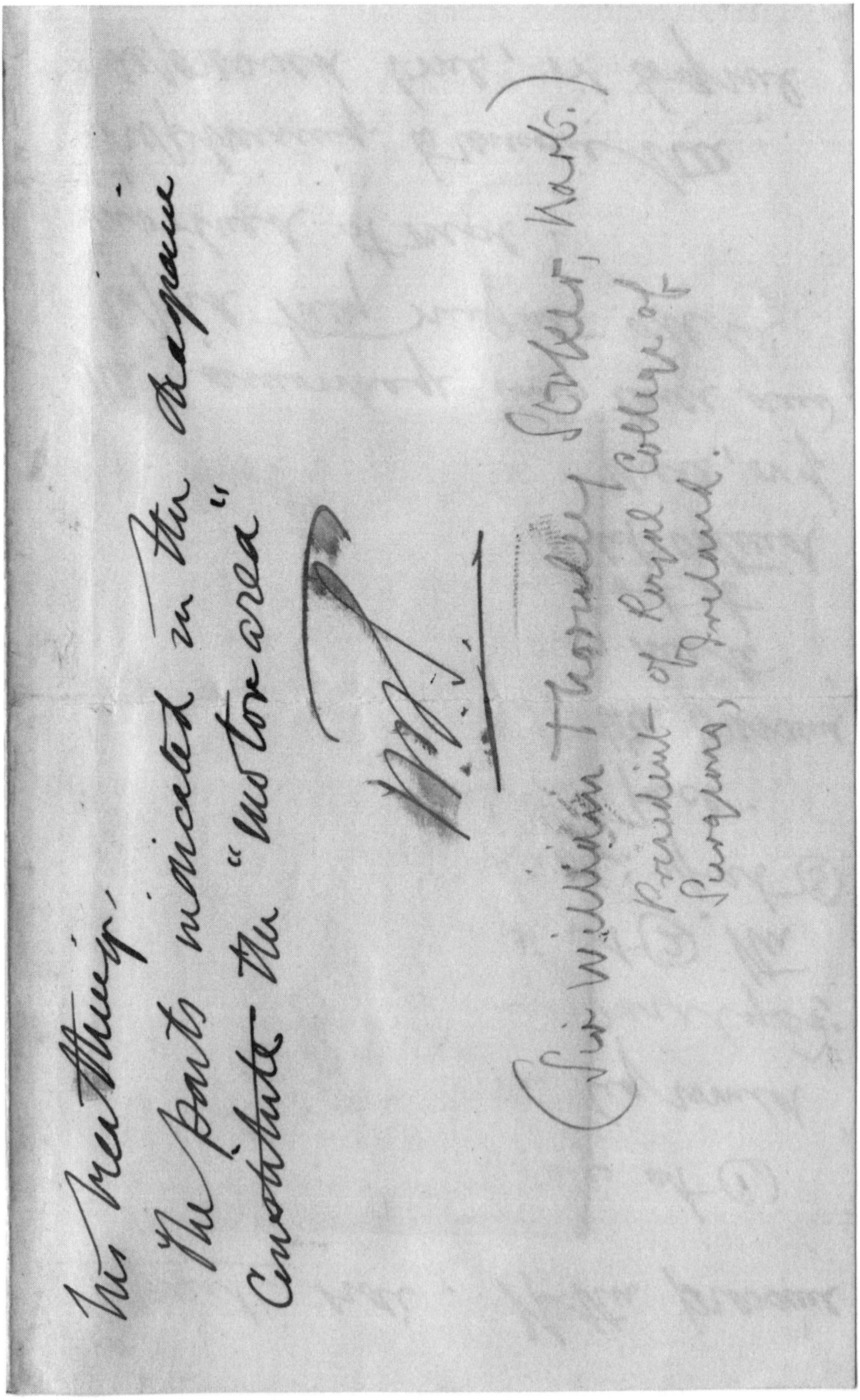

his meeting.
The parts indicated in the diagram
constitute the "motor area"
W. T.
(Sir William Thornley Stoker, Bart.
President of Royal College of
Surgeons, Ireland.)

Page 84. Rosenbach #45a. Size: 5 × 8. Landscape.

his breathing.[303]

The parts indicated in the diagram constitute the "motor area."
W.T.S.

(Sir William Thornley Stoker, Bart.)[304]
President of Royal College of Surgeons, Ireland

Sir William Thornley Stoker (*Illustrograph*, Dublin, Midsummer 1895).

303. Dr. Seward writes, "When I came to Renfield's room I found him lying on the floor on his left side in a glittering pool of blood. When I went to move him, it became at once apparent that he had received some terrible injuries; there seemed none of that unity of purpose between the parts of the body which marks even lethargic sanity. As the face was exposed I could see that it was horribly bruised, as though it had been beaten against the floor....

"The patient was now breathing stertorously, and it was easy to see that he had suffered some terrible injury. Van Helsing returned with extraordinary celerity, bearing with him a surgical case....

"The wounds of the face were superficial; the real injury was a depressed fracture of the skull, extending right up through the motor area. The Professor thought for a moment and said: 'We must reduce the pressure and get back to normal conditions, as far as can be; the rapidity of the suffusion shows the terrible nature of his injury. The whole motor area seems affected. The suffusion of the brain will increase quickly, so we must trephine at once or it may be too late.'...

"The poor man's breathing came in uncertain gasps. Each instant he seemed as though he would open his eyes and speak; but then would follow a prolonged stertorous breath, and he would relapse into a more fixed insensibility....

"Without another word [Van Helsing] made the operation. For a few moments the breathing continued to be stertorous. Then there came a breath so prolonged that it seemed as though it would tear open his chest. Suddenly his eyes opened, and became fixed in a wild, helpless stare" (21:282–285).

304. William Thornley Stoker and Henry Irving were both knighted by Queen Victoria in 1895. "Bart" is an abbreviation for "Baronet." This title was bestowed on Thornley in June 1911. We do not know who added these two lines, or when they were added.

VAMPIRES IN NEW ENGLAND.

46v

Dead Bodies Dug Up and Their Hearts Burned to Prevent Disease.

STRANGE SUPERSTITION OF LONG AGO.

The Old Belief Was that Ghostly Monsters Sucked the Blood of Their Living Relatives.

RECENT ethnological research has disclosed something very extraordinary in Rhode Island. It appears that the ancient vampire superstition still survives in that State, and within the last few years many people have been digging up the dead bodies of relatives for the purpose of burning their hearts.

Near Newport scores of such exhumations have been made, the purpose being to prevent the dead from preying upon the living. The belief entertained is that a person who has died of consumption is likely to rise from the grave at night and suck the blood of surviving members of his or her family, thus dooming them to a similar fate.

The discovery of the survival in highly educated New England of a superstition dating back to the days of Sardanapalus and Nebuchadnezzar has been made by George R. Stetson, an ethnologist of repute. He has found it rampant in a district which includes the towns of Exeter, Foster, Kingstown, East Greenwich and many scattered hamlets. This region, where abandoned farms are numerous, is the tramping-ground of the book agent, the chromo peddler and the patent medicine man. The social isolation is as complete as it was two centuries ago.

Here Cotton Mather and the host of medical, clerical and lay believers in the uncanny ideas of bygone centuries could still hold high carnival. Not merely the out-of-the-way agricultural folk, but the more intelligent people of the urban communities are strong in their belief in vampirism. One case noted was that of an intelligent and well-to-do head of a family who some years ago lost several of his children by consumption. After they were buried he dug them up and burned them in order to save the lives of their surviving brothers and sisters.

TWO TYPICAL CASES.

There is one small village distant fifteen miles from Newport, where within the last few years there have been at least half a dozen resurrections on this account. The most recent was made two years ago in a family where the mother and four children had already succumbed to consumption. The last of these children was exhumed and the heart was burned.

Another instance was noted in a seashore town, not far from Newport, possessing a summer hotel and a few cottages of hot-weather residents. An intelligent man, by trade a mason, informed Mr. Stetson that he had lost two brothers by consumption. On the death of the second brother, his father was advised to take up the body and burn the heart. He refused to do so, and consequently he was attacked by the disease. Finally he died of it. His heart was burned, and in this way the rest of the family escaped.

This frightful superstition is said to prevail in all of the isolated districts of Southern Rhode Island, and it survives to some extent in the large centres of population. Sometimes the body is burned, not merely the heart, and the ashes are scattered.

In some parts of Europe the belief still has a hold on the popular mind. On the Continent from 1727 to 1735 there prevailed an epidemic of vampires. Thousands of people died, as was supposed, from having their blood sucked by creatures that came to their bedsides at night with goggling eyes and lips eager for the life fluid of the victim. In Servia it was understood that the demon might be destroyed by digging up the body and piercing it through with a sharp instrument, after which it was decapitated and burned. Relief was found in eating the earth of the vampire's grave. In the Levant the corpse was cut to pieces and boiled in wine.

VAMPIRISM A PLAGUE.

There was no hope for a person once chosen as a prey by a vampire. Slowly but surely he or she was destined to fade and sicken, receiving meanwhile nightly visits from the monster. Even death was no relief, for—and here was the most horrible part of the superstition—the victim, once dead and laid in the grave, was compelled to become a vampire and in his turn to take up the business of preying on the living. Thus vampirism was indefinitely propagated.

Realize, if you please, that at that period, when science was hardly born and no knowledge had been spread among the people to fight off superstition, belief in the reality of this fearful thing was absolute. Its existence was officially recognized, and military commissions were appointed for the purpose of opening the graves of suspected vampires and taking such measures as were necessary for destroying the latter.

Vampirism became a plague, more dreaded than any form of disease. Everywhere people were dying from the attacks of the blood-sucking monsters, each victim becoming in turn a night-prowler in pursuit of human prey. Terror of the mysterious and unearthly peril filled all hearts.

Evidence enough as to the prevalence of the mischief was afforded by the condition of many of the bodies that were dug up by the commissions appointed for the purpose. In many instances corpses which had been buried for weeks and even months were found fresh and lifelike. Sometimes fresh blood was actually discovered on their lips. What proof could be more convincing, inasmuch, as was well known, the buried body of a vampire is preserved and nourished by its nightly repasts? The blood on the lips, of course, was that of the victim of the night before.

The faith in vampirism entertained by the public at large was as complete as that which is felt in a discovery of modern science. It was an actual epidemic that threatened the people, spreading rapidly and only to be checked by the adoption of most drastic measures.

46v→

The contents of every suspected grave were investigated, and many corpses found in such a condition as that described were promptly subjected to "treatment." This meant that a stake
vas driven through the chest, and t
heart, being taken out, was eith
burned or chopped into small piec
For in this way only could a vamp
be deprived of power to do mischi
In one case a man who was unburi
sat up in his coffin, with fresh blood
his lips. The official in charge of t
ceremonies held a crucifix before
face and, saying, "Do you recogni
your Saviour?" chopped the unfort
nate's head off. This person presum
bly had been buried alive in a catalep
trance.

WERE THEY BURIED ALIVE?

How is the phenomenon to be a
counted for? Nobody can say with c
tainty, but it may be that the frig
into which people were thrown by t
epidemic had the effect of predisposi
nervous persons to catalepsy. In
word, people were buried alive in
condition where, the vital functions
ing suspended, they remained as it w
dead for a while. It is a common thi
for a cataleptic to bleed at the mou
just before returning to consciousne
According to the popular superstitio
the vampire left his or her body in t
grave while engaged in noctur
prowls.

The epidemic prevailed all over sou
eastern Europe, being at its worst
Hungary and Servia. It is supposed
have originated in Greece, where a
lief was entertained to the effect th
Latin Christians buried in that count
could not decay in their graves, bei
under the ban of the Greek Church. T
cheerful notion was that they got o
of their graves at night and pursued t
occupation of ghouls. The superstiti
as to ghouls is very ancient and u
doubtedly of Oriental origin. Genera
speaking, however, a ghoul is just t
opposite of a vampire, being a livi
person who preys on dead bodies, wh
a vampire is a dead person that fee
on the blood of the living. If you h
your choice, which would you rather
a vampire or a ghoul?

One of the most familiar of the stor
of the Arabian Nights tells of a wom
who annoyed her husband very mu
by refusing food. Nothing more th
a few grains of rice would she e
at meals. He discovered that she w
in the habit of stealing away from
side in the night, and, following h
on one such occasion, he found her e
gaged in digging up and devouring
corpse.

Among the numerous folk tales abo
vampires is one relating to a fie
named Dakanavar, who dwelt in a ca
in Armenia. He would not permit an
body to penetrate into the mountains
Ulmish Altotem or to count their v
leys. Every one who attempted t
had in the night the blood sucked by t
monster from the soles of his feet un
he died.

At last, however, he was outwitt
by two cunning fellows. They began
count the valleys, and when night ca
they lay down to sleep, taking care
place themselves with the feet of ea
under the head of the other. In t
night the monster came, felt as us
and found a head. Then he felt at t
other end and found a head there also

"Well!" cried he, "I have gone throu
all of the three hundred and sixty-s
valleys of these mountains and ha
sucked the blood of people without e
but never yet did I find one with t
heads and no feet!" So saying he r
away, and never more was seen in th
country, but ever since people ha
known that the mountains have th
hundred and sixty-six valleys.

Belief in the vampire bats is mo
modern. For a long time it was ri
culed by science as a delusion, but
has been proved to be founded correc
upon fact. It was the famous natur
ist Darwin who settled this questi
One night he was camping with a pa
near Coquimbo, in Chili, and it happen
that a servant noticed the restlessn
of one of the horses. The man went
to tha horse and actually caught a
in the act of sucking blood from t
flank of the animal.

While many kind of bats have be
ignorantly accused of the blood-sucki
habit, only one species is really a va
pire. It constitutes a genus all by
self. Just as a man is the only spec
of the genus homo, so the vampire
is the only species of the genus desn
dus. Fortunately, it is not very lar
having a spread of only two feet. T
is not much for a bat. The so-cal
"flying foxes" of the old world, wh
go about in flocks and ravage orchar
are of much greater size, and there is
bat of Java, known as the "kalon
that has a spread of five feet from w
tip to wing tip. The body of the t
vampire bat weighs only a few ounce

Page 85. Rosenbach #46 verso.

New York World
(Sunday 2 February, 1896)[305]

Vampires in New England[306]

Dead Bodies Dug Up and Their Hearts Burned to Prevent Disease

Strange Superstition of Long Ago

The Old Belief Was that Ghostly Monsters Sucked the Blood of Their Living Relatives

Recent ethnological research has disclosed something very extraordinary in Rhode Island. It appears that the ancient vampire superstition still survives in that State, and within the last few years many people have been digging up the dead bodies of relatives for the purpose of burning their hearts.

Near Newport scores of such exhumations have been made, the purpose being to prevent the dead from preying upon the living. The belief entertained is that a person who has died of consumption is likely to rise from the grave at night and suck the blood of surviving members of his or her family, thus dooming them to a similar fate.

The discovery of the survival in highly educated New England of a superstition dating back to the days of Sardanapalus and Nebuchadnezzar has been made by George R. Stotson, an ethnologist of repute. He has found it rampant in a district which includes the towns of Exeter, Foster, Kingstown, East Greenwich and many scattered hamlets. This region, where abandoned farms are numerous, is the tramping-ground of the book agent, the chromo peddler and the patent medicine man. The social isolation is as complete as it was two centuries ago.

Here Cotton Mather and the host of medical, clerical and lay believers in the uncanny ideas of bygone centuries could still hold high carnival. Not merely the out-of-the-way agricultural folk, but the more intelligent people of the urban communities are strong in their belief in vampirism. One case noted was that of an intelligent and well-to-do head of a family who some years ago lost several of his children by consumption. After they were buried he dug them up and burned them in order to save the lives of their surviving brothers and sisters.

TWO TYPICAL CASES

There is one small village distant fifteen miles from Newport, where within the last few years there have been at least half a dozen resurrections on this account. The most recent was made two years ago in a family where the mother and four children had already succumbed to consumption. The last of these children was exhumed and the heart was burned.

Another instance was noted in a seashore town, not far from Newport, possessing a summer hotel and a few cottages of hot-weather residents. An intelligent man, by trade a mason,

notes continue on page 189

305. Bram Stoker probably found this article during his trip to New York in the winter of 1896.

306. "The Sunday newspaper feature from which the following passages are taken is important in at least two respects. I found it among Bram Stoker's working papers for *Dracula* (1897), and to my knowledge it has never previously been reprinted in whole or in part by any other vampire devotee. Moreover, since it is the only newspaper clipping among the *Dracula* papers, it seems safe to assume that Stoker's notions about vampires were to some degree influenced by it" (McNally, *A Clutch of Vampires* 163).

An illustration for Stoker's story, "The Invisible Giant" (*Under the Sunset*, 1881/1882).

informed Mr. Stotson that he had lost two brothers by consumption. On the death of the second brother, his father was advised to take up the body and burn the heart. He refused to do so and consequently he was attacked by the disease. Finally he died of it. His heart was burned, and in this way the rest of the family escaped.

This frightful superstition is said to prevail in all of the isolated districts of Southern Rhode Island, and it survives to some extent in the large centres of population. Sometimes the body is burned, not merely the heart, and the ashes are scattered.

In some parts of Europe the belief still has a hold on the popular mind. On the Continent from 1727 to 1735 there prevailed an epidemic of vampires. Thousands of people died, as was supposed, from having their blood sucked by creatures that came to their bedsides at night with goggling eyes and lips eager for the life fluid of the victim. In Servia it was understood that the demon might be destroyed by digging up the body and piercing it through with a sharp instrument, after which it was decapitated and burned. Relief was found in eating the earth of the vampire's grave. In the Levant the corpse was cut to pieces and boiled in wine.

VAMPIRISM: A PLAGUE

There was no hope for a person once chosen as a prey by a vampire. Slowly but surely he or she was destined to fade and sicken, receiving meanwhile nightly visits from the monster. Even death was no relief, for — and here was the most horrible part of the superstition — the victim, once dead and laid in the grave, was compelled to become a vampire and in his turn to take up the business of preying on the living. Thus vampirism was indefinitely propagated.

Realize, if you please, that at that period, when science was hardly born and no knowledge had been spread among the people to fight off superstition, belief in the reality of this fearful thing was absolute. Its existence was officially recognized, and military commissions were appointed for the purpose of opening the graves of suspected vampires and taking such measures as were necessary for destroying the latter.

Vampirism became a plague, more dreaded than any form of disease. Everywhere people were dying from the attacks of the blood-sucking monsters, each victim becoming in turn a night-prowler in pursuit of human prey. Terror of the mysterious and unearthly peril filled all hearts.

Evidence enough as to the prevalence of the mischief was afforded by the condition of many of the bodies that were dug up by the commissions appointed for the purpose. In many instances corpses which had been buried for weeks and even months were found fresh and lifelike. Sometimes fresh blood was actually discovered on their lips. What proof could be more convincing, inasmuch, as was well known, the buried body of a vampire is preserved and nourished by its nightly repasts? The blood on the lips, of course, was that of the victim of the night before.

The faith in vampirism entertained by the public at large was as complete as that which is felt in a discovery of modern science. It was an actual epidemic that threatened people, spreading rapidly and only to be checked by the adoption of most drastic measures.

The contents of every suspected grave were investigated, and many corpses found in such a condition as that described were promptly subjected to "treatment." This meant that a stake was driven through the chest, and the heart, being taken out, was either burned or chopped into small pieces. For in this way only could a vampire be deprived of power to do mischief. In one case a man who was unburied sat up in his coffin, with fresh blood on his lips. The

notes continue on page 191

Cover of 1901 edition of *Dracula*.

official in charge of the ceremonies held a crucifix before his face and, saying, "Do you recognize your Saviour?" chopped the unfortunate's head off. This person presumably had been buried alive in a cataleptic trance.

WERE THEY BURIED ALIVE?

How is the phenomenon to be accounted for? Nobody can say with certainty, but it may be that the fright into which people were thrown by the epidemic had the effect of predisposing nervous persons to catalepsy. In a word, people were buried alive in a condition where, the vital functions being suspended, they remained as it were dead for a while. It is a common thing for a cataleptic to bleed at the mouth just before returning to consciousness. According to the popular superstition, the vampire left his or her body in the grave while engaged in nocturnal prowls.

The epidemic prevailed all over south-eastern Europe, being at its worst in Hungary and Servia. It is supposed to have originated in Greece, where a belief was entertained to the effect that Latin Christians buried in that country could not decay in their graves, being under the ban of the Greek Church. The cheerful notion was that they got out of their graves at night and pursued the occupation of ghouls. The superstition as to ghouls is very ancient and undoubtedly of Oriental origin. Generally speaking, however, a ghoul is just the opposite of a vampire, being a living person who preys on dead bodies, while a vampire is a dead person that feeds on the blood of the living. If you had your choice, which would you rather be, a vampire or a ghoul?

One of the most familiar of the stories of the Arabian Nights tells of a woman who annoyed her husband very much by refusing food. Nothing more than a few grains of rice would she eat at meals. He discovered that she was in the habit of stealing away from his side in the night, and, following her on one such occasion, he found her engaged in digging up and devouring a corpse.

Among the numerous folk tales about vampires is one relating to a fiend named Dakanavar, who dwelt in a cave in Armenia. He would not permit anybody to penetrate into the mountains of Ulmish Altotem to count their valleys. Everyone who attempted this had in the night the blood sucked from the soles of his feet until he died.

At last, however, he was outwitted by two cunning fellows. They began to count the valleys, and when night came they lay down to sleep, taking care to place themselves with the feet of each under the head of the other. In the night the monster came, felt as usual and found a head. Then he felt at the other end and found a head there also.

"Well!" cried he, "I have gone through all of the three hundred and sixty-six valleys of these mountains and have sucked the blood of people without end, but never yet did I find one with two heads and no feet!" So saying he ran away, and never more was seen in that country, but ever since people have known that the mountains have three hundred and sixty-six valleys.

Belief in the vampire bats is more modern. For a long time it was ridiculed by science as a delusion, but it has been proved to be founded correctly upon fact. It was the famous naturalist Darwin who settled this question. One night he was camping with a party near Coquimbo, in Chili, and it happened that a servant noticed the restlessness of one of the horses. The man went up to the horse and actually caught a bat in the act of sucking blood from the flank of the animal.

While many kinds of bats have been ignorantly accused of the blood-sucking habit, only

notes continue on page 193

Bram Stoker, drawn by Alfred Bryan in 1885.

one species is really a vampire. It constitutes a genus all by itself. Just as a man is the only species of the genus homo, so the vampire bat is the only species of the genus desmodus. Fortunately, it is not very large, having a spread of only two feet. This is not much for a bat. The so-called "flying foxes" of the old world, which go about in flocks and ravage orchards are of much greater size, and there is a bat of Java, known as the "kalong," that has a spread of five feet from wing tip to wing tip. The body of the true vampire bat weighs only a few ounces.

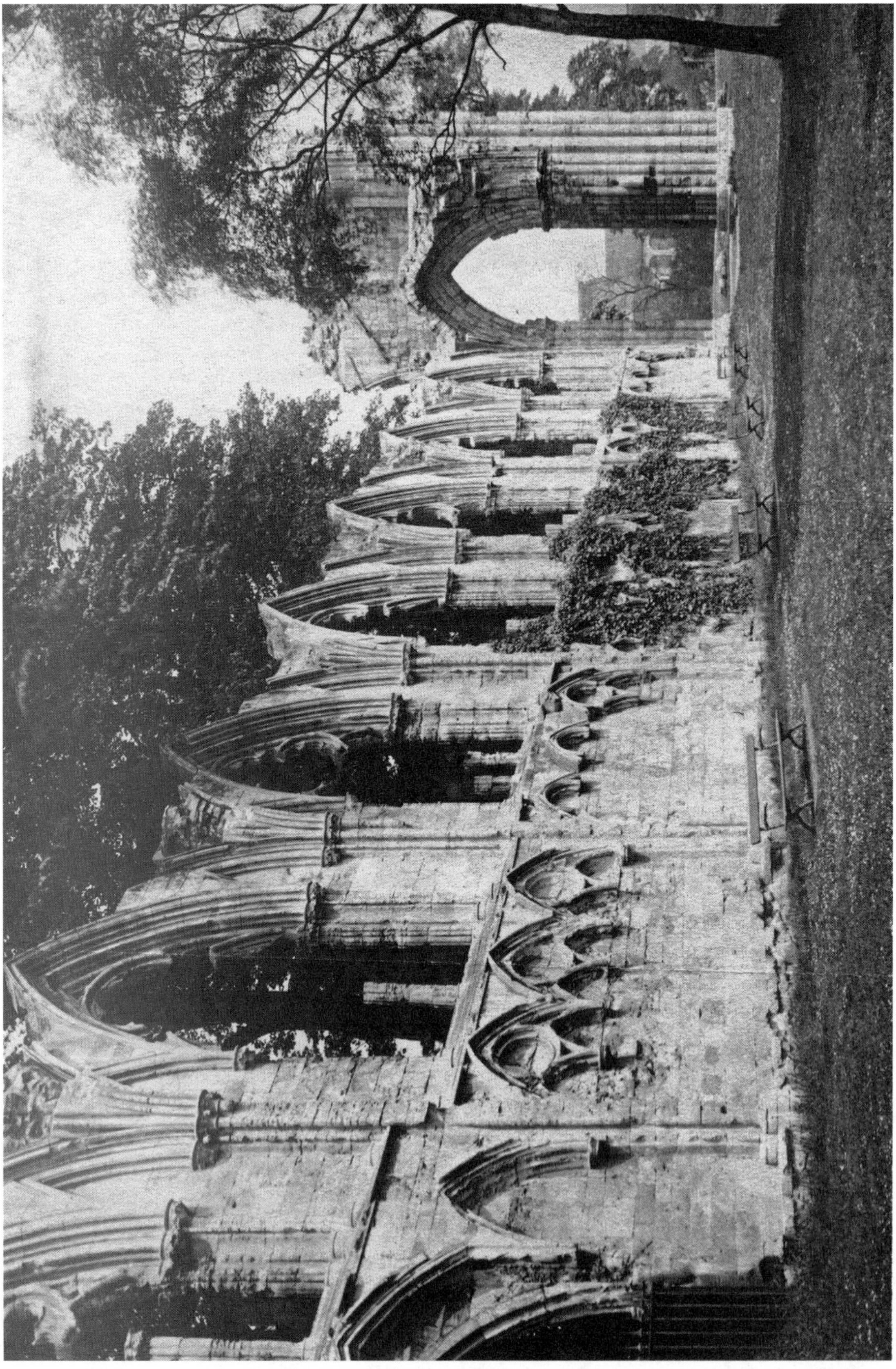

Page 86. Rosenbach #45 verso.

Photograph

[Photo a. of Whitby Abbey]

Page 87. Rosenbach #46.

Photograph

[Photo b. of Whitby Abbey]

Part III

Typed Research Notes ("'Dracula' Notes, etc.")

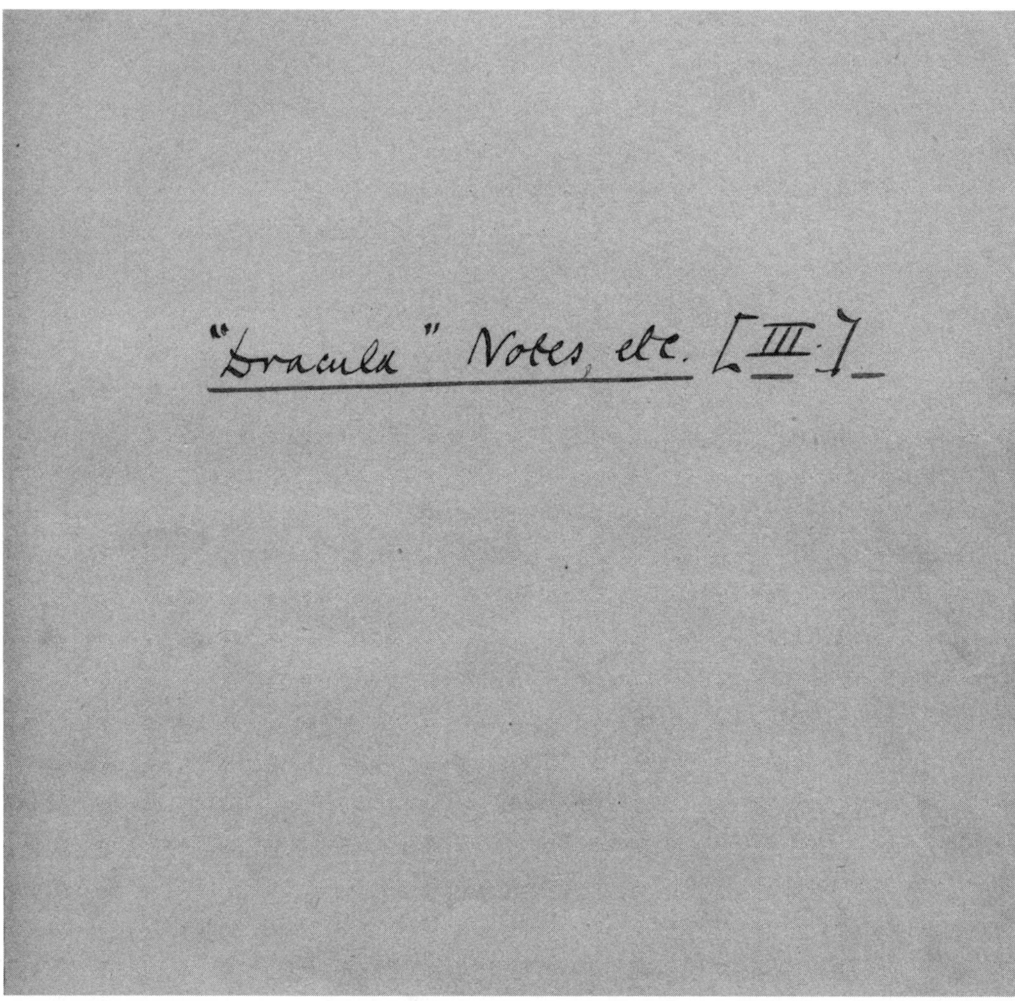

49

1

MAGYARLAND.

By a Fellow of the Carpathian Society.

Sampson Low 1881.

"PAPRIKA HENDL"

"szegény legény" = Poor lads" = robbers

Fogado = inn.

South east of Northern Carpathians are Rusniaks or Ruthenians-

"Where the Turk treads no grass grows."

"Blats"- Swamp or marsh.

Grasses 8 or 10 feet hegh near L. Balaton

MAGYAR is pronounced MAD-YAR.

B.45. Max Muller traces Magyars to Ural Mountains stretching up to Artic Ocean. Close affinity of language to idiom of **Finnish race east of Volga**. Says Magyars are 4th branch of Finnish stock viz. the Ugric - in 4th century were called Ugrogs [see Max Muller's Science of Language] (mem wehr wolf legend through Fins)

HUNS under Attila came between 3rd and 4th centuries-

Page 88. Rosenbach #49.

A Fellow of the Carpathian Society[307]
Magyarland
London: Sampson Low, 1881

"PAPRIKA HENDL"

"szégény légény" = "Poor lads" = robbers

Fogado = inn

South east <xxx> of Northern Carpathians are Rusniaks or Ruthenians–

"Where the Turk treads no grass grows."

"Blats"—swamp or marsh

Grasses 8 or 10 feet high near L. Balaton

MAGYAR is pronounced MAD-YAR

P. 45

Max Muller[308] traces Magyars to Ural Mountains stretching up to Arctic Ocean. Close affinity of language to idiom of Finnish race east of Volga. Says Magyars are 4th branch of Finnish stock viz. the Ugric—in 4th century were called Ugrogs. (See: Max Muller's "Science of Language.")
(Memo: werewolf legend through Finns.)

HUNS under Attila came between 3rd and 4th centuries—

307. The anonymous author of *Magyarland* has been identified as Nina Elizabeth Mazuchelli.
308. Max Muller may have been the model for Professor Van Helsing.

50

2

MAGYARLAND.

a Century or two later came the Avars also of Northern race.
Then came Magyars under Arpád.

P.53. "FARAS NÉPEK"= King Pharoah's people= Gypsies= Czigány.

P.57 The "HONFOGLALAS"= Conquest of Hungarians fatherland by Arpád in 9th century.

P.75. "DÉLI-BÁB"= Mirage seen in the Hungarian plains= "Fairy of the South".

P.77. "ÖRDÖG"----Satan.
"POKOL"----Hell.
"KIS"------Little.
"NAGY"-----Great.
"SZÓHORDÓK"= "word-bearers"= bench outside peasants' house.

The "ALFÖLD" is the great Hungarian plain.

[Man leeches - attracted to Count D, and then repelled - develop idea.]

P.113. "KÖDMÖNY"= Short sheepskin embroideried on smooth side bright coloured silk or vool.

P.169. Ròcr STRACENA" - Slav word for "vanished"

Page 89. Rosenbach #50.

a century or two later came the Avars also of Northern race. Then came Magyars under Arpad.

P. 53

"FARAS NEPEK" = King Pharaoh's people = Gypsies = Czigány.

P. 57

The "HONFOGLALAS" = Conquest of Hungarian fatherland by Arpad in 9th century.

P. 75

"DÉLI-BÁB" = Mirage seen in the Hungarian plains = "Fairy of the South."

P. 77

"ORDÖG"----- Satan.
"POKOL"----- Hell.[309]
"KIS"----- Little.
"NAGY"----- Great.
"SZÓHORDÓK" = "word-bearers" = bench outside peasant's house.

The "ALFÖLD" is the great Hungarian plain.

(Mem: leeches—attracted to Count D, and then repelled—develop idea.)[310]

P. 113

"KÖDMÖNY" = Short sheepskin embroidered on smooth side bright coloured silk or wool.

P. 169

River "STRACENA"—Slav word for "vanished."

309. Jonathan Harker repeatedly hears the words "Ordog" and "pokol" in Bistritz. His memo to "ask the Count about these superstitions" (1:6) is tinged with irony.

310. Occasionally, Stoker inserts plot-related memos into his research notes. The memo about leeches is not developed any further but, in chapter 4, Harker likens Dracula to a leech: "There lay the Count.... It seemed as if the whole awful creature were simply gorged with blood; he lay like a filthy leech, exhausted with his repletion. I shuddered as I bent over to touch him..." (4:52).

3

MAGYARLAND.

P.190.1. 470,000 Rusniaks in N.E. portion of Hungary, supposed descendents of band of Russians who came in with Arpád. Wear ponderous capes of black curly sheepskin.

Rusniaks and Slovaks wear

P.191. loose jackets, large trousers of coarse wool, once white,— round waist enormous belts leather more than ½ inch thick 12 to 16 inches broad, studded with brass headed nails in various patterns. In these belts they keep knives, scissors, tobacco pouch, light box. &c

P.262. Rusniaks are called "Ruthenians" in Gallicia [Poland] and are, like Slavoks, of Greek Church.

P.316. "TÓT NEM EMBER" — "Not a man of all" a saying of Magyars regarding Slovak.

Page 90. Rosenbach #51.

P. 190–1

470,000 Rusniaks in N.E. portion of Hungary, supposed descendants of band of Russians who came in with Arpad. Wear ponderous capes of black curly sheepskin.

P. 191

Rusniaks and <xxx> Slovaks wear loose jacket, large trousers of coarse wool, once white — round waist enormous belts leather more than ½ inch thick 12 to 16 inches broad, studded with brass headed nails in various patterns. In these belts, they keep knives, scissors, tobacco pouch, light box etc.

P. 262

Rusniaks are called "Ruthenians" in Gallacia (Poland) and are, like Slovaks, of Greek Church.

P. 316

"TÓT NEM EMBER" = "Not a man of all" — a saying of Magyars regarding Slovak.

1

I have never heard in any country of such universal belief in devils, familiars, omens, ghosts, sorceries, and witchcrafts. The Malays have many queer notions about tigers, and usually only speak of them in whispers, because they think that certain souls of human beings who have departed this life have taken up their abode in these beasts, and in some places for this reason, they will not kill a tiger unless he commits some specially bad aggression. They also believe that some men a tigers by night and men by day!

The pelisit, the bad spirit which rode on the tail of Mr Maxwell's horse, is supposed to be the ghost of a woman who has died in childbirth. In the form of a large bird uttering a harsh cry it is believed to haunt forests and burial-grounds and to afflict children. The Malays have a bottle-imp, the polong, which will take no other sustenance than the blood of its owner, but it will reward him by aiding him to carry out revengeful purposes. The harmless owl has strange superstitions attaching to it, and is called the "spectre bird," you may remember that the fear of encountering it was one of the reasons why the ~~Permantang-~~ Permantang Pasir men would not go with through the jungle of Rassa.

A vile fiend called the penangalan takes possession of the forms

Page 91. Rosenbach #52.

Isabella L. Bird
The Golden Chersonese
London: John Murray, 1883

(pp. 353–55)

I have never heard in any country of such universal belief in devils, familiars, omens, ghosts, sorceries, and witchcrafts. The Malays have many queer notions about tigers, and usually only speak of them in whispers, because they think that certain souls of human beings who have departed this life have taken up their abode in these beasts, and in some places for this reason, they will not kill a tiger unless he commits some especially bad aggression. They also believe that some men are tigers by night and men by day.

The pelisit, the bad spirit which rode on the tail of Mr. Maxwell's horse, is supposed to be the ghost of a woman who has died in childbirth. In the form of a large bird uttering a harsh cry it is believed to haunt forests and burial-grounds and to afflict children. The Malays have a bottle-imp, the polong, which will take no other sustenance than the blood of its owner, but it will reward him by aiding him to carry out revengeful purposes. The harmless owl has strange superstitions attaching to it, and is called the "spectre bird"; you may recall that the fear of encountering it was one of the reasons why the <Permantagg> Permantang Pasir men would not go through the jungle of Rassa.

A vile fiend called the penangalan takes possession of the forms

2

of women, turnes them into witches, and compels them to quit the greater part of their bodies, and fly away by night to gratify a vampire craving for human blood. This is very like one of the ghoul stories in the Arabian Nights Entertainments. Then they have a spectre huntsman with demon dogs who roams the forests, and a storm fiend who rides the whirlwind, and spirits borrowed from Persia and Arabia. It almost seems as if the severe monotheism to which they have been converted compels them to create a gigantic demonology.

From miss Bird's "Goldon Chersonese." pages 353.

Page 92. Rosenbach #53.

of women, turns them into witches, and compels them to quit the greater part of their bodies, and fly away by night to gratify a vampire craving for human blood. This is very like one of the ghoul stories in the Arabian Nights Entertainments. Then they have a spectre huntsman with demon dogs who roams the forests, and a storm fiend who rides the whirl-wind, and spirits borrowed from Persia and Arabia. It almost seems as if the severe monotheism to which they have been converted compels them to create a giant demonology.

THE
ROUNDS ABOUT CARPATHIANS.

A F Crosse. Blackwoods.1878.

(E) P.7. Houses [Hungarian] Separate, Blank gable to road.

(E) P.5. Horses four abreast and small

P.8. SLIVOVITZ= plum brandy.

P.84. "Robber steak" bits of beef bacon and onion strung on stick, seasoned with paprika and salt, and roasted over a fire; lower end of stick being rolled backwards and forwards between palms as you hold it over the embers.

P.89. CZARDAS- dances of Maygar peasant.

(E) P-91. Hayricks in trees.

(E) -102 dogs in Hungary dangerous.

(E) - 106. LEITERWAGEN - ladderwagon, long cart without springs with a snake like vertebrae which adapts itself to inequalities of road.

(E) - 108. Weeping birch trees in Southern Carpathians .

Page 93. Rosenbach #54.

A. F. Crosse
Round About the Carpathians
London: Blackwoods, 1878[311]

P. 7

Houses (Hungarian) Separate. Blank gable to road.[312]

P. 5

Horses four abreast and small[313]

P. 8

SLIVOVITZ = plum brandy.[314]

P. 84

"Robber steak" bits of beef bacon and onion strung on stick, seasoned with paprika and salt, and roasted over a fire[315]; lower end of stick being rolled backwards and forwards between palms as you hold it over the embers.

P. 89

CZARDAS = dances of Magyar peasant.

P. 91

Hayricks in trees.[316]

P. 102

dogs in Hungary dangerous.

P. 106

LEITERWAGEN = ladderwagon, long cart without springs with a snake like vertebrae which adapts itself to inequalities of road.[317]

P. 108

Weeping birch trees in Southern Carpathians.[318]

---

311. Crosse is one of Stoker's most important sources of information about Transylvania. Contrary to popular opinion, Stoker never ventured into "The Land Beyond the Forest."

312. Jonathan describes the scene en route to the Borgo Pass: "Before us lay a green sloping land full of forests and woods, with here and there steep hills, crowned with clumps of trees or with farmhouses, the blank gable end to the road" (1:7).

313. "Then our driver, whose wide linen drawers covered the whole front of the box-seat—'gotza' they call them—cracked his big whip over his four small horses, which ran abreast, and we set off on our journey" (1:6).

314. "The night is chill, mein Herr, and my master the Count bade me take all care of you. There is a flask of slivovitz (the plum brandy of the country) underneath the seat, if you should require it" (1:11).

315. Before leaving Bistritz, Jonathan Harker dined at the Golden Krone hotel: "I dined on what they call 'robber steak'—bits of bacon, onion, and beef, seasoned with red pepper, and strung on sticks and roasted over the fire, in the simple style of the London cat's meat" (1:6).

316. "There were many things new to me: for instance, hay-ricks in the trees..." (1:8).

317. "Now and again we passed a leiter-wagon—the ordinary peasant's cart, with its long, snakelike vertebra, calculated to suit the inequalities of the road" (1:8).

318. "...and here and there very beautiful masses of weeping birch, their white stems shining like silver through the delicate green of the leaves" (1:8).

(Round about Carpathians)
2

55

(E)

P.110. Grey moss in abundant festoons from fir trees, a weird and solemn.

" 120. golden Mediasch, one of the best Translyvanian wines produces an agreeable pricking on tongue called by Germans "tschirpsen"

" 141. Maize variously cooked, water melons paprika handl and "gulgas" [sort of Irish stew]

\+

" 141. Czigany = gypsies. 150,000 in Hungary.

(D)

\+

" 146. Gypsies hang on to Magyar castles, and call themselves by names of the owner and profess his faith, whatever it be.

(F)

" 149. In Hungarian the Christian name comes last Buda Adam not Adam Buda.

" MEM. see "The birds of Translyvania." Danford and Brown. 1875.

P.159. Matthias Corvinus King of Hungary, son of Hunyadi, saying "King Matthias is dead and justice with him!"

do. Capestrano was the monk who carried Cross to raise the

Page 94. Rosenbach #55.

P. 110

Grey moss in abundant festoons from fir trees — weird and solemn.

P. 120

golden Mediasch, one of the best Transylvanian wines produces an agreeable pricking on tongue — called by Germans "tschirpsen"

P. 141

Maize variously cooked — water melons — paprika hendl and "gulyas" (sort of Irish stew).

P. 141

Czigany = gypsies. 150,000 in Hungary.

P. 146

Gypsies hang on to Magyar castles, and call themselves by names of the owner and profess his faith, whatever it be.

P. 149

In Hungarian the Christian name comes last — Buda Adam not Adam Buda.[319]

MEM. see "The Birds of Transylvania." Danforth and Brown, 1875.[320]

P. 159

Matthias Corvinus — King of Hungary, son of Hunyadi. Saying "King Matthias is dead and justice with him!"

Capestrano was the monk who carried Cross to raise the

319. We are reminded that Dracula's native tongue is Hungarian, not Romanian, when he exclaims, "my friend Harker Jonathan — nay, pardon me, I fall into my country's habit of putting your patronymic first…" (2:23).

320. We do not know if Stoker read this book or took any notes from it.

(Round about Carpathians)
3

Hungarians against Moslems.

MEM. Horses to be disturbed at approach of Count Dracula and smell blood!

P.171. Old Saxon fortress-churches.

-' 187. In Cox's Travels in Sweden, mentioned that Sainovitz Hungarian Jesuit went to Lapland 1775. to see Transit of Venus; said Lapland and Hungarian idioms were the same.

-' 202. Kronstadt. picturesque inn-yard seen through wide arched doorway. open arcade surrounds it oleander trees in green tubs in centre. long wagons four horses abreast, peasantry with snow-white sheepskins or embroi-derie, white leather coats lined with black fur, flat caps, peaked hats, drum-shaped hats for girls— matrons wear close twisted white kerchiefs.

-' 205. SZEKLERS -' 1 of 4 Translyvanian races— are of Turanian origin, like Maygar but older branch. Whem Maygars over-ran Pannonia in the 10th. Century under Arpad the found Szeklers in possession of part of the vast Carpathian horse-shoe— that part known as the Transylvanian frontier of Moldaria. They claim to have come there in 4th Century. Descended from Huns.

MEM. Valley - belt of dark fir and then snow, late Spring— and early Autumn.

(E) P223 "grim phantom-haunted clouds"

Page 95. Rosenbach #56

Hungarians against Moslems.

MEM. Horses to be disturbed at approach of Count Dracula and smell blood![321]

P. 171

Old Saxon fortress — churches.

P. 187

In Cox's Travels in Sweden, mentioned that Sainovitz a Hungarian Jesuit went to Lapland 1775 to see Transit of Venus; said Lapland and Hungarian idioms were the same.

P. 202

Kronstadt. Picturesque inn-yard seen through wide arched doorway — open arcade surrounds it — oleander trees in green tubs in centre, long wagons four horses abreast, peasantry with snow-white sheepskins or embroidery, white leather coats lined with black fur, flat caps, peaked hats, drum-shaped hats for girls — matrons wear close twisted <xxx> white kerchiefs.

P. 205

SZEKLERS —1 of 4 Transylvanian races — are of Turanian origin, like Magyar but older branch. When Magyars overran Pannonia in the 10th Century under Arpad they found Szeklers in possession of part of the vast Carpathian horse-shoe — that part known as the Transylvanian frontier of Moldavia. They claim to have come there in the 4th Century. Descended from Huns.

MEM. Valley — belt of dark fir and then snow, late Spring and early Autumn.

P. 223

"grim phantom-haunted clouds."

321. This is another intriguing scrap that Stoker did not use in the novel, but a resonance remains: "[T]he horses began to neigh and snort and plunge wildly, so that the driver had to hold them up. Then, amongst a chorus of screams from the peasants and a universal crossing of themselves, a calèche, with four horses, drove up behind us, overtook us, and drew up beside the coach.... They were driven by a tall man, with a long brown beard and a great black hat, which seemed to hide his face from us. I could only see the gleam of a pair of very bright eyes, which seemed red in the lamplight, as he turned to us" (1:10). In the final chapter, Van Helsing records that as they neared Castle Dracula, "the horses began to scream, and tore at their tethers till I came to them and quieted them" (27:377).

(Round about Carpathians)
4

(E) P. 243. Oak, Beech, Pine. Plenty water.

- 264. At St Miklos popn. mostly Armenians.

- 271. "It is curious to notice sometimes in the higher Carpathians how the clouds march continously through the winding valleys." (E)

-286. Forest near Toplicza - Giant trees, Oaks, and many burned and fallen.

- 294. MAROS VASARHELY - is central place of Szeklers.

- 298. "A lord is a lord even in Hell". Peasant saying in time of forced labour.

MEM. Read "The New Landlord" Hungarian novel. G.Jokai.

P.312. MEM - Robber incident, lady entertains robbers, and trusts their honour - they leave.

- 345. RUSNIACKS - descended from Russian settlers - very savage.

- 359. SLOVACKS - Shaggy coats of black sheepskin and usual long staff with axe at end. (E)

Page 96. Rosenbach #57

P. 243

Oak, Beech, Pine. Plenty water.

P. 264

At St. Miklos population mostly Armenians.

P. 271

"It is curious to notice sometimes in the higher Carpathians how the clouds march continuously through the winding valleys."

P. 286

Forest near Toplicza — Giant trees, Oaks and many burned and fallen.

P. 294

MAROS VASARHELY — is central place of Szeklers.

P. 298

"A lord is a lord even in Hell." Peasant saying in time of forced labour.

MEM. Read "The New Landlord" Hungarian novel. G. Jokai.[322]

P. 312

MEM. — Robber incident, lady entertains robbers, and trusts their honour — they leave.

P. 345

RUSNIACKS — descended from Russian settlers — very savage.

P. 359

SLOVACKS — Shaggy coats of black sheepskin and usual long staff with axe at end.

322. There is no indication that he read Jokai.

(Round about Carpathians)

5

58

P.366 Sometimes Tokay (wine) gets sick in Spring - the time when the sap rises in living plants. (mem. Guess cause.)

- 373. Harvest operations begin end of June and last 6 weeks - Vintage [Tokay] 3 or4th week in Oct.

mem Count Dracula in prison picks out murderer.

Page 97. Rosenbach #58.

P. 366

Sometimes Tokay wine gets sick in Spring — the time when the sap rises in living plants. (Mem. Guess cause.)

P. 373

Harvest operations begin end of June and last 6 weeks — Vintage (Tokay) 3 or 4th week in Oct.

Mem. Count Dracula in prison picks out murderer.[323]

323. This idea was not used in the novel.

" ON THE TRACK OF THE CRESCENT."

My Major C.Johnson. Hurst & Blackett 1885.

Name of people GETÆ changed to DACIANS after defeat by Alexander the Great 4th Century B.C.

H +

P. 105.6. In 376. A.D. Huns subdued Dacia driving out the Goths- Huns at Attila's death 543 A.D.by the Gepidae - a tribe of Goths. Country was afterwards held by Lombards, Avars and Bulgars. last named driven out of Thessaly etc. and back to Dacia where obtained ascendency over Avars. 678.680.

See Samuelson's Roumania.P.146.

+

P. 107. Hungarians annexed Translyvania A.D.1008. under Stephen. Afterwards ruled by Voivodes.

E

P.118-19. Roumanian women loose-sleeved white undergarment or chemisette, and over this coloured apron called a CATRINTSA which descended before and behind fitting so tightly as to show the figure - also wore necklaces and large earrings, white cloths on head, which descended to the back of the neck, coloured stockings and ankle boots. Some of these wore what afterwards saw in Translyvania — a broad belt or girdle called an OBRESKA tightly bound round the waist handsomely embroideried in various colours

Page 98. Rosenbach #59.

Major E. C. Johnson
On the Track of the Crescent
London: Hurst & Blackett, 1885

Name of people GETAE changed to DACIANS after defeat by Alexander the Great. 4th Century B.C.

P. 105–6

In 376 A.D. Huns subdued Dacia driving out the Goths — Huns at Attila's death 543 A.D. by the Gepidae — a tribe of Goths. Country was afterward held by Lombards, Avars and Bulgars. Last named driven out of Thessaly etc. and back to Dacia where obtained ascendancy over Avars. 678–680. See Samuelson's Roumania. P. 146.

P. 107

Hungarians annexed Transylvania A.D. 1008 under Stephen. Afterwards ruled by Voivodes.

P. 118–19

Roumanian women loose-sleeved white undergarment or chemisette, and over this coloured apron called a CATRINTSA which descended before and behind fitting so tightly as to show the figure — also wore necklaces and large earrings. White cloths on head, which descended to the back of the neck, coloured stockings and ankle boots. Some of those wore what afterwards saw in Transylvania — a broad belt or a girdle called an OBRESKA tightly bound round the waist, handsomely embroidered in various colours

"On the track of the Crescent"

2

and had a thick fringe of black and red pendent from it to bottom of skirt — as if the other apron had been cut into stripes. The wearers of this costume had coloured handkerchiefs instead of the white head cloth.

P.119 Roumanians of better class had tight chemisette with short skirt showing embroidered shoes and open sleeves which hung from the elbow, and above this a very fine cambric or muslin overskirt covered with spangles and beautifully worked by hand - Aprons also richly worked with spangles were sometimes worn both before and behind - Chemisette open at neck - no stays.

P.120. Favourite dish of peasant "Mamaliga" maize flour stirred in water and consistency of hasty pudding and eaten with salt - Egg plant stuffed with chopped meat is National dish and called "UA IMPLETATA".

Roumanian white wine "ODOBESTI"; also red wine made at Berleta. Sturgeon is staple fish, Sterlet and Danube Carp.

P.205-6 WALLACHIA.

Men in Tartar fur caps, sheepskin jackets - fur outwards, shirts with tails outside white trousers, and Russian boots or trousers tucked into garters made of rough cloth over which sandals are bound - Women with white kerchief

Page 99. Rosenbach #60

and had thick fringe of black and red pendent from it to bottom of skirt — as if the other apron had been cut into strips. The wearers of this costume had coloured handkerchiefs instead of the white head cloth.

P. 119

Roumanians of better class had tight chemisette with short skirt showing embroidered shoes and open sleeves which hung from the elbow and above this a very fine cambric or muslin overskirt covered with spangles and beautifully worked by hand. Aprons also richly worked with spangles were sometimes worn both before and behind. Chemisette open at neck — no stays.

P. 120

Favourite dish of peasant "Mamaliga" — maize flour stirred in water and consistency of hasty pudding and eaten with salt. Egg plant stuffed with chopped meat is National dish and called "UA IMPLETATA."

Roumanian white wine "ODOBESTI"; also red wine made at Berleta. Sturgeon is staple fish, Sterlet and Danube Carp.

P. 205–6

WALLACHIA.

Men in Tartar fur caps, sheepskin jackets — fur outwards, shirts with tails outside white trousers, and Russian boots or trousers tucked into garters made of rough cloth over which sandals are bound — Women with white kerchief

"On the track of the Crescent"

3

on head loose chemise with baggy sleeves . tucked up at elbow - reaching to ankle, open down to waist : has strings to fasten at neck and waist - and belt or girdle from which is suspended the OBRESKA - with fringe of black and scarlet reaching to ankle

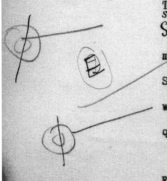

TRANSLYVANIA inhabited by Magyars, Saxons, Wallachs, and Szekelys — Magyars to West — Saxons South. — Szekelys East and North. Wallachs [descendents of Dacians] mixed with Saxons.

Szekelys claim to be descended from Attila and the Huns, who were found settled on Eastern frontier when country conquered by Magyars in 11th Century.

From 11th Century till 1526 Translyvania was part of Hungary, governed by an official appointed by the King of Hungary.

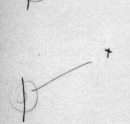

After battle of Mohacs which extinguished Hungarian independence Transylvania became Turkish who made it an independent principality governed by Princes elected by people with approval of the Sultan.

P.205.6. No Szekely or Saxon elected to office of prince which was reserved for Hungarian nobility. Protection of Turkey withdrawn, 1699, when after much civil war all parties, except Wallachs and Gypsies, got equal rights; and in 1791. Diet lost right of electing princes.

Page 100. Rosenbach #61

on head loose chemise with baggy sleeves — tucked up at elbow — reaching to ankle, open down to waist has strings to fasten at neck and waist — and belt or girdle from which is suspended the OBRESKA — with fringe of black and scarlet reaching to ankle.

TRANSYLVANIA inhabited by Magyars, Saxons, Wallachs, and Szekelys. Magyars to West — Saxons South — Szekelys East and North — Wallachs (descendents of Dacians) mixed with Saxons.[324]

Szekelys claim to be descended from Attila and the Huns, who were found settled on Eastern frontier when country conquered by Magyars in 11th Century.[325]

From 11th Century till 1526 Transylvania was part of Hungary, governed by an official appointed by the King of Hungary.

After battle of Mohacs which extinguished Hungarian independence Transylvania became Turkish who made it an independent principality governed by Princes elected by people with approval of the Sultan.

P. 205–6

No Szekely or Saxon elected to office of prince which was reserved for Hungarian nobility. Protection of Turkey withdrawn, 1699, when after much civil war all parties, except Wallachs and Gypsies, got equal rights; and in 1791 Diet lost right of electing princes.

324. All of this material can be found in Harker's Journal: "In the population of Transylvania there are four distinct nationalities: Saxons in the south, and mixed with them the Wallachs, who are the descendants of the Dacians; Magyars in the west, and Szekelys in the east and north" (1:2). Stoker makes Count Dracula a Szekely (Szekler). As the Count exclaims, "We Szekelys have a right to be proud, for in our veins flows the blood of many brave races..." (3:29).

325. Dracula asks Harker, "What devil or what witch was ever so great as Attila, whose blood is in these veins?" (3:30).

(on the track of the Crescent)

P. 207. Hungary and Translyvania though nominally, not really united until 1848. Transylvania sends 69 delegates to Pesth, finally united, after rebellion, in 1867.

P.207. Rivers rise in Translyvania flowing through Moldavia, Wallachia and Hungary.

P.228. Formerly only Nobles could hold lands in Hungary - paid no taxes but were obliged to flock with retainers to Kings standard on receipt of the "bloody sword" as a signal of national emergency.

P.234. The Szekelys played important part in Hungary and Translyvania. The Szekelys were recognized as kindred by the Magyars on first entering Hungary and have remained allies since. Szekelys received privileges for guarding frontier towards Moldavia and "Turkey land"; also speak purest Hungarian. In 1848. joined National force against Austrians.

"Ban" means "Lord".

P.238. Many women wear only one loose garment, sleeves tucked up and Obreska round waist fringe of it blowing in breeze. Most had handkerchiefs twisted round head.

P238-9 Full costume of Hungarian peasant very ancient. Summer - loose embroideried shirt - immense linen drawers "GATZA": those of ~~seated~~ coachman cover front of box. Shirt has voluminous sleeves like bishops'. high boots

Page 101. Rosenbach #62.

P. 207

Hungary and Transylvania, though nominally, not really united until 1848. Transylvania sends 69 delegates to Pseth. Finally united, after rebellion, in 1867.

P. 207

Rivers rise in Transylvania flowing through Moldavia, Wallachia and Hungary.

P. 228

Formerly only nobles could hold lands in Hungary—paid no taxes but were obliged to flock with retainers to king's standard on receipt of the "bloody sword" as a signal of national emergency.

P. 234

The Szekelys played important part in Hungary and Transylvania. The Szekelys were recognized as kindred by the Magyars on first entering Hungary and have remained allies since. Szekelys receive privileges for guarding frontier towards Moldavia and "Turkey land"[326]; also speak purest Hungarian. In 1848, joined National force against Austrians.

"Ban" means "lord."

P. 238

Many women wear only one loose garment, sleeves tucked up and Obreska round waist fringe of it blowing in breeze. Most had handkerchiefs twisted round head.

P. 238–9

Full costume of Hungarian peasant very ancient. Summer—loose embroidered shirt—immense linen drawers "GATZA"—those of seated coachman cover front of box. Shirt has voluminous sleeves like bishops'—high boots

326. "And when the Hungarian flood swept eastward, the Szekelys were claimed as kindred by the victorious Magyars, and to us for centuries was trusted the guarding of the frontier of Turkey-land" (3:30).

(on the track of the Crescent)
5

63

and pork pie hat with feather

P.238.9. Winter . tight cloth panteloons "Nadrag" over loose drawers - very tight, Sleeveless embroideried waistcoat fastened up to throat, silver buttons close together down front, embroideried huzzar jacket and immense cloak, reaching to heels, made of sheepskin and called a "Bunda". When no boots, cloth bound with strips of leather

P.240. Girls' hair bound with piece of silk. Married women like chignons . chemisette embroidered coloured worsted in front and sleeves body dress, startling colours, laced in front like Swiss. full, short dark calico petticoat; high boots or cloth sandals, and handkerchief on head fastened under chin - Peasants even in Summer wear when going to church thick cloaks with fur inside. Women short blue pelisses, fur lined, heavy top boots black or yellow leather red heels - handkerchiefs on head. Hungarian magnates gala dress [Translyvanian] embroi-deried tunic- loose frogs - fitting tight . tight "Nadrag" [pantaloons] embroidered - Polish busby, feather fastened with spray of diamonds - high patent leather boots :- slung on shoulder tight sleeved Polish pelisse . lined with silk. massive embroidery - chain in front - Curved scimitar with velvet sheath and studded with jewels and gold . Sometimes an "ATTILA" or large overcloak

Page 102. Rosenbach #63.

and "pork pie" hat with feather.

P. 238–9

Winter — tight cloth pantaloons "Nadrag" over loose drawers — very tight, sleeveless embroidered waistcoat fastened up to the throat, silver buttons close together down front, embroidered huzzar jacket and immense cloak, reaching to heels, made of sheepskin and called a "Bunda." When no boots, cloth bound with strips of leather.

P. 240

Girls' hair bound with piece of silk. Married women like chignons. Chemisette embroidered coloured worsted in front and sleeves body dress, startling colours, laced in front like Swiss. Full, short, dark, calico petticoat: high boots or cloth sandals, and handkerchief on head fastened under chin. Peasants even in Summer wear when going to church thick cloaks with fur inside. Women short blue pelisses, fur lined, heavy top boots black or yellow leather red heels — handkerchiefs on head. Hungarian magnates gala dress (Transylvanian) embroidered tunic — loose frogs —fitting tight — tight "Nadrag" (pantaloons) embroidered — Polish busby, feather fastened with spray of diamonds — high patent leather boots — slung on shoulder tight sleeved Polish pelisse. Lined with silk. Massive embroidery — chain in front — Curved scimitar with velvet sheath and studded with jewels and gold. Sometimes an "ATTILA" or large overcloak

("On the track of The Crescent")
6

coloured velvet lined with satin.

(E) P.244. SLOVAKS [Translyvanian peasants] white linen shirts, loose white trousers enormous broad leather belts - long straight hair about shoulders, heavy black moustaches immense hats. Knee boots.

P.246. Translyvanians house usually built, two wings with central archway main entrance - upper room open stone corridors, staircases, floors etc. and furniture polished oak - strips of carpet by bedside rest of floor uncovered.

(E) P-249. Many Crosses by roadside.

P.258. Torture tower narrow windows.

(E) P.261. CARPATHIANS. interminable forest up to base of mountains, brilliant in shades of blue brown and dusky purple - rocky crags towered range on range till crowned by mighty "Isten - Szek" ["God's Seat"] the abode of eternal snow.

(E) Carpathians. towering aloft in savage grandeur — steep and rocky sides cut by immense chasms through which descend waters which fertilize Translyvania.

(E) P.269. Carpathians — highest snow peaks had flesh tints as sun sank.

Page 103. Rosenbach #64.

coloured velvet lined with satin.

P. 244

SLOVAKS (Transylvanian peasants) white linen shirts, loose white trousers enormous broad leather belts — long straight hair about shoulders, heavy black moustaches immense hats. Knee boots.

P. 246

Transylvanians <home> house usually built two wings with central archway main entrance — upper room open stone corridors, staircases, floors etc. and furniture polished oak — strips of carpet by bedside rest of floor uncovered.

P. 249

Many crosses by roadside.

P. 258

Torture tower narrow windows.

P. 261

CARPATHIANS. interminable forest up to base of mountains, brilliant in shades of blue brown and dusky purple — rocky crags towered range on range till crowned by mighty "Isten-Szek" ("God's Seat") the abode of eternal snow.

Carpathians towering aloft in savage grandeur — steep and rocky sides cut by immense chasms through which descend waters which fertilize Transylvania.[327]

P. 269

Carpathians — highest snow peaks had flesh tints as sun sank.

327. Having never visited the Carpathians, Stoker relied on research for passages such as this: "...an endless perspective of jagged rock and pointed crags ... where the snowy peaks rose grandly. Here and there seemed mighty rifts in the mountains, through which, as the sun began to sink, we saw now and again the white gleam of falling water. One of my companions touched my arm as we swept round the base of a hill.... 'Look! Isten szek!— God's seat!'" (1:8).

("on the track of the Crescent"=)

65

P.271. PAPRIKAS CZIRKE = Chicken and cayenne pepper.

P.275. ferry boat propelled by pole at stern.

P.286. Old Berlin for carriage. Translyvanians call such covered carriages "GELEGENBEITEN" = ["opportunities"]

P.295- "KOLOZSVAR" = "Klausenburg" six gulden for drive 12/-.

P.295. In Szamos. 25,000 Magyars and Szekelys. Houses of German character.

Mathias Hunyadi born here. large Squares and wide streets

P.168-70 Dinner at Pesth

"fogas" [pronounced "fogush"], fish of Barlaton lake,

Spatchcock with red pepper ("Paprika")

Töltött Kaposzta (cabbage filled with rice, meat and spice) delicious but dyspeptic.

Water melon, green outside..red inside —

Bottle of Neszmelyi, between Hock and Chablis —

121312

Page 104. Rosenbach #65.

P. 271

PAPRIKAS SZIRKE = chicken and cayenne pepper.

P. 275

ferry boat propelled by pole at stern.

P. 286

Old Berlin for carriage. Transylvanians call such covered carriages "GELEGEN-BEITEN" = ("opportunities")

P. 295

"KOLOZSVAR" = "Klausenburg" six gulden for drive 12/-.

P. 295

In Szamos. 25,000 Magyars and Szekelys. Houses of German character.

Mathias Hunyadi born here — large Squares and wide streets.

P. 168–70

Dinner at Pesth

fogas (pronounced "fogush"), fish of Balaton Lake, spatchcock with red pepper ("Paprika")

Toltott Kaposzta (cabbage filled with rice, meat and spice) delicious but dyspeptic.

Water melon — green outside, red inside

Bottle of Neszmelyi — between Hock and Chablis

THE THEORY OF DREAMS.

2 vols. F.C. &JRivington . 62. St Paul's Churchyard1808.

1

P.P.3.to 8.

MACROBIUS{ (1) Ονειρος – Somnium –' a figurative and mysterious representation that requires to be interpreted, vision – seeing things which come to pass. (2) Οραμα – (3) Χρηματισμος – oraculum – oracular (4) Ενυπνιον – Insomnium –' Some solicitude as when awake affecting us when asleep. (5) Phantasm called 'visio' by Cicero – that which takes place between sleeping and waking

P.14. Simonides buried a body and was advised by it in a dream not to start next day : He took advice and all those who sailed were lost. Told by the Stoics

P.86. Pliny gives Amphyction son of Deucalion as first skilful interpreter of dreams, but Trogus Pompeius gives the honour to Joseph son of Jacob; and Philo Judaeus gives it to Abraham.

Page 105. Rosenbach #66.

F. C. & J. Rivington
The Theory of Dreams. 2 vol.
London: 62 St. Paul's Churchyard, 1808

P. 3 to 8

MACROBIUS[328] (1) [GREEK][329]—Somnium—a figurative and mysterious representation that requires to be interpreted (2) [GREEK][330]—vision—seeing things which come to pass. (3) [GREEK][331]—oraculum—oracular (4) [GREEK][332]—Insomnium—Some solicitude as when awake affecting us when we sleep. (5) Phantasm called "visio" by Cicero—that which takes place between sleeping and waking.

P. 14

Simonides buried a body and was advised by it in a dream not to start next day. He took advice and all those who sailed were lost. Told by the Stoics.

P. 86

Pliny gives Amphyction son of Deucalion as first skilful interpreter of dreams, but Trogus Pompeius gives the honour to Joseph son of Jacob; and Philo Juddeas gives it to Abraham.

328. Ambrosius Theodosius Macrobius was a fifth-century Roman grammarian and philosopher who is best-known for *Saturnalia*. These fragments come from his commentary on Cicero's *Somnium Scipionis*.
329. Greek: "oneiras"; a symbolic dream, which requires interpretation.
330. Greek: "orama"; the foretelling of future events.
331. Greek: "chrematismos"; direct prophecies received in a dream.
332. Greek: "enypnion"; nightmare.

("The Theory of Dreams")

P.9. Amongst authors with theories of dreams Aristotle, Themistius, Artemidorus, Domocritus, Lucretius etc.

P.30. "RELIGIO MEDICI" B 11. § 12.

Sir Thomas Brown.

"It [sleep] is a death whereby we live. A middle moderating point between life and death, and so like death, ~~and as like death~~ I dare not trust it without my prayers, and an half adieu to the world, and take my farewell in a colloquy with God. After which I close my eyes in security, content to take my leave of him, and sleep unto the resurrection."

Garth's "Dispensary."

P.32. "The memory retains the colouring of the day."

P.41.2. In "Considerations sur un sommeil extraordinaire, Mem. de l'Academie de Berlin" is given a case drawn up by Mons. Gualtier at request of King of Sweden of a woman named Guasser who got kind of catalepsy twice a day, limbs grew hard like stone, little pulse but respiration as in sleep, had no feeling though flesh scarified, recovery gradually convulsive, this character sometimes lasted six months or a year, and finally 2½ years, at last being only once a day. She was married and had healthy

Page 106. Rosenbach #67.

P. 97

Amongst authors with theories of dreams — Aristotle, Themistius, Artemidorus, Domocritus, Lucretius etc.

P. 30

"RELIGICO MEDICI" B 11 & 12

Sir Thomas Browne[333]

"It (sleep) is a death whereby we live. A middle moderating point between life and death, and so like death <and as like death> I dare not trust it without my prayers, and an half adieu to the world, and take my farewell in a colloquy with God. After which, I close my eyes in security, content to take my leave of him, and sleep unto the resurrection."

P. 32

Garth's "Dispensary"[334]

"The memory retains the colouring of the day."

P. 41–2

In "Considerations sur un sommeil extraordinaire, Mem. de l'Academie de Berlin" is given a case drawn up by Mons. Gaultier at request of King of Sweden of a woman named Guasser who got kind of catalepsy twice a day, limbs grew hard like stone, little pulse but respiration as in sleep, had no feeling though flesh scarified, recovery gradually convulsive, this character sometimes lasted six months or a year, and finally 2½ years — at last being only once a day. She was married and had healthy

333. Sir Thomas Browne's best-known work, *Religio Medici*, attempted to reconcile science and religion.

334. Rivington is referring to *The Dispensary* (1706), a satirical poem by Sir Samuel Garth about a dispute between physicians and apothecaries regarding the provision of cheap medicine to the poor.

("Theory of Dreams")
3

child during the malady and died at 80. 1746.

P.43. See "Cheyne's English Malady" where Col. Townshend who had ~~[illegible]~~ nephritic complaint had power of dying and coming to life at pleasure. Dr. Cheyne, Dr. Baynard and Mr. Skrine saw this at Bath when for half an hour he died. No motion of heart. Mirror held over mouth not even soiled etc.

Page 107. Rosenbach #68.

child during the malady and died at 80. 1746.

P. 43

See "Cheyne's English Malady"[335] where Col. Townshend who had <xxx> nephritic complaint had power of dying and coming to life at pleasure. Dr. Cheyne, Dr. Baynard and Mr. Skrine saw this at Bath when for half an hour he died. No motion of heart. Mirror held over mouth not even soiled etc.

335. George Cheyne, *The English Malady; or, A Treatise of Nervous Diseases of All Kinds, as Spleen, Vapours, Lowness of Spirits, Hypochondreacal and Hysterical Distempers, etc.* (London, 1733).

1

TRANSLYVANIA.

Charles Bonner.

Longmans.1865.

P.66. Wallacks or as they call themselves "ROMANEN" [Roumains] are descendents of original settlers in Translyvania, as distinguished from Wallachians = inhabitants of Wallachia.

P.377. From 1836 to 1850. 5 general conflagrations in Bistritz. In former days its frontiers were exposed to devastations of Mongols and Tarters. In 1602. twenty days' seige, foe, famine and disease carried off 13,000 poeple. In war of 1564 between Translyvania and Austria, Bistritz had to furnish 3000 men armed with arquebuses. War contribution of that year was 30,000 florins and 200 horses.

P.406. Dancing in villages went on in street. Youths went to invite girls and carried white wands. Danced in moonlight. Intense cold, snow around, girls with only shift and coloured Kratsina and youths in shirt sleeves. Went on till 5.a.m.

P.417. BORGOS PRUND. to E. of Bistritz.

P.418. "MITTEL LAND" a ridge of low hills rising in the Vale

Page 108. Rosenbach #69.

Charles Boner
Transylvania: Its Products and Its People
London: Longman's, 1865

P. 66

Wallachs or as they call themselves "ROMANEN" (Roumains) are descendents of original settlers in Transylvania, as distinguished from Wallachians = inhabitants of Wallachia.

P. 377

From 1836 to 1850. 5 general conflagrations in Bistritz. In former days its frontiers were exposed to devastations of Mongols and Tartars. In 1602, twenty days' siege, foe, famine and disease carried off 13,000 people. In war of 1564 <xxx> between Transylvania and Austria, Bistritz had to furnish 3000 men armed with arquebuses <xxx>. War contribution of that year was 30,000 florins and 200 horses.[336]

P. 405

Dancing in villages went on in street. Youths went to invite girls and carried white wands. Danced in moonlight. Intense cold, snow around, girls with only <xxx> shift and coloured Kratsina and youths in shirt sleeves. Went on till 5 A.M.

P. 417

BORGO PRUND. To E. of Bistritz.

P. 418

"MITTEL LAND" a <xxx> ridge of low hills rising in the vale

336. Harker writes this of Bistritz: "Fifty years ago a series of great fires took place, which made terrible havoc on five separate occasions. At the very beginning of the seventeenth century it underwent a siege of three weeks and lost 13,000 people..." (1:3).

2

TRANSLYVANIA

between the highest mountains. Bold forms and gentle slopes most attractive.

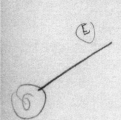

P.419. Further on, Pass into Moldavia, scenery increases in picturesqueness - good road. Near Prund is a territory continously fought for by Wallachians and Saxons.

(E)

(6)

Page 109. Rosenbach #70.

between the highest mountains. Bold forms and gentle slopes most attractive.

P. 419

Further on Pass into Moldavia, scenery increases in picturesqueness — good road. Near Prund is a territory continuously fought for by Wallachians and Saxons.[337]

337. Dracula tells Harker that the region of the Borgo Pass was "fought over for centuries by the Wallachian, the Saxon, and the Turk" (2:22).

ACCOUNT OF THE PRINCIPALITIES OF WALLACHIA AND MOLDAVIA.ETC.

Wm.Wilkinson late consul of Bukorest.Longmans.1820 Whitby Library.0.1097

P.19. DRACULA in Wallachian language means DEVIL. Wallachians were accustomed to give it as a surname to any person who rendered himself conspicuous by courage, cruel actions or cunning.

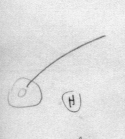

P.18.19.The Wallachians joined Hungarians in 1448.and made war on Turkey, being defeated at battle of Cassova in Bulgaria and finding it impossible to make stand against the Turks submitted to annual tribute which they paid until 1460.when Sultan Mahomet II. being occupied in completing conquest of islands in Archipelogo gave opportunity of shaking off yoke. Their VOIVODE [DRACULA] crossed Danube and attacked Turkish troops Only momentarily success. Mahomet drove him back to Wallachia where pursued and defeated him. The VOIVODE escaped into Hungary and the Sultan caused his brother Bladus received in his place. He made treaty with Bladus finding Wallachians to perpetual tribute and laid the foundations of that slavery not yet abolished.[1820]

Page 110. Rosenbach #71.

William Wilkinson
An Account of the Principalities of Wallachia and Moldavia[338]
London: Longmans, 1820

Whitby Library 0.1097.[339]

P. 19[340]

DRACULA[341] in Wallachian language means DEVIL.[342] Wallachians were accustomed to give it as a surname to any person who rendered himself conspicuous by courage, cruel actions or cunning.

P. 18–19

The Wallachians joined Hungarians in 1448 and made war on Turkey being defeated at battle of Cassova in Bulgaria and finding it impossible to make stand against the Turks submitted to annual tribute which they paid until 1460 when Sultan Mahomet II being occupied in completing conquest of islands in Archipelago gave opportunity of shaking off yoke. Their VOIVODE (DRACULA) crossed Danube and attacked Turkish troops. Only momentary success. Mahomet drove him back to Wallachia where pursued and defeated him. The VOIVODE escaped into Hungary and the Sultan caused his brother <Bladuss> Bladus[343] received in his place. He made treaty with Bladus binding Wallachians to perpetual tribute and laid the foundations of that slavery not yet abolished. (1820) <p. 18–19>

338. Many scholars consider this book Stoker's most important source, for it is most likely where he found the name "Dracula."

339. This is a shelf mark from the library in Whitby, where Stoker found a copy of Wilkinson's book.

340. In Wilkinson, this is a footnote. Stoker highlights it by placing it at the top of the page. What apparently attracted him was the connection with the devil.

341. This excerpt from Wilkinson contains the only references to the historical Dracula in Stoker's Notes. Nor is there any other information about him in any of the sources that we know Stoker consulted. The role of the historical Dracula (Vlad the Impaler) in Stoker's conception of *Dracula* has been grossly overstated. (This topic is examined in Miller, *Dracula: Sense & Nonsense*, chapter 5.)

342. Neither "Dracula" nor "devil" is in capital letters in the original text.

343. I.e., Radu.

[Wilkinson's Wallachia, Moldavia &c.] 72

2

Ancient Kingdom of DACIA = Wallachia, Moldavia, Transylvania, and Temesvar -finally conquered by Romans.

P.26. 1600. after abdication of Sigismund of Translyvania, this principality became tributary to Emperor Rodolphus who appointed Michael VOÏVODE. Translyvanians revolted & wished to recall Sigismund but were defeatedby Austrians and whole province subjugated.

P.32. 1695. Sultan Ahmet declared war against the Emperor and Voïvode Constantine Barancovano Bessarabba of Wallachia directed to form an army - did not help and at peace of Carlowitz Emperor Leopold made him Prince of Roman Empire and gave him landed estates in Translyvania.

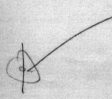

P.57. THORNTON= Present State of Turkey[P.116] says Boyars of ancient family assert descendants of the Slavi and are distinct race from offspring of Dacians and Romans.

P.79. Galatz is in Moldavian close to Wallachia at broadest & deepest pa of Danube 60 miles from Black Sea and 72 from BuKorest .

P.91. Boyars use German Caleche chiefly - gaudy carriage with poor harness and horses and Gypsy driver in rags is common.

P.92-3. No coaches to be hired - but posting quick, but bad - like , Crate of earthenware on 4 small wheels by wooden pegs

Page 111. Rosenbach #72.

Ancient kingdom of DACIA = Wallachia, Moldavia, Transylvania, and Temesvar—finally conquered by Romans.

p. 26

1600. After abdication of Sigismund of Transylvania, this principality became tributary to Emperor Rodolphus who appointed Michael VOIVODE. Transylvanians revolted & wished to recall Sigismund but were defeated by Austrians and whole province subjugated.

p. 32

1695. Sultan Ahmet declared war against the Emperor and Voivode Constantine Brancovano Bessarabba of Wallachia directed to form an army—did not help and at peace of Carlowitz Emperor Leopold made him Prince of Roman Empire and gave him landed estates in Transylvania.

p. 57

THORNTON = Present State of Turkey (P. 116) says Boyars of ancient family assert descendents of the Slavs and are distinct race from offspring of Dacians and Romans.

p. 79

Galatz[344] is in Moldavia close to Wallachia at broadest & deepest part of Danube 60 miles from Black Sea and 72 from Bucharest.

p. 91

Boyars use German caleche chiefly—gaudy carriage with poor harness and horses and Gypsy driver in rags is common.

p. 92–3

No coaches to be hired—but posting quick though bad—like crate of earthenware on 4 small wheels by wooden pegs

344. The port of Galatz plays a part in Count Dracula's retreat to his homeland.

(Wilkinson's Wallachia Moldavia &c.)

3

hardly higher than wheelbarrows, filled with straw, and traveller sits in middle keeping body erect and with difficulty cramming away his legs. Four horses are attached with cords - whole of harness - and driven by one postillion on horseback, gallops all way to next post house.

P.126-7 Much rain in summer. June and July storms frequent and recurrent at same hour each day - nights cold - Summer heat sets in at once beginning of May very little Spring.

P.161. All the best lands in Translyvania in hands of Hungarians, Szecklers and Saxons.

(E) P.166. Carpathian roads almost impossible in winter. mud and great stones rolled down and on brink of precipice etc.

(E) P.166. Hospodars neglect to repair roads. for fear of making Turks think they wish to facilitate entry of foreign troops.

(E) P.167. Inhabitants have goitre.

(G) P.213. In Wallachian tongue "STREGOICA" Italian STREGA = A WITCH

P.214. KATANDISSIT - Modern Greek καταντισμενος = -Reduced in circumstances.

Page 112. Rosenbach #73.

hardly higher than wheelbarrow, filled with straw and traveller sits in middle keeping body erect and with difficulty cramming away his legs. Four horses are attached with cords — whole of harness — and driven by one postillion on horseback gallops all way to next post house.

p. 126–7

Much rain in summer — June and July storms frequent and recurrent at same hour each day — nights cold — Summer heat sets in at once beginning of May with very little Spring.

p. 161

All the best lands in Transylvania in hands of Hungarians, Szeklers and Saxons.

p. 166

Carpathian roads almost impossible in winter. Mud and great stones rolled down and on brink of precipice etc.

p. 166

Hospodars neglect to repair roads for fear of making Turks think they wish to facilitate entry of foreign troops.[345]

p. 167

Inhabitants have goitre.

p. 213

Wallachian tongue "STREGOICA" — Italian STREGA = A WITCH

p. 214

KATANDISSIT — Modern Greek [GREEK][346] reduced in circumstances.

345. "Of old the Hospodars would not repair [the roads], lest the Turk should think that they were preparing to bring in foreign troops" (1:7) is an example of how Stoker borrowed from his sources almost verbatim.

346. Greek: "katandisnos"; to fall on hard times.

(Wilkinson's Wallachia Moldavia &c)

4

(H)

(10)

P.232. "Water sleeps, and Enemy is sleepless" Turkish proverb.

P.234. "The Serpent kills a man in Egypt whilst the Teryac [an article of Venetian trade - supposed to be remedy against Snake bites.] is coming from Venice.

Page 113. Rosenbach #74.

p. 232

"Water sleeps, and Enemy is sleepless" Turkish proverb.

p. 234

"The Serpent kills a man in Egypt whilst the Teryac (an article of Venetian trade—supposed to be a remedy against snake bites) is coming from Venice.

Tombstones. Whitby Churchyard on Cliff.

(Note M.M. means Master Mariner

Thomas Davison

Drowned on Coast of Holland 24th. Dec. 1811, 29 aet.

John Robinson drowned Haseborough Sand

1st. March 1814. aet 18.

In church. John Braithwaite, Master Mariner who died at Stanchio, one of the Grecian Islands 21 st. July 1826. aet. 38.

Church

Cornelius Usherwood M.M. died at St Domingo 30th June 1798. aet. 37.

Steward Usherwood. Lost at sea 27th April 1790. aet. 17.

John Usherwood M.M. who with most of his ships Company was drowned on Haisbro' Sand 1st March 1814. aet. 27.

William Noble aet. 33 who was drowned on the Cotton Beach

Page 114. Rosenbach #75.

Tombstones — Whitby Churchyard on Cliff[347]

(Note M.M. means Master Mariner)

Thomas Davison
Drowned on Coast of Holland 24th December 1811. 29 aet.[348]

John Robinson drowned Haseborough Sand
1st March 1814. aet.18.

In church. John Braithwaite Master Mariner who died at Stanchio, one of the Grecian Islands 21st July 1826. aet. 38.

Church
Cornelius Usherwood M.M. died at St Domingo 30th June 1798. aet. 37.

Steward Usherwood. Lost at sea 27th April 1790. aet. 17.

John Usherwood M.M. who with most of his ships company was drowned on Haisbro Sand 1st March 1814. aet. 27.

William Noble aet. 33 who was drowned on the Coiton Beach

347. Apparently, Stoker strolled through the graveyard with notebook in hand.
348. "[A]et." is an abbreviation of the Latin word for age.

(Whitby Tombstones. 2)

from "The Peggy" on 5th January 1857.

William Johnson M.M. lost on passage from Honduras March 1810.aet.45.

John Yeoman buried on "La Fayette".New Orleans 25th April 1787.

John Barritt.Pilot,drowned off Whitby 29th Dec 1845. aet.57.

Joseph Weatherell drowned on passage from America 25th January 1854. aet 20.

John Foxton M.M. drowned in the "Bellona" near Brest on the coast of France. Janry 21. 1814. aet 29.

Ann Swales. 6th Feb.1795. aet 100.

Braithwaite Lowrey lost in the ship "Lively" that foundere

Page 115. Rosenbach #76.

from "The Peggy" on 5th January 1857.

William Johnson M.M. lost on passage from Honduras March 1810. aet. 45.

John Yeoman buried on "La Fayette." New Orleans 25th April 1787.

John Barritt. Pilot, drowned off Whitby 29th December 1845. aet. 57.

Joseph Weatherell drowned on passage from America 25th January 1854. aet. 20.

John Foxton M.M. drowned in the "Bellona" near Brest on the coast of France. January 21 1814. aet. 29.

Ann Swales, 6th February 1795. aet. 100.[349]

Braithwaite Lowrey lost in the ship "Lively" that foundered

349. This is apparently the source of the name "Swales." Other headstones furnish the names and obituaries of sailors who are buried in Whitby.

(Whitby Tombstones 3)

at Greenland 18th April 1820.aet 29.

Andrew Woodehouse drowned in the Greenland Seas. 16th April.1777.aet 19.

Samuel Tully M.M. perished with all crew of the "King George" of Whitby" on the passage from New York 2nd Janry 1782.aged 33.

John Paxton drowned off Cape Farewell 4th April 1778.

Christopher Pearson drowned at Malton. 16th June 1806. aet.27.

James Armstrong lost in the ship "Atlas" from Calcutta [illegible] 1817. aet 30.

Robert Walker, drowned, upsetting lifeboat, 6th Oct.1841.

Wm.Wright M.M. drowned Cromer 22nd Nov. 1840.aet 48.

Page 116. Rosenbach #77.

at Greenland 18th April 1820. aet. 29.[350]

Andrew Woodhouse drowned in the Greenland Seas. 16th April 1777. aet. 19.[351]

Samuel Tully M. M. perished with all crew of the "King George" of Whitby on the passage from New York 2nd January 1782. aged 33.

John Paxton drowned off Cape Farewell 4th April 1778.[352]

Christopher Pearson drowned at Malton. 16th June 1806. aet. 27.

James Armstrong lost in the ship "Atlas" from Calcutta 1817. aet. 30.

Robert Walker drowned, upsetting lifeboat, 6th October 1841.

Wm. Wright M. M. drowned Cromer 22nd November 1840. aet 48.

350. "This Braithwaite Lowery—I knew his father, lost in the *Lively* off Greenland in '20" (6:68).
351. "Andrew Woodhouse, drowned in the same seas in 1777" (6:68).
352. "John Paxton, drowned off Cape Farewell" (6:68).

(Whitby Tombstones 4)

Also his son Lawson drowned with him.

Lawson Wright M.M. lost with all hands in brig "Norma" Ystad to London 2nd Decr. 1867. aet 27.

William Brown drowned at sea. 10th Novr.1825. aet 24.

Robert Jackson drowned Dingle Bay 17th Janry. 1819. aet 19.
John Truman M.M. brother-in-law of above do do.aet 26.

George Beaument drowned Coast of Shetland 13th Decr. 1817. aged 26.

Thomas Britton drowned off Coast off Calabria 1808.

Robert Barrett Master of the "Bess" of Stockton perished at Shields to Gothenburg, 1809. aet. 43.
Also son Robert, perished with him.

Thomas Benjamin Page M.M., lost with all hands schooner "Ware" 25th Sept. 1851. aet. 31.
Also George Dick Page drowned Whitby Harbour 22nd May 1829. aet 3.

Jas.Elder drowned Hartlepool 12th Nov 1813. aet 12.

Page 117. Rosenbach #78.

Also his son Lawson drowned with him.

Lawson Wright M. M. lost with all hands in brig "Norma" Ystad to London 2nd December 1867. aet 27.

William Brown drowned at sea. 10th November 1825. aet. 24.

Robert Jackson drowned Dingle Bay 17th January 1819. aet. 19.
John Truman M. M. brother-in-law of above, ditto. aet. 26.

George Beaumont drowned Coast of Shetland, 13th December 1817. aged 26.

Thomas Britton drowned off coast of Calabria, 1808.

Robert Barrett Master of the "Bess" of Stockton perished at sea Shields to Gothenburg, 1809. aet. 43.
Also son Robert perished with him.

Thomas Benjamin Page M. M., lost with all hands, schooner "Ware" 25th September 1851. aet. 31.
Also George Dick Page drowned Whitby Harbour 22nd May 1829. aet. 3.

Jas. Elder drowned Hartlepool 12th November 1813. aet. 12.

(Whitby Tombstones 5)

Fredk Matthew Woodhouse, wife, child and all hands

S.S. "Milanecia" Autumn of 1888.

John Burn drowned in R. St Lawrence. Sept. 20th 1840 aged 15.

James Burn drowned in river Eske 22nd June 1840 .aet. 11.

2

Rippon Lorains drowned on passage to Plymouth. 15th April

1829 aet 30. Also his son George died on passage from

London. 26th August 1849. aet 25.

Francis Garthsides drowned at sea 30th Decr. 1811. aet 22.

John do drowned in Thames 26th Dec. 1815. aet. 30.

William Hebbron Medd. lost off Coast of Holland in trans-

\+ port "Centurion" [with H.M.S."Hero"] 24th Decr. 1811 aet. 22.

John Jackson M.M. lost London to Dalhousie. 1846, aet. 31.

James Watson drowned Oct. 22th 1837.

George Harrison Cussons, drowned Gravesend Reach 18th June

1873. aet. 23.

8

George Thomas Wood M.M. drowned at Malden 4th. Janry 1842.

aet 24.

George Sinclair M.M. drowned passage from New York to

Page 118. Rosenbach #79.

Fredk Matthew Woodhouse, wife, child and all hands S.S. "Milanecia" Autumn of 1888.

John Burn drowned in R. St. Lawrence September 20th 184<x>. aet 15.

James Burn drowned in river Esk 22nd June 1840. aet. 11.

Rippon Lorains drowned on passage to Plymouth. 15th April 1829. aet 30. Also his son George died on passage from London, 26th August 1849. aet 25.

Francis Garthsides drowned at sea 30th December 1811. aet 22.

John Garthsides drowned in Thames 26th December 1815 aet.30.

William Hebbron Medd lost off Coast of Holland in transport "Centurion" (with H.M.S. "Hero") 24th December 1811 aet. 22.

John Jackson M. M. lost London to Dalhousie 1846. aet. 31.

James Watson drowned October 22th 1837.

George Harrison-Cussons drowned Gravesend Reach 18th June 1873. aet. 23.

George Thomas Wood M. M. drowned at Malden 4th January 1842. aet 24.

George Sinclair M. M. drowned passage from New York to

(Whitby Tombstones. 6)

Queenstown. 1862. aet. 29.

Henry Ord M.M. lost at Haseborough Sand 13th Sept. 1836. aet. 32.

Joseph Mead drowned off Runswick 30th Janry 1825. aet 27.

Wm Edward Turner. drowned 15/2/66. aet. 30.

Richard Leng drowned at Leba [buried at Krokow] 27th March 1863. aet. 49.

Mark Leadley died on passage from India 26th Sept 1825. aet 25.

Robt Boys lost in Brig "Dowson" of Stockton 1833.

John Millburn drowned off Harwich, 31th Decr. 1849. aet. 19.

George Millburn drowned 4.1.27 aet 21.
Robert do drowned near Alfred, Lincoln. 25/4/34. aet. 33.

Joseph Wray drowned River Somme, 26.2.52.

George Trueman drowned from Hamburgh 24th Decr. 1852.

Thomas Mills M.M. drowned Lynn to Ireland Oct 1815. aet 43.

Page 119. Rosenbach #80.

Queenstown. 1862. aet 29.

Henry Ord M. M. lost at Haseborough Sand 13th September 1836. aet. 32.

Joseph Mead drowned off Runswick 30th January 1825. aet. 27.

Wm Edward Turner drowned 15/2/66. aet. 30.

Richard Long drowned at Leba (buried at Krokow) 27th March 1863. aet. 49.

Mark Leadley died on passage from India 26th September 1825. aet. 25.

Robert Boys lost in Brig "Dowson" of Stockton 1833.

John Millburn drowned off Harwich 31st December 1849. aet. 19.

George Millburn drowned 4.1.27. aet. 21.
Robert Millburn drowned near Alfred, Lincoln. 25/4/34. aet. 33.

Joseph <xxx> drowned River Somme. 26.2.52.

George Trueman drowned from Hamburg 24th December 1852.

Thomas Mills M. M. drowned Lynn to Ireland October 1815. aet. 43.

(Whitby Tombstones 7)

his son William lost with him.

1 John Rawling drowned Gulf of Finland Novr 1850. aet 61.

Wm Anderson drowned Kamrish Bay, 11th July 1856. aged 20.

Wm Appleby drowned in Thames 2nd Decr 1850. aet 21.

Wm Tyerman, drowned English Channel 18th March 1841. aet 23.

Wm do [grandson] upsetting lifeboat 9th Feb. 1861. aet 27.

Joseph Tyerman M.M. lost all hands brig "Mariam" 1867.

+ John Readshaw drowned to Quebec, 30th April 1820. aet 32.
+ His son James Readshaw drowned Liverpool 16/12/34. aet 18.

Wm Noble drowned in Thames Sept 27th 1822. aet 19.

Robert Coates. drowned 1825.

g Edward Spencelayh M.M. murdered by pirates, Coast of Andreas 12th April 1854. aet 30.

James Reed. drowned Liverpool 7/1/59 aet 23.

Wm Bedlington drowned 1817. aet 18.

Page 120. Rosenbach #81.

His son William lost with him.

John Rawling drowned Gulf of Finland November 1850. aet. 61.[353]

Wm. Anderson drowned Kamrish Bay. 11th July 1856. aged 20.

Wm. Appleby drowned in Thames 2nd December 1850. aet. 21.

Wm. Tyerman drowned English Channel 18th March 1841. aet. 23.

Wm. Tyerman (grandson) upsetting lifeboat 9th February 1861. aet. 27.

Joseph Tyerman M. M. lost all hands brig "Miriam" 1867.

John Readshaw drowned to Quebec 30th April 1820. aet. 32.
His son James Readshaw drowned Liverpool 16/12/34. aet. 18.

Wm. Noble drowned in Thames September 27th 1822. aet. 19.

Robert Coates, drowned 1825.

Edward Spencelagh M. M. murdered by pirates, Coast of Andres 12th April 1854. aet. 30.[354]

James Reed, drowned Liverpool 7/1/59. aet. 23.

Wm Bedlington drowned 1817. aet. 18.

353. "John Rawlings, whose grandfather sailed with me, drowned in the Gulf of Finland in '50" (6:68).

354. Mina reads, "Edward Spencelagh, master mariner, murdered by pirates off the coast of Andres, April, 1854, aet. 30" (6:67).

(Whitby Tombstones 8)

Robert Slater, drowned Decr. 1792. aet 31.

Thomas Douglas drowned off Whitby. 4th Oct 1853. aet 43.

Philip Lawson 11th June 1833. aet 104.

Wm Garbutt M.M. with wife and child lost in brig "Canton" on Briam Island Oct. 1837.

Henry Charter drowned on passage from East Indies 14th March 1810. aet 17.

Danied Yollop, drowned in Whitby Harbour 2nd August 1854 aet 15.

+ Joseph Smith M.M. drowned Rio Janeiro Augt. 11th 1815. aet 37.

George Smith M.M. drowned Novr. 1790. aet 50.

Richard Purvis M.M. drowned East Hartlepool 25th Augt. 1874. aet 65.

+ John Wetherell drowned at sea 1789.

John Foster Lindsley drowned in the "Esk" near Marsk 7 Sept. 1826. aet 20.

+ Wm Wilson drowned in the Baltic. 13th April 1830. aet 46.

Page 121. Rosenbach #82.

Robert Slater, drowned December 1792. aet. 31.

Thomas Douglas drowned off Whitby. 4th October 1853. aet. 43.

Philip Lawson 11th June 1833. aet. 104.

Wm. Garbutt M. M. with wife and child lost in brig "Canton" on Brian Island October 1837.

Henry Charter drowned on passage from East Indies 14th March 1810. aet. 17.

Daniel Yollop, drowned in Whitby Harbour 2nd August 1854. aet. 15.

Joseph Smith M. M. drowned Rio Janeiro August 11th 1815. aet. 37.

George Smith M. M. drowned November 1790. aet. 50.

Richard Purvis M. M. drowned East Hartlepool 25th August 1874. aet. 65.

John Wetherell drowned at sea 1789.

John Foster Lindsley drowned in the "Esk" near Marsk 7 September 1826. aet. 20.

Wm. Wilson drowned in the Baltic 13th April 1830. aet. 46.

(Whitby Tombstones 9)

43

THomas Wilson M.M. lost with all hands near Yarmouth

Novr 1864. aet 32.

+ Marmaduke Blackburn drowned in the Western Ocean Sept 11.

1796. aet 32.

Richard Ramsden drowned [no date.]

Henry Bockin M.M. lost Whitby 1823.

Page 122. Rosenbach #83.

Thomas Wilson M. M. lost with all hands near Yarmouth November 1864. aet. 32.

Marmaduke Blackburn drowned in the Western Ocean September 11, 1796. aet. 32.

Richard Ramsden drowned (no date.)

Henry Bockin M. M. lost Whitby 1823.

(Whitby Tombstones)
10

SACRED

to the Memory of

THOMAS BAXTER

Who was killed on board of

H.M.S. SCOUT

by a shot from a Spanish Gunboat

Off Cape Trafalgar Novr.2nd 1807

ALSO

JOHN ROBINSON who

died Aug. 3rd 1827. aged 36 years

This Stone was erected out of

Affectionate remembrance by

Mary their surviving Widow.

ALSO

the above Mary their

Wife who died Oct.27. 1833.

Aged 36 years.

Page 123. Rosenbach #84.

SACRED
to the Memory of
THOMAS BAXTER
Who was killed on board of
H.M.S. SCOUT
by a shot from a Spanish Gunboat
Off Cape Trafalgar Novr 2nd 1807

ALSO
JOHN ROBINSON who
died Aug. 3rd 1827. aged 36 years
This Stone was erected out of
Affectionate remembrance by
Mary their surviving widow.

ALSO
The above Mary their
Wife who died Oct. 27, 1833.
Aged 36 years.

DEGREES OF WIND.

"Beaufort's Scale of Wind force."

0-- CALM.

1-- LIGHT AIR. . . . Steerage way only

2-- LIGHT BREEZE. . . 1 to 2 Knots

3-- GENTLE BREEZE. 3 to 4. do

4-- MODERATE BREEZE. 5 to 6. . . do

(Lines 2–4, bracketed: What a well appointed Man of war frigate about 1806 all sail set and clean hull would go in smooth water)

5-- FRESH BREEZE .----Royals.

~~MODERATE GALE~~. .

6-- STRONG BREEZE.----Single reefed Topsails & Topgallant sails

7-- MODERATE GALE. . . . Double reefed Topsails, Jibs &c

8-- FRESH GALE . . . . . Triple reefed Topsails

9-- STRONG GALE. - - - . Close reefed Topsails & Courses

(Lines 5–9, bracketed: That which she could just carry in chase, full & by)

10- WHOLE GALE. . . . . . Scarcely bear close reefed Main Topsail & reefed Foresail

11- STORM. ----------- Reduce her to Storm Stay sails.

12- HURRICANE.---------NO Canvas - bare poles.

Page 124. Rosenbach #85.

Degrees of Wind

"Beaufort's Scale of Wind force."[355]

0—CALM

1—LIGHT AIR... steerage way only

2—LIGHT BREEZE... 1 to 2 knots

3—GENTLE BREEZE... 3 to 4 knots

4—MODERATE BREEZE... 5 to 6 knots

(What a well appointed man of war frigate about 1806 all sail set and clean hull would go in smooth water)

5—FRESH BREEZE... Royals

<6—MODERATE GALE>

6—STRONG BREEZE... Single reefed Topsails & Top gallant sails

7—MODERATE GALE... Double reefed Topsails, Jibs etc

8—FRESH GALE... Triple reefed Topsails

9—STRONG GALE ... Close reefed Topsails & Courses

(That which she could just carry in chase, full & by)

10—WHOLE GALE... scarcely bear close reefed Main Topsail & reefed foresail

11—STORM... Reduce her to Storm Stay sails.

12—HURRICANE... No canvas—bare poles.

355. Beaufort's Wind Scale was introduced in 1805 to help sailors estimate the force of winds by visual observations. Sir Francis Beaufort's scale, which ranges from 0 to 12, is still in use.

Overview

In his introduction to the first Oxford World Classics edition of *Dracula*, A. N. Wilson concedes, "It would seem likely that he [Stoker] did some — but very little — research for his fantasy" (x).[356] The Notes put the lie to Wilson's remark. Research from diverse sources combined with incessant revisions and emendations testify to a fervor and commitment that elevate Bram Stoker's immortal masterpiece to a level none of his other works aspire to. As Martin Tropp points out, "After their first appearance in nineteenth century England, three [horror stories] quickly became classic tales of terror, the modern equivalent of myths: Mary Shelley's *Frankenstein*, Robert Louis Stevenson's *Dr. Jekyll and Mr. Hyde*, and Bram Stoker's *Dracula*" (1). The Notes leave no doubt that Stoker had begun writing *Dracula* by 8 March 1890 and continued researching and restructuring various outlines until at least 5 April 1896. Granted, his research was neither exhaustive nor meticulous; he often mixed bits and pieces from divergent sources into his stew with contradictory results. However, he was not a scholar. He was a part-time author who, for eight golden years, was caught up in the process of creating a villain who people in every part of the world can identify as a "vampire" from "Transylvania."

Method of Narration

The first three lines of the Notes see a lawyer purchase an old town house for an unnamed client. The following page continues with correspondence between various lawyers and a "Count." Less than a week later, these messages become the first of a proposed twenty-eight chapters (p. 8). By page 9, a revised series of letters concludes with Dracula's injunction to Peter Hawkins to "let Harker start for Munich." A new, more extensive outline of the plot begins on page 10.

Dracula is a potpourri of journal entries, letters and other forms of communication. The Notes leave no doubt that Stoker intended to use this form of storytelling from the beginning. The first four chapters of the novel consist of entries from Jonathan Harker's journal. He is the "reluctant hero" who guides us from the familiar world of the West into mysteries of the East and introduces us to Transylvania, Count Dracula and the "awful women" in the castle who are waiting to suck his blood. Our access to his journal tells us vampires exist long before most of the human protagonists are aware that "the devil and his children still walk with earthly feet!" (1:54).

In *The Diary Novel*, Lorna Martens explains,

---

356. Christopher Frayling quips, "Evidently, A. N. Wilson had done *some* research for his anaemic contribution — but very little" (297).

> The first-person account is a useful device in narratives where the author wants to withhold information and thereby prolong suspense. The reader is given a partial view of the situation, yet is left as mystified as the character himself about the true situation. Bram Stoker's *Dracula* (1897) is a celebrated example of a work that uses multiple diaries to unfold the story. Journals kept by Count Dracula's victims and others reveal the vampire's devious plan to purchase an English estate, his sinister voyage from Transylvania and melodramatic arrival on English soil, his nightly visits to Lucy Westenra's room, and finally his attacks on Mina Harker, his flight back to Transylvania, and the successful campaign to annihilate him [112].

These documents take many forms. Accounts are written by hand, entered in shorthand, recorded on a gramophone, transcribed with a typewriter and sent by wire. Jennifer Wicke calls *Dracula* a "textually ... au courant" fusion of nineteenth-century diaristic and epistolary narrative modes with "cutting-edge technology" (470). Multiple perspectives help to establish the veracity of fantastic tales. In *Dracula*, the fact that most of the narrators have professional credentials — a solicitor, a doctor, a professor and an assistant schoolmistress — buttresses the credibility of their testimonies. Carol Senf points out that this amalgamation of voices "represents the collective wisdom of the late nineteenth century — male and female, Catholic and Protestant, science and law" (32).

The omniscient reader participates in the adventure on every page and, like the protagonists, learns what other people think, feel and do as the story unfolds. Entries such as "Mina undertakes to typewrite Seward's phonograph" or "Van Helsing tells the story which Mina has arranged" pepper the Notes. More and more documents are brought together until every scrap of information rests in Van Helsing's hands. Collaborative narration serves as the textual equivalent of collective action by the human participants. Dracula, and the supernatural menace he embodies so magnificently, will be foiled by a band of mortals who have sworn "to find out the author of all this our sorrow and to stamp him out" (16:222). In contrast to his enemies, Dracula does not love, he does not share and he does not serve. All of his actions serve his own foul purposes. The Count is the only important character who does not share his innermost thoughts and feelings with the reader or describe other people from his point of view.[357]

Narrative Time

The untitled preface that introduces the novel contributes to the misconception that *Dracula* is set in 1897, the year the first edition was published.[358] Its anonymous (i.e., unidentified) author assures us, "There is throughout no record of past things wherein memory may err, for all the records chosen are exactly contemporary, given from the standpoints and within the range of knowledge of those who made them" (n.p.). In the first annotated edition of *Dracula* (1975), Leonard Wolf proposes that 1889 is the "probable date for the events in this book, but a reader is cautioned not to believe in it too precisely. Any five-year period before or after 1887 will do to account for the phases of the moon as Stoker has given them to us" (343).[359] Four years later, Raymond McNally and Radu Florescu's "discovery" of the Notes allowed them to conclude that

357. The first book in Fred Saberhagen's Dracula series provides new, often amusing, explanations for many of events in the novel. For instance, Dracula explains, "Lucy I did not kill. It was not *I* who hammered the great stake through her heart.... [Nor] would she ever have become a vampire were it not for the idiot Van Helsing and his work" (*The Dracula Tape* 7).

358. Every edition of *Dracula* that was published before Permabooks' edition of 1957 states "1897" on its copyright page.

359. This is not the case; full moons occur whenever the author commands them to.

"After studying Whitaker's Almanac for 1893 ... we found that these dates and days of the week coincided with 1893" (25). The novel supports this claim:

1. Mr. Swales has sat on George Canon's tombstone "off an' on for nigh twenty years past" (6:69). The fact that this monument was dated "29 July 1873" (6:68) means the story cannot have taken place *before* 1893.

2. A newspaper cited in chapter 13, *The Westminster Gazette*, was established in 1893.

3. The term the "New Woman" appears twice in chapter 8. According to Michele Tusan, this term was coined in "The Social Standing of the New Woman" which was published in the feminist newspaper, *The Woman's Herald*, on 17 August 1893.

4. When Jonathan Harker spies Dracula in Piccadilly, he exclaims, "It is the man himself!" (13:175). This encounter happened on 21 September, which, Mina recalls, was a "Thursday" (14:188). In 1893, 21 September fell on a Thursday.[360]

5. Jean-Martin Charcot, an expert in neurology and hypnosis, died on 16 August 1893.[361] On 26 September, Van Helsing regrets that "the great Charcot ... is no more" (14:195).

The Construction of the Plot

The first 51 pages show how the plot evolved over a period of more than seven years.[362] The earliest form of *Dracula* can be found in the first five pages of notes. It includes the purchase of a house for a foreign nobleman, a series of letters about this purchase, the Count's arrival at Dover and a dinner party at a mad doctor's house. Many of the twists and turns in these pages disappear, but Jonathan Harker's journey to the castle, his encounter with three vampire women and the Count's imperious "This man belongs to me" become important parts of the published text.

The first outline of the entire book appears on page 8, which is dated 14 March 1890. At this time, the author planned to present his story in a series of Books headed "Styria to London," "Tragedy," "Discovery" and "Punishment." "Many scholars suggest that Stoker's division of the novel resembles four acts of a play, each with seven scenes, further evidence that he had a theatrical production in mind when writing *Dracula*" (*Bram Stoker's Dracula* 18). The Notes continue with a chapter-by-chapter outline (p. 10–29) that reworks and expands material from page 8. This outline ends abruptly with Book III, Chapter 7. Bits and pieces were jettisoned, but parts of it emerged in a new plan for the book that has three sections with nine chapters each (p. 34).

The calendar of events (p. 39–47) takes a new direction. With the exception of material for two deleted chapters (p. 39 and 40), most of what happens in the calendar is carried over to the novel. Christopher Frayling points out that "The whole of this detailed breakdown of the story into dates and times was evidently written after Stoker had made up his mind about the details of the story itself" (315). He probably had this calendar close at hand when he composed the first complete draft of his masterpiece.[363] Four additional pages (p. 48–51) about the

360. 21 September also fell on a Thursday in 1882 and 1899.

361. The neurologist, Jean-Martin Charcot (1825–1893), was one of Freud's most important teachers.

362. The fact that Stoker worked on *Dracula* intermittently while meeting the demands of full-time job and an exacting employer may explain why the finished novel has so many inconsistencies. (See Miller, *Dracula: Sense & Nonsense* 100–105.)

363. This was probably a handwritten draft that preceded the first version of the typescript which is, in turn, a hybrid assemblage of previous typed drafts.

final chapters are relatively skimpy, while notations for chapters 26 and 27 will be expanded as the last six chapters of the novel.[364]

"Dracula's Guest"

Shortly before his death in 1912, Bram Stoker planned to publish a three-volume collection of his stories. Two years later, his widow Florence brought out one of these volumes with an additional tale. In her preface to *Dracula's Guest: And Other Weird Stories* she informs readers that "To his original list of stories in this book, I have added an hitherto unpublished episode from 'Dracula.' It was originally excised owing to the length of the book, and may prove of interest to the many readers of what is considered my husband's most remarkable work" (n.p.).

The title story, "Dracula's Guest,"[365] takes place on the outskirts of Munich. Despite numerous warnings, an unnamed Englishman sets out on foot to explore a deserted village on Walpurgis Night.[366] When a storm forces him to seek shelter in Countess Dolingen's tomb, a flash of lightning reveals a beautiful woman who appears to be "sleeping" on a bier.[367] The narrator is hurled from the tomb by a powerful unseen hand just before lightning destroys the woman and the tomb. When he regains consciousness, he finds a great wolf lying on him, licking his throat.[368] It protects him from the storm until its howls attract a band of soldiers who have been sent to look for him.

The origin of the story and its relation to *Dracula* have been controversial. Opinions run the gamut from accepting it unquestionably as part of the novel to dismissing it as a hoax. Critics have argued that the story is a self-contained narrative of unknown origin or that it is part of an early draft which was abandoned during the planning stage. The most widespread misconception may be that it was once the first chapter of the novel.[369]

"Dracula's Guest" was not included in the typescript, and there is no known copy of the final draft. However, the Notes indicate that it was once an integral part of the novel. An entry for chapter 2, "Harker's Diary Munich — wolf" (p. 30), shows that Jonathan Harker is the protagonist and narrator of this tale. Chapter 3 continues with his adventures in the "Dead House." Eventually, the word "wolf" is expanded to the phrase "adventure snow storm and wolf" (p. 40). This was to occur on Thursday 27 April, which was changed to Sunday 30 April (Walpurgis Night), dovetailing into the opening line of the novel in which Harker "Left Munich at 8.35 P.M. on 1st May" (1:1). Florence Stoker refers to "Dracula's Guest" as an "episode" rather than a story. This is not surprising, for the material that she passed down to us begins *in medias res* (in the middle of the action). As we have seen, the first segment originally consisted of correspondence between Count Dracula and his lawyers. These letters were followed by bits and pieces about Harker's adventures in Munich — including a dead house, a night at the opera, a trip to a museum and a snowstorm and a wolf. The typescript proves that Bram continued to fiddle with the opening section until the final draft.

---

364. At one point, Stoker planned 31 chapters.

365. In addition to its original title, the story has been reprinted as: "The Curse of Dracula," "Dracula's Curse," "Dracula's Daughter," "The Dream in the Dead House" and "Walpurgis Night."

366. Walpurgis Night (Walpurgisnacht) occurs on 30 April. In German folklore, this was one of the times witches held their revels.

367. The "sleeping beauty" motif is found in fairy tales throughout the world.

368. "A wolf— and yet not a wolf" (14) suggests that the creature may be a vampire or a werewolf.

369. Even today, authors such as Lisa Hopkins refer to it as the "deleted first chapter" or "the original beginning to *Dracula*" (*Bram Stoker: A Literary Life* 7 and 84).

The phrase "owing to the length of the book" refers to a time when the first section of the typescript was 101 pages longer than the final draft. Eventually, most of the original introductory material was deleted or moved to chapters 5, 6 and 7. The "missing" chapters included parts of the Whitby and London narratives. For example, page 30 calls Seward, Renfield and Morris into action *before* Harker arrives at the castle. The decision to begin the novel with Harker's adventures in Transylvania was a stroke of genius! As Montague Summers remarked many years ago, "The first part, 'Jonathan Harker's Journal,' which consists of the first four chapters is most admirably done, and could the whole story have been sustained at so high a level we should have had a complete masterpiece" (*The Vampire: His Kith and Kin* 333).[370]

In the novel, Jonathan Harker's coach is surrounded by wolves on the way to the castle. He exclaims, "It is only when a man feels himself face to face with such horrors that he can understand their true import" (1:13). The typescript continues as follows: "and my experience in the storm near Munich was not calculated to ease my mind. As I looked at them I unconsciously put my hand to my throat which was still sore from the licking of the grey wolf's file-like tongue" (121). In chapter 2, the sentence "During the time I was eating [supper] the Count asked me many questions as to my journey, and I told him by degrees all I had experienced" (2:18) is followed by "He [Dracula] seemed very interested especially in my adventures in Munich. When I told him of the coming of the soldiers he appeared quite excited...."[371] In addition, John McLaughlin presents us with a deleted passage that "refers to the events in the excised chaper, from page 60, the seduction of Harker by the weird sisters: 'As she spoke I was looking at the fair woman and it suddenly dawned on me that she was the woman — or her image — that I had seen in the tomb of Walpurgis Night'" (n.p.). It follows that "the beautiful woman, with rounded cheeks and red lips, seemingly sleeping on a bier" in "Dracula's Guest" (11) is the "fair" woman in Dracula's castle.

Florence does not tell us when "Dracula's Guest" was cut or who deleted it but there can no doubt that Bram Stoker, rather than an anonymous editor, completed the task, for he wove parts of this "episode" into chapters 1–4 and 27. The old man and woman who manage the Golden Krone hotel in Bistritz serve a similar function to Herr Delbrück, who is the maitre d'hotel of the Quatre Saisons in "Dracula's Guest." His question "for you know what night it is" (1) is placed in their mouths as "but do you know what day it is" (1:5). The coachman in "Dracula's Guest" (Johann) is also reincarnated as the unnamed coachman in *Dracula*: both men consult their watches — "Then he took out his watch..." (1) becomes "looking at his watch..." (1:10) — and both men hurry their horses "to make up for lost time" (2) or as if "bent on losing no time" (1:7). The innkeepers also assume some of Johann's functions. "Then he stretched out his hands appealingly to me, and implored me not to go" (2) becomes "Finally, she went down on her knees and implored me not to go..." (1:5). "Dracula's Guest" inters "Countess Dolingen of Gratz" (9) in a mausoleum that bears the motto "The dead travel fast" (10). In the typescript, the phrase "Denn die Todten reiten Schnell" is inserted in pen before the typed line "('For the dead travel fast.')" (115). This excerpt from Burger's "Lenore" resurfaces as an aside by a passenger in Harker's coach (1:10).

The opening of "Dracula's Guest" echoes Sabine Baring-Gould's introduction to *The Book*

370. "Let your story begin intimately, involving only a few principal characters. But as the telling moves forward, allow their actions to ramify outward into the world around them, touching and changing the lives of more and more people. Not all at once. Rather, spread the effect gradually through the progressions" (Robert McKee, *Story* 294).

371. Cited in Leslie S. Klinger, ed. *The New Annotated Dracula*. New York: W. W. Norton, 2008. Advance reading copy.

of Were-Wolves, which was one of Bram Stoker's earliest and most important sources. Its opening line "I shall never forget the walk I took one night in Vienna..." (1) may have inspired the narrator's fateful stroll in the woods outside Munich. Baring-Gould had difficulty making himself understood, for "Few in the place could speak French..." (2), while Harker found that "There was just enough English mixed with his German for me to understand the drift of his talk" (2). Baring-Gould ignores this warning: "Monsieur can never go back to-night across the flats, because of the — the — and his voice dropped; 'the loups-garoux'" and, like the Englishman in "Dracula's Guest," sets off, armed with a "strong stick" (4). Baring-Gould's conclusion, "This was my first introduction to were-wolves" (5), foreshadows Harker's initial encounter with vampires.

Characters

The Notes include three casts of characters. The lists on pages 1 and 7 were drawn up during the first few months. The former list does not include any names; characters are identified by their occupation or their relationship with other people. The latter assigns names to many of these characters and introduces new faces, including "Count ___ [Wampyr] Dracula" and "A Texan." The list on page 38 was drawn up later, but it seems to pre-date the calendar of events in which Quincey is surnamed "Morris." It includes Count Dracula, Peter Hawkins, Jonathan Harker, Mina Murray, John Seward, Lucy Westenra and Quincey P. Adams [the Texan] and adds Arthur Holmwood, Mrs. Westenra and Dr. Vincent. The "mad patient" does not appear here, but he participates in various plots.

All of the major characters evolve throughout the Notes:

Jonathan Harker

He enters the fray as a "lawyer's clerk" who has both a name and a fiancée (Mina). There are numerous details about his journey to Transylvania and his adventures in the castle. The name "Jonathan Harker" is a nod to Joseph Harker, who was a set designer at the Lyceum Theatre. *In Studio and Stage*, Harker mentions "My friend, Bram Stoker, who, incidentally, one day announced to me that he had appropriated my surname for one of his characters in 'Dracula'..." (135).

The Vampire Women

The earliest dated page proclaims "young man goes out sees girls one tries to kiss him not on lips but throat" but "Old Count interferes" saying "This man belongs to me I want him" (p. 2). These "girls" become the three vampire women who reside in Dracula's castle. A week later, Stoker refers to "the kiss" again (p. 8) and repeats "This man belongs to me." Eventually, the kiss becomes "woman stoops to kiss him" but "suddenly Count turns her away — 'This man belongs to me'" (p. 12). This scene must have been embedded in Stoker's imagination from the start, for it emerges again and again like a recurring dream.

These "terrible women" may have reminded Stoker's contemporaries of the prostitutes who inhabited the squalid tenements of London's East End, for they exhibit a similar aggressive and promiscuous sexuality. These "lost souls controlled by inhuman appetites" (Judith Weissman 74) are a central part of many psychosexual readings of the text in which "vampirism is linked with stifled, obsessive sexuality, all the more urgent because forbidden; and this sexuality is represented as female" (Gail Griffin 139).

A deleted passage in the typescript compares these sirens to the witches in *Macbeth*. Harker remarks, "For I feared to see those weird sisters. <How right was Shakespeare, no one would believe that after three hundred years one could see in this fastness of Europe the counterpart of the witches of Macbeth>" (174).

Mina (Murray) Harker

"Wilhelmina Murray (called Mina)" debuts on page 7, but her name could have been added to the first draft of this page on a later, unknown date. There is no convincing evidence about the origin of her name, but her character seems to be based on Laura, the heroine of "Carmilla." Both women write letters, and each of them was the last victim of a vampire who invaded their bedrooms and "seduced" them in a series of irresistible, erotic encounters. The fate of their friends — Bertha Spielsdorf or Lucy Westenra as the case may be — emphasizes the danger they are in and awakens our sympathy. Laura and Mina put their fates in God's hands, and both of them survive with the help of family and friends who, fortunately, call in an occult detective-cum-vampire hunter.

Lucy Westenra (a.k.a. the "bloofer lady")

Lucy was initially Dr. Seward's fiancée and a "schoolfellow of Miss Murray." Her vulnerability, seduction, illness and death weave their way through the Notes. Her adventures include encounters with Dracula in Whitby (p. 17–18), sleepwalking (p. 8 and 31), a mysterious wound on her throat (p. 18), illness and subsequent transfusions (p. 45) and her death and final destruction (p. 46).

Lucy's name links her with "Lucifer," but Stoker may have had a specific "Lucy" in mind. Salli Kline compares Lucy to Mary Elizabeth Braddon's Lady Audley:

> As a woman with "tainted blood" and thus predestined to crime, Lucy closely resembles another woman in English fiction with the same first name: Lady Lucy Audley, the anti-heroine of Mary Elizabeth Braddon's sensation-causing *Lady Audley's Secret* (1862) who is, all in one, a demoniac Dora Copperfield, a true kitsch version of the Pre-Raphaelite Lilith and a schizophrenic degenerate through heredity (her secret is the "hereditary taint" that is in her blood). Next to *The Woman in White* and *East Lynne*, Braddon's novel was one of the most influential bestsellers of the 1860s, and Stoker was certainly among the many other famous authors who were influenced by it [117].[372]

Her surname, "Westenra" could be a pun on "West End," for both Lucy and Mina, who inhabit the fashionable part of London are contrasted with the vixens from the East who resemble the prostitutes in the East End. Nina Auerbach contends that Lucy is modeled on George du Maurier's heroine, for "Like Trilby, Lucy Westenra has two selves. She is all silly sweetness in the daylight, but as Dracula's powers invade her, she becomes a florid predator at night. Like Trilby, too, she longs to marry three men" ("Mayhem and Maidens" 27).

In *Dracula*, Lucy is referred to as the "bloofer lady" after she becomes a vampire. This term may have originated in *Our Mutual Friend* where Dickens uses the very similar "boofer lady" as a child-like rendering of "beautiful lady."

Lucy's relationship with Mina resembles that of Mariora Slobozianu and the gypsy, Zamfira, in *Captain Vampire*. The pretty and coquettish Mariora, who "has the charming faults and caprices of a noble lady of Bucharest" (30) explains that she has befriended Zamfira, who is two

372. Braddon published a vampire story titled "Good Lady Ducayne" in 1896. Her note to Stoker on 23 June 1897, complimented him on *Dracula*. (See Miller, *Dracula: A Documentary Volume* 264).

years older than and neither rich nor pretty, "first of all, because she loves me ... and then because she's good" (41).

Dr. John Seward (a.k.a. Jack)

Dr. Seward is present from the beginning, first as a "mad doctor" (p. 1 and 5) then as the "doctor of mad house" (p. 7). His surname, which is also given on page 7, appears to have been added later. "John" appears on page 38, but "Jack," his nickname in the novel, is not found in the Notes. Initially he is in love with a "girl" [Lucy] who becomes his "fiancée."

"Dr. John Seward" may be a variation of "Dr. George Savage," the psychologist in "A Thirst for Blood," whose patients include a young boy who pulls the wings off flies. Dr. Seward, who continuously praises the virtues and wisdom of his friend and teacher, Professor Van Helsing, fills much the same role as another well-known doctor named John who chronicles the adventures of his mentor, Sherlock Holmes.

R. M. Renfield (a.k.a. the "fly patient" and "the Flyman")

Renfield's peculiar eating habits are hinted at on the first page of notes, and developed on pages 42 and 43. Neither the name "Renfield" nor the initials R. M. appear in the Notes. *The Undead* points out that, in the typescript, "the name of Renfield ... has been typed only in the later portions of the novel. Prior to those appearances he is referred to variously as The Flyman, Renfold [sic], or simply as a blank space reserved for the later insertion of his name" (n.p.).

The novel imbues Renfield with all of the characteristics of the original mad patient, including an ambiguous relationship with Dracula. However, the Notes neither cite his catch phrase, "The blood is the life," nor mention the episode in which Dracula attacks and kills Renfield.[373]

Rheinfeldt in "Carmilla" has been cited as the possible origin of his name. In addition, McNally and Florescu suggest that "Renfield, Dracula's minion, played the role which Stoker did in real life for the actor Sir Henry Irving, as his manager" (*Essential Dracula* 22).

After consulting prominent psychologists, the anonymous author of "A Thirst for Blood" informed readers that "Dr. Savage gives a ghastly instance of a child who commenced his career ... by pulling off the wings of flies. After a time this amusement palled, and the pleasing child took to baking frogs. He next turned his young intelligence to capturing birds and boring out their eyes. And later on nothing would satisfy him but ill-treating other children." Even people who have never read *Dracula* may see this child as the prototype of Stoker's fly-eating madman who tries to obtain immortality by eating his way up the evolutionary tree. In the novel, Dr. Seward observes that his patient "disgusted me much while with him, for when a horrid blow-fly, bloated with some carrion food, buzzed into the room, he caught it, held it exultantly for a few moments between his finger and thumb, and, before I knew what he was going to do, put it in his mouth and ate it" (6:70–71). Eventually, he "managed to get a sparrow" (6:71). Like the unnamed child who progressed from flies to birds to acts of violence against his playmates, Renfield soon escapes from his cell and attacks his custodian with a dinner knife, cutting his wrist.

Quincey P. Morris (a.k.a. The Texan)

Morris is a tribute to America and Americans. Following Lucy's death, Dr. Seward exclaims, "What a fine fellow is Quincey! I believe in my heart of hearts that he suffered as much about

373. However, Bram consulted his brother, William Thornley, for details about the nature and treatment of head injuries (p. 81–84).

Lucy's death as any of us; but he bore himself through it like a moral Viking. If America can go on breeding men like that, she will be a power in the world indeed" (13:177). There is no doubt that Stoker intended to include "a Texan" from the beginning. Morris' earliest name was Brutus M. Marix (p. 7), but he is often referred to as the "Texan." Eventually, he becomes Quincey P. Adams but, by the time Stoker composed the calendar of events, he was christened "Quincey Morris." Like Dracula, he once had a heftier role in the plot: "Texan to go to Transylvania" (p. 8), "Texan in Transylvania" (p. 8), "two visitors — Count Dracula and the Texan" (p. 19), "consult the Texan" (p. 24), and "return of the Texan — new light on Dracula" (p. 29). However, he is not cast as one of Lucy's rejected suitors.

Louis Warren argues convincingly that Morris is a parody of Buffalo Bill. The Texan also resembles a gun-toting American in Stoker's "The Squaw" with "his quaint speech and his wonderful stock of adventures" (87). They have the same middle initial — P. — and both men meet a tragic end.[374] Grizzly Dick, the protagonist of *The Shoulder of Shasta*, who, like Morris, totes a Winchester and a bowie knife, may be another early incarnation of the Texan.

Arthur Holmwood (a.k.a. Lord Godalming)

Arthur does not appear until quite late in the Notes (p. 38). In the novel, he is Lucy's third suitor and the man she chooses. He is selected as her first blood donor when she becomes ill and, when the men destroy the vampire Lucy, Arthur is chosen to drive the "mercy-bearing stake" through her heart.

Professor Abraham Van Helsing

The name "Van Helsing" appears in the list of characters on page 38. The Professor may be an amalgam of three characters from the first two lists: a Philosophic historian, a German Professor of History, a detective inspector (p. 1); Detective, Psychical Research Agent, German Professor (p. 7). The Notes hint at some of his roles: providing medical assistance to Lucy, solving the mystery of her demise, providing others (and the reader) with information about vampires, and leading in the destruction of the Count.

Bram Stoker and his father were both named "Abraham," for "Bram" is a diminutive of Abraham. In "Loving You All Ways," Robert Tracy sees Van Helsing as "an idealized self-portrait" (44). Two suggestions have been put forth as the source of his surname: Dr. Hesselius, the fictional narrator of Joseph Sheridan Le Fanu's collection, *In a Glass Darkly* (which includes "Carmilla") and Van Helmont, an alchemist who is mentioned in T. J. Pettigrew's *On Superstitions Connected with the History and Nature of Medicine and Surgery*, one of Stoker's sources. Soon after the novel was published, Stoker confided that the professor "is based on a real character" (Jane Stoddard 487). He reiterated this in his preface to the Icelandic edition of *Dracula* in 1901 where he confides that "the highly respected scientist, who appears here under a pseudonym, will also be too famous all over the educated world for his real name ... to be hidden from people" (8). If there was a live model for Van Helsing, a case can be made for a contemporary German professor at Oxford, Max Muller,[375] while the Notes champion Bram's brother William Thornley as a candidate. We do not know when or why Stoker decided to make the professor a Dutchman. However, David B. Dickens argues that Van Helsing is not Dutch, but German (34–37).

---

374. "The Squaw" was published in 1893, while Bram Stoker was working on *Dracula*.

375. According to *Personal Reminiscences of Henry Irving*, Stoker met Muller in the Beefsteak Room at the Lyceum and at Oxford University (v2.146; v2.252). Many scholars believe that this professor from Germany, who lectured in mythology and religion, inspired the character of Van Helsing.

Vampires

Stoker did more writing and research on vampires before his vacation in Whitby than many people have assumed. The Notes confirm that he began working on a vampire novel before he discovered the name "Dracula" or chose Transylvania as the monster's homeland.

In an interview for *British Weekly* in 1897, he responded to the question "Is there any historical basis for the [vampire] legend?" with "It rested, I imagine, on some such case as this. A person may have fallen into a death-like trance and been buried before the time. Afterwards the body may have been dug up and found alive, and from this a horror seized upon the people, and in their ignorance they imagined that a vampire was about" (Stoddard 486). He may have been familiar with Calmet's accounts of vampires or seen an article about vampire sightings in the *Encyclopædia Britannica* of 1888.[376]

For Transylvania, Stoker borrows liberally from Emily Gerard's article, "Transylvanian Superstitions," which includes many folk beliefs and customs. The following passage certainly caught his eye:

> More decidedly evil, however, is the vampire, or *nosferatu*, in whom every Roumenian peasant believes as firmly as he does in heaven or hell ... every person killed by a *nosferatu* becomes likewise a vampire after death, and will continue to suck the blood of other innocent people till the spirit has been exorcised, either by opening the grave of the person suspected and driving a stake through the corpse, or firing a pistol shot into the coffin. In very obstinate cases it is further recommended to cut off the head and replace it in the coffin with the mouth filled with garlic, or to extract the heart and burn it, strewing the ashes over the grave [142].

This is where Stoker found the word "nosferatu," which Gerard claims, erroneously, is a synonym for "vampire."[377] This passage may also be the source of the ritual in which Lucy's head is cut off and her mouth is stuffed with garlic.

The Rev. Sabine Baring-Gould's *The Book of Were-Wolves* contains numerous descriptions which Stoker appropriated for his vampire: canine teeth, pointed nails, hairy palms and the ability to change form. Isabella Bird's *The Golden Chersonese* includes a short note about vampires, which Stoker typed almost verbatim into his Notes.

Many readers are dismayed by the paucity of information about how Dracula became a vampire. The novel contains two references to the "Scholomance," the Devil's school that Dracula attended. This could explain how he became a vampire who is armed with an arsenal of supernatural powers. Another possibility is implicit in Van Helsing's exhortation:

> With this one, all the forces of nature that are occult and deep and strong must have worked together in some wondrous way. The very place, where he have been alive, Un-dead for all these centuries, is full of strangeness of the geologic and chemical world. There are deep caverns and fissures that reach none know whither. There have been volcanoes, some of whose openings still send out waters of strange properties, and gases that kill or make to vivify. Doubtless, there is something magnetic or electric in some of these combinations of occult forces which work for physical life in strange way; and in himself were from the first some great qualities [24:329].

This passage evokes images of caverns in which H. Rider Haggard's "She" bathed in the light of immortality.

376. See Appendix V.
377. There is no such word in the Romanian language. Gerard must have misinterpreted a word such as "nosophoros" (which is Greek for plague-carrier) or "necuratul" (a Romanian synonym for "the devil").

Naming the Count

Early references to the vampire who would become Count Dracula do not give him a name. Page 1 contains the phrases "Count's servants in London" and "in power of Count." The earliest dated page (p. 2) and the "Historiae Personae" (p. 7) refer to him as "Count ___" but, at some point, the *aide-memoire* "Count Wampyr" is inserted. It would be ludicrous to use it as a name. If a lawyer received a letter from "Count Wampyr," would he bother to answer it? And would any sensible solicitor go to a foreign country to visit a client who advertised his wares?

Bram Stoker followed the literary convention of making his anti-hero a member of the aristocracy. A cursory survey of Gothic literature yields a plethora of nasty Counts: Morano in Radcliffe's *The Mysteries of Udolpho*, de Bruno in Radcliffe's *The Italian*, Doni in Polidori's *Ernestus Berchtold*, Cenci in Shelley's *The Cenci*, Montonio in Maturin's *The Fatal Response*, Byron's Manfred and Collins' Count Fosco. Gothic fiction often links the temporal power of aristocrats, especially foreign lords, with supernatural powers. Count Azzo von Klatka in "The Mysterious Stranger" and Countess Karnstein in Le Fanu's "Carmilla" also pre-date *Dracula*.

Stoker discovered the name he would make famous (or, more correctly, which would make him famous) in William Wilkinson's *An Account of the Principalities of Wallachia and Moldavia* in the local library in Whitby. The fact that all of his notes about "voivode Dracula" are copied almost verbatim from Wilkinson's text makes its meager references extremely important:

> Wallachia continued to pay it [tribute] until the year 1444; when Ladislas King of Hungary, preparing to make war against the Turks, engaged the Voivode Dracula to form an alliance with him. The Hungarian troops marched through the principality and were joined by four thousand Wallachians under the command of Dracula's son [17].

And,

> Their Voivode, also named Dracula,* did not remain satisfied with mere prudent measures of defence: with an army he crossed the Danube and attacked the few Turkish troops that were stationed in his neighbourhood; but this attempt, like those of his predecessors, was only attended with momentary success. Mahomet, having turned his arms against him, drove him back to Wallachia, whither he pursued and defeated him. The Voivode escaped into Hungary, and the Sultan caused his brother Bladus to be named in his place. He made a treaty with Bladus, by which he bound the Wallachians to perpetual tribute... [19].
>
> *Dracula in the Wallachian language means Devil. The Wallachians were, at that time, as they are at present, used to give this as a surname to any person who rendered himself conspicuous either by courage, cruel actions, or cunning.

These three references to "Dracula" along with the footnote are the only occurrences of the name in all of the sources we know Stoker consulted.[378] Note that Wilkinson is vague about which Dracula is which. The first paragraph refers to Vlad's father, Vlad Dracul. Wilkinson refers to "Dracula" and "Voïvode," but never to "Vlad," "Vlad Ţepeş" or "the Impaler" and he does not bring up any of Vlad's atrocities. It is unlikely that Stoker did any more research on the historical Dracula, for his novel does not contain any additional information about him or his family.

Bram Stoker may have been aware of how a notorious nom de plume drew world-wide attention to a series of gruesome murders in Whitechapel in 1888. Philip Sugden's *The Complete History of Jack the Ripper* testifies to the power of the name "Jack the Ripper!" He points out that "Few names in history are as instantly recognizable. Fewer still could evoke such vivid images: noisome courts and alleys, hansom cabs and gaslights, swirling fog, prostitutes decked

378. Gerard's article makes it clear that the root word Drak- means Devil: "Gregnyia Drakuluj" (devil's garden), "Gania Drakuluj" (devil's mountain) and "Yadu Drakuluj" (devil's hell or abyss) (131).

out in the tawdriest of finery, the shrill cries of newsboys—'Whitechapel! Another 'orrible murder! Mutilation!'—and silent, cruel death, personified in the cape-shrouded figure of a faceless prowler of the night, armed with a long knife and carrying a black Gladstone bag" (1).

The decision to make "*Dracula*" the title of the novel was made at the last minute. When the typescript was submitted to the publisher in the spring of 1897, it still bore the title *The Un-Dead*. The dramatic reading held at the Lyceum in May moved a step closer, with *Dracula: or, The Un-Dead*. Just over a week later,[379] the book appeared with the title—*Dracula*. As Skal points out, "the decision was fortuitous—the one-word title itself, the three sinister syllables that crack and undulate on the tongue, ambiguous, foreign, and somehow alluring, was certainly a component of the book's initial and continued mystique" (22).

The Count's Physical Appearance

Many people come to the novel with preconceived ideas about what Count Dracula looks like, often based on how he is portrayed in various movies. Here is a summary of how Stoker portrayed him:

Height and build: tall and thin
Skin tone: "extraordinary pallor"; "waxen"
Age: "old" (although, after feeding, he may appear to be younger)
Nose: "aquiline ... high bridge ... thin nose ... peculiarly arched nostrils"
Hair: scanty around temples, profuse elsewhere
Eyebrows: very massive "almost meeting over the nose"
Eyes: red
Moustache: heavy, concealing much of the mouth
Mouth: "fixed and rather cruel-looking" with ruddy red lips
Teeth: "sharp white teeth [that] protruded over the lips"
Ears: pale, with "extremely pointed" tops
Hands: coarse, "broad, with squat fingers," hairs in centre of palm, long and sharp fingernails
Odor: fetid breath
Clothing: "clad in black from head to foot"

The Notes provide a few clues about the origin of these traits. The first hint appears on page 2: "describe old dead man made alive—waxen colour—dead dark eyes—what fire in them—not human—hell fire," along with later allusions to his "white moustache" (p. 3) and "red eyes" (p. 17).

Of course, Stoker could have been inspired by a variety of sources, including folk vampires, literary vampires and his own stories.[380] A likely influence is Henry Irving. Dracula's diabolical demeanor may have been inspired by Irving's stage presence. Stoker observed that Irving's private recitation of "The Dream of Eugene Aram" captured "the awful horror on the murderer's face" and "the fixed face—set as doom, with eyes as inflexible as Fate" (*Personal Reminiscences* v1.30). Maurice Richardson adds, "Irving's saturnine appearance and the savage hiss ... [may have] inspired the character of Dracula" (421). Irving's ability to capture the facial expressions of the great villains comes through on many occasions. Some of his most famous roles may have

379. The most widely accepted publication date for *Dracula* is 26 May 1897.

380. In "The Judge's House" Malcolm Malcolmson is unnerved by the villain's portrait, whose "face was strong and merciless, evil, crafty and vindictive, with a sensual mouth, hooked nose of ruddy colour, and shaped like the beak of a bird of prey. The rest of the face was a cadaverous colour" (38–39).

flashed across Stoker's mind as he was writing the novel: how as Shylock his eyes did "flash like lurid fire"; his features in Don Quixote "heightened by the resources of art to an exaggerated aquiline"; and his exaggeration in speaking.

In one of the most dramatic scenes in the novel, the vampire hunters break down the door of Mina's bedroom and confront the Count, who attacks them. Seward records the incident: "But by this time the Professor had gained his feet, and was holding towards him the envelope which contained the Sacred Wafer. The Count suddenly stopped, just as poor Lucy had done outside the tomb, and cowered back" (21:290). A deleted sentence in the typescript adds this allusion: "Even then at that awful moment with such a tragedy before my eyes, the figure of Mephistopheles in the Opera cowering before Margaret's lifted cross swam up before me and for an instant, I wondered if I were mad" (416). In 1897, any reference to *Faust* would have reminded Bram Stoker's contemporaries of Henry Irving, famous for his portrayal of Mephistopheles, a role he reportedly performed 792 times.

While several of Dracula's characteristics signify supernatural traits, most of them present a figure who is recognizably human.[381] This is one reason for the perennial popularity of vampire fiction. Unlike werewolves, mummies or incarnations of Frankenstein's monster, vampires are sufficiently similar to human beings to allow metaphors to operate on many levels.

Castle Dracula

Castle Dracula is one of the most infamous pieces of real estate in horror literature. References to a "castle" appear on pages 2 and 8. Although Stoker reminds himself to "describe" the castle, there is no such description in the Notes. Castles are a staple of Gothic fiction. They are usually located in remote mountainous regions, and have towering battlements, hidden rooms, secret passages, gloomy dungeons and creaking doors.

As he approaches the castle, Harker remarks, "I must have been asleep, for certainly if I had been fully awake I must have noticed the approach of such a remarkable place. In the gloom the courtyard looked of considerable size, and several dark ways led from it under great round arches" (2:15).

Earlier, at the Golden Krone, the innkeeper handed Harker a letter with instructions from Count Dracula: "At three to-morrow the diligence will start for Bukovina; a place on it is kept for you. At the Borgo Pass my carriage will await you and will bring you to me" (1:4). The Notes show that Stoker found "Borgo Prund" in Boner's book on Transylvania.[382] He then borrowed a description of mountains in other parts of the Carpathians—"rocky crags towered range on range," "savage grandeur," "the abode of eternal snow," and "steep and rocky sides cut by chasms"—and attached them to his immortal version of the Borgo Pass.

Although no specific castle is cited in the Notes, many Dracula enthusiasts claim to have visited *the* castle, be it Bran Castle or Poenari in Romania, or Slains Castle in Cruden Bay.[383]

381. In spite of claims to the contrary, it is unlikely that Vlad the Impaler was the model for any of Dracula's physical traits. There is no evidence that Stoker either saw a portrait or read a description of Vlad.

382. The same information would have been available in Baedeker, where the "Borgo Pass" appears both in print (407) and on a map.

383. The argument for Slains Castle in Cruden Bay relies on a comment Florence Stoker made in an interview in 1927: "When he [Stoker] was at work on *Dracula* we were all frightened of him. It was up on a lonely part of the east coast of Scotland, and he seemed to get obsessed by the spirit of the thing. There he would sit for hours, like a great bat, perched on the rocks of the shore or wander alone up and down the sandhills, thinking it out" (qtd. in Dalby, "Introduction" 7).

It is unlikely that Stoker used any particular castle as a model, for castles dot the landscapes of England and Ireland. "The Castle of the King," which is one of his earliest stories, is distinguished by an illustration of a castle.

Whitby

The Notes contain more material on Whitby than on any other topic. Only 3 of 27 chapters are set there, but the town plays an important and memorable role in the plot. Many of the most vivid passages in the novel — the view across the harbor to East Cliff, the graveyard and the tombstones, the ruins of Whitby Abbey, the cliffs where the "Demeter" comes ashore, the local dialect, and the weather — are set in this seaport in Yorkshire on the northeast coast of England.

Although Bram Stoker never visited Transylvania, he was familiar with Whitby.[384] He, his wife Florence and their son Noel, vacationed there during the summer of 1890. They arrived in late July and stayed for at least three weeks. By this time, he had begun his novel and outlined his villain. He had originally planned to have his vampire enter England via Dover but, by the time he returned to London, he had found a name for his vampire, had a new location for his villain's arrival in England as well as a picturesque background for Lucy's defilement.

The events at Whitby were originally to have taken place between 17 July and 18 August, when the story switches to London. This corresponds to the time Stoker spent in Whitby with his family. He adhered to this time-line as the story developed. In the novel, the Whitby segment of the plot ranges from 24 July, when Lucy meets Mina at the train station, to 19 August, when Mina leaves for Budapest.

The first references to Whitby in the Notes are on page 8:

Book II, Ch. 1: "Whitby — argument uncanny things"
Book II, Ch. 2: "Whitby — the storm — ship arrives"
Book II, Ch. 2: "Whitby. Lucy walks in sleep — bloody"

In this outline, dated 14 March 1890, these events replaced an earlier sketch about "The auctioneer," "The Doctor," and "The lawyer's clerk." These details are fleshed out in outlines for the first three chapters of Book II (p. 16, 17, 18). The following plot points (or variations of them) survive as a unit that shapes chapters 6, 7 and 8:

Mina and Lucy on the cliff chat with three old fishermen
the storm and a newspaper report on a derelict ship that runs aground
newspaper report — ship full of clay, cargo shipped to London
Lucy on the cliff: a strange man with red eyes amongst tombstones
Lucy sleepwalks, Mina pursues her to graveyard
Mina sees dark shape, resembling both man and wolf
Mina finds Lucy asleep on bench, wound on throat seemingly caused by brooch

Many of the notes he made in Whitby were expanded and worked into the novel:

1. The earliest note, a memo of a conversation with three old fishermen about local lore, becomes the basis of Mina and Lucy's chats with Mr. Swales.

2. Ten pages of inscriptions from tombstones in the graveyard on the East Cliff. The novel uses many of the names on these tombstones, while one surname, that of "Ann Swales," is bestowed on the cantankerous Mr. Swales.

---

384. He also vacationed in Cruden Bay on the northeast coast of Scotland. Although this town is not mentioned in the Notes, we know that he worked on *Dracula* there during the summers of 1893 or 1896.

3. Ten pages of words in the Yorkshire dialect. Mr. Swales uses dozens of these words in conversations with Mina and Lucy.

4. A note about a conversation with Coast Guard William Petherick. This is where Stoker heard about the Russian ship, the "Dimitry," that ran ashore in Whitby harbor in 1885 (p. 61). In the novel, this ship becomes the "Demeter."

5. Sundry notes about weather conditions, wind velocity, grey land- and sea-scapes, etc.

The novel takes many passages from the Notes almost verbatim, often preserving minute details. For example, as Bram Stoker looked down on the town from one of the cliffs on 18 August at 9 P.M., he recorded, "sheep and lambs bleating — clatter of donkey's hoofs up paved road. Band on pier harsh waltz. Salvation Army in street" (p. 71). The novel includes all of these details, even the time of day: Mina tells us, "the clock has just struck nine" (6:69).

Another important set of Notes is linked to Whitby — typewritten excerpts from William Wilkinson's book, which contains the name "Dracula." After he returned to London, Stoker made an additional note about Whitby (p. 76). This tidbit, which is dated 15 October, describes a large dog coming off a ship. Readers who are familiar with the details of Dracula's arrival in England will recognize this episode immediately.

Had Stoker not spent his summer vacation in Whitby in 1890, the book we know as *Dracula* would have taken a different form.

The Myth of *Dracula*

Many literary critics are baffled by *Dracula*'s undying popularity. Glen St. John Barclay realizes "No book could possibly have been so successful without possessing some extraordinary features," (40) yet he maintains that "the people in the story are totally unconvincing" (44) while the novel "exhibits amazing depths of incompetence" (45). After stating that "No one in their right mind would think of Stoker as a 'great writer,'" A. N. Wilson wonders, "How can someone who is not a great writer be said to have written a classic?" (xiv). Like other great works of art, *Dracula* defies attempts to analyze, criticize or dismiss it.

Explanations (and apologies) for the novel's appeal have concentrated on a plethora of psychosexual interpretations, the changing mores of Victorian England, the historical Vlad the Impaler and numerous other themes. But *Dracula* is more than a horror novel with elements of mystery, romance and eroticism; a deeper level of meaning is embedded in the text. As James B. Twitchell remarks, "If *Dracula*'s claim on our attention is not its historical importance or its artistic merit, then its power is derived from something below the surface, something carried within the myth itself. *Dracula* is the consummate retelling of the vampire story; all the pieces are used and all the pieces fit" (134). Claude Levi-Straus' classic study of myths offers plausible hypotheses for *Dracula*'s ongoing success. His theories begin with the principle that myths are created by language, for "to be known, myth has to be told; it is part of human speech" (209). Hence, in myths, "anything is likely to happen" (208)[385]

On the surface, *Dracula* is a study in oppositions. As the story unfolds, readers are confronted with an array of polarities that permeate the text: angel vs. demon; attraction vs. repulsion; civilization vs. barbarism; conscious vs. unconscious; creation vs. destruction; day vs. night; evolution vs. degeneration; England vs. Transylvania; fact vs. fiction; faith vs. doubt; familiar vs. foreign; fight vs. flight; free will vs. determinism; freedom vs. restraint; friend vs. foe; God vs. Satan[386]; good vs. evil; heaven vs. hell; human vs. animal; innocence vs. guilt; life vs. death; liberal vs. conservative; love vs. hate; master vs. slave; moral vs. immoral; mortal vs. immortal; mortality vs. immortality; natural vs. supernatural; natural vs. unnatural; new vs. old; order vs. chaos; peace vs. war[387]; pleasure vs. pain; predator vs. prey; order vs. chaos; reality vs. illusion; sacred vs. profane; salvation vs. damnation; sanity vs. madness; science vs. super-

385. In a similar vein, Tzvetan Todorov determined that fantastic literature "permits the description of a fantastic universe, one that has no reality outside language; the description and what are described are not of a different nature" (92).

386. Jan L. Perkowski points out that, in modern culture, "Dracula the Vampire has become our folkloric devil and in this role is opposed to the godlike Santa Claus..." (15).

387. "Blood is too precious a thing in these days of dishonourable peace; and the glories of the great races are as a tale that is told" (3:31).

stition; selfishness vs. altruism; technology vs. magic[388]; urban vs. rural; us vs. them; virgin vs. whore[389]; and young vs. old.

The fantastic elements in stories often conceal a more complicated level of order. Their mythical elements are encoded in the text by series of oppositions that are repeated over and over again in different ways.[390] Once we uncover the underlying repetitive elements in a text, we can begin to understand its mythic meaning by analyzing the relationships that are created by these bundles. When we study *Dracula* in this way, it becomes apparent that its dominant theme is human vs. vampire. "Human" represents everything that is natural, life-affirming and good, while "vampire" serves as a metaphor for the supernatural, the abnormal and the evil forces that threaten or deny life. As the story progresses, conflicts between these dualities are resolved or transcended. These oppositions occur on many levels. The Notes tell how the tensions arising from Jonathan Harker's trip to Transylvania and magnified by Dracula's voyage to England — the age-old fear that the dead may arise from their graves and overthrow the kingdom of the living — are reawakened in us. These dramas are resolved when the vampire hunters pursue their quarry back to his native land for a "final" confrontation.

Jonathan Harker's remark, "I was not able to light on any map or work giving the exact locality of the Castle Dracula" (1:2), serves the same function as the phrase "Once upon a time" does in fairy tales, for it invites us to accompany the narrator to a realm that has no place and no time. Harker's adventures in Transylvania initiate us into the dream time of folk lore and mythology. His escape from the castle completes the first octave of the myth, but the essential elements in the opening chapters are repeated again and again as the story progresses. One by one, each of the human protagonists will be forced to admit that vampires exist. Their survival will depend on the ability to understand, predict and control a supernatural menace. Each of these heroes acts out the age-old drama of good versus evil as they are forced to battle a vampire or vampire-like entity. In contrast to the "weird sisters" in Dracula's castle, Lucy and Mina are the virgins and treasures of Bram Stoker's macabre fairy tale. Their fates take different paths after Dracula attacks Lucy.[391] Lucy Westenra succumbs to Dracula's embrace to become a feminine version of the Count, but Mina resists his advances (and the promise of immortality). Each of Lucy's suitors fights a version of Dracula. Dr. Seward is bound to the human vampire, Renfield. He not only introduces us to Renfield and functions as his biographer, but is at his side to comforts him when he dies. Quincey Morris is plagued by vampire bats, while Arthur must drive a stake through his former fiancée's heart.

> The thing in the coffin writhed; and a hideous, blood-curdling screech came from the opened red lips. The body shook and quivered and twisted in wild contortions; the sharp white champed together till the lips were cut, and the mouth was smeared with a crimson foam. But Arthur never faltered. He looked like a figure of Thor as his untrembling arm rose and fell, driving deeper and deeper the mercy-bearing stake, whilst the blood from the pierced heart welled and spurted up around it [16:220].

388. Ronald Morrison alerts us to the "tension between gothic, supernatural elements and the scientific advances of the late Victorian age" (25).

389. Martin Tropp observes that "Stoker was no crusader for equal rights.... But he does show, whether he is aware of it or not, that the contradictory images of women as angel or whore are irreconcilable and self-destructive, that some new model of women would have to take their place" (166).

390. Levi-Strauss labeled these elements "gross constituent units" or "mythemes."

391. The first hint of the danger that awaits the girls occurs soon after Dracula's arrival in England: "We had a lovely walk. Lucy, after a while, was in gay spirits, owing, I think, to some dear cows who came nosing towards us in a field close to the lighthouse, and frightened the wits out of us" (8:91).

After his ordeal, his beloved's "sweetness and purity" return to her face and a "holy calm" washes over the vampire hunters.

After Dracula lands in Whitby and begins to prey on Lucy, Professor Abraham Van Helsing is called in to diagnose her mysterious, wasting illness. This scientist/priest/shaman — whose credentials bridge the gap between natural and supernatural reality — is often portrayed as the hero of the novel or the vampire's chief antagonist. But attempts to reduce *Dracula* to a story about vampires, victims and vampire hunters miss the point.

The climax of the story begins with Count Dracula's attacks on Mina, and reaches a crescendo with her "baptism of blood" in chapter 21. The Count's preface to Mina's initiation — "And you, their best beloved one, are now to me, flesh of my flesh; blood of my blood; kin of my kin; my bountiful wine-press for a while; and shall be later on my companion and my helper" (21:295) — reflects Adam's words when he first saw Eve: "This is now bone of my bones, and flesh of my flesh" (Genesis 2:23) and renders this coupling a blasphemous marriage ceremony. Dracula's newest "bride" repeats the story from her point of view:

> With that he pulled open his shirt, and with his long sharp nails opened a vein in his breast. When the blood began to spurt out, he took my hands in one of his, holding them tight, and with the other seized my neck and pressed my mouth to the wound, so that I must either suffocate or swallow some of the — Oh my God! my God! what have I done? What have I done to deserve such a fate, I who have tried to walk in meekness and righteousness all my days [21:296].

The vampire hunters burst into Mina's bedroom as the Count completes the ritual and ward him off with their crucifixes.

Following Mina's ordeal, Van Helsing touches a Sacred Wafer to her forehead. His blessing is cut short by a scream as it sears into her flesh, leaving a scar. Mina's lament, "Unclean! Unclean! Even the Almighty shuns my polluted flesh! I must bear this mark of shame upon my forehead until the Judgment Day" (22:305) reveals the depth of her despair. Mina's ability to transcend her "baptism of blood" elevates Dracula to a status few works have achieved. After the men return from their confrontation with Dracula, she reminds them, "That poor soul who has wrought all of this misery is the saddest case of all.... You must be pitiful to him too, though it may not hold your hands from his destruction" (23:317).

The first part of the tale introduced us to the vampires, whose ongoing association with animals is a token of primitive levels of consciousness. In the second part, the heroes distinguished themselves by rising above their base instincts. In the finale, the "outer" layer of the story revolves around the mechanics of the hunt, while the "inner" story concerns Mina's descent into the dark night of her soul and her eventual transcendence.

All of the characters can be interpreted by how they contribute to Mina's victory. Her ability to resist the horror of Dracula's lips upon her throat was foreshadowed by Jonathan's salvation from the vampire women in chapter 3, while her empathy for Dracula contradicts Lucy's dream-like acceptance of the Count's embrace and Renfield's servile craving for his master's gifts.

The story concludes in a flurry of action as the vampire hunters converge on Dracula's box. After overcoming Dracula's forces Jonathan's knife shears through the vampire's throat, beheading him, while Quincey's knife plunges into his heart. Mina exclaims, "It was like a miracle; but before our very eyes, and almost in the drawing of a breath, the whole body crumbled into dust and passed from our sight" (27:388). Their efforts are rewarded by Mina's observation: "I shall be glad as long as I live that even in the moment of final dissolution, there was in the face a look of peace, such as I never could have imagined might have rested there" (27:388). Upon his death, Mina's curse is lifted and the scar that united her with Dracula disappears.

An epilogue takes us back to Transylvania:

> Seven years ago we all went through the flames; and the happiness of some of us since then is, we think, well worth the pain we endured. It is an added joy to Mina and me that our boy's birthday is the same day as that on which Quincey Morris died. His mother holds, I know, the secret belief that some of our brave friend's spirit has passed into him. His bundle of names links all our little band of men together; but we call him Quincey [27:389].

Dracula suggests that stories about "immortality" refer to heightened states of consciousness, rather than the supernaturally prolonged existence of the ego. As the novel comes to a close, Dracula and all of the characters who craved physical immortality have died, while its heroes live on in the records and effects of their deeds and in the lives of their children. Bram Stoker's symphony of shadows has returned us to the world of everyday life with a renewed appreciation of the treasures it offers us.

Dracula and his followers continue to rise from the grave in books and films. Yet we are reassured that the world "will not be given over to monsters" (24:329) while, as Madam Mina reminds us all, "The world seems full of good men — even if there are monsters in it" (17:229).

Bram Stoker's Notes for *Dracula* not only reveal the genesis of a novel but serve as the first tentative steps in the creation of a modern myth. They provide a wealth of insights into this tale of "spiritual pathology" (10:122), which transcends its author's talents as a writer to speak to us today in the timeless language of myth.

Appendix I. The Rosenbach Page Numbers

The notes came to the Rosenbach in 1970 in the solander case in which they were sold in 1913. The pages in sections I and II, which are of widely-varying size and shape, were mounted singly or in groups of two or three on larger sheets of paper, but these leaves were not bound together. Most of the pages were mounted on one side of the sheet. Each section was preceded by another leaf with a section heading [I, II, and III] written in an unidentified hand. These leaves [Rosenbach pages A, 37, and 48] are not integral parts of the Notes. They may be the work of Bram Stoker's literary executor who, according to Ludlam, was named "Jarvis" (151)—or of someone at Sotheby, Wilkinson & Hodge who prepared the papers for auction on 7 July 1913.[392]

In the following chart, the Rosenbach page numbers are followed by their corresponding Eighteen-Bisang/Miller numbers and a brief description of each page.

R#	*EM#*	*Description*
A		*Bram Stoker's Original Foundation Notes & Data for His "Dracula." / [This remarkable book, which has already run into nine editions, has been aptly / described as "the very weirdest of weird tales."]*
1	7	Cast of characters. "Historiae Personae"
2	8	Plot. Books I, II, III and IV (dated 14/3/90)

392. Neither the original pages of the manuscript nor the leaves they were mounted on were numbered in any way. Page numbers were added by the Rosenbach staff between 1984 and 1990. In sections I and II the numbers were written on the leaves rather than the manuscript but, if a leaf had more than one page on it, the letters a, b, and c were written on the upper right corners of each page. Hence, these are not page numbers per se, but folio numbers.

The recto, or front, of the first leaf was numbered 1, the recto of the second leaf was 2, and so on. This was reasonable because most of the original pages were inscribed on one side and could be mounted on one side of one leaf. The exceptions can be confusing. For example, leaf 42 had two pages on each side—a recto and verso. The second page on the recto of the leaf is "42b," so the verso of this page is "42b verso," while (the recto of) the second page on the verso of this leaf is "42 verso b." When the Notes were conserved in 1997 and the pages were detached from the leaves, the existing numbers had been used in internal records and published citations. Therefore, the numbers were transferred from the album to the manuscript, and prefixed to any letters that were already there.

The Rosenbach prefers that the Notes be cited with their call number as Bram Stoker. Dracula: notes and outline, [ca. 1890–ca. 1896]. Rosenbach Museum & Library EL3 f.S874d MS.

R#	*EM#*	*Description*
3	77	History. Centuries 1–19
4	6	Characteristics of vampires. "goes through fog by instinct"
5	9	Plot. Book I: Chap. 1
6	10	_____. Book I: Chap. 2
7	11	_____. Book I: Chap. 3
8	12	_____. Book I: Chap. 4
9	13	_____. Book I: Chap. 5
10	14	_____. Book I: Chap. 6
11	15	_____. Book I: Chap. 7
12	16	_____. Book II: Chap. 1
13	17	_____. Book II: Chap. 2
14	18	_____. Book II: Chap. 3
15	19	_____. Book II: Chap. 4
16	20	_____. Book II: Chap. 5
17	21	_____. Book II: Chap. 6
18	22	_____. Book II: Chap. 7
19	23	_____. Book III: Chap. 1
20	24	_____. Book III: Chap. 2
21	25	_____. Book III: Chap. 3
22	26	_____. Book III: Chap. 4
23	27	_____. Book III: Chap. 5
24	28	_____. Book III: Chap. 6
25	29	_____. Book III: Chap. 7
26a	39	Calendar of events. (6 March–2 April)
26b	40	_____. (3 April–30 April)
27a	41	_____. (1 May–28 May)
27b	42	_____. (29 May–25 June)
28a	43	_____. (26 June–23 July)
28b	44	_____. (24 July–20 August)
29a	45	_____. (21 August–17 September)
29b	46	_____. (18 September–15 October)
30a	47	_____. (16 October–12 November)
30b	__	_____. No entries. Dates listed: Nov. 13–Dec. 10
31a	__	_____. No entries. Dates listed: Dec. 11–Jan. 7
31b	__	_____. No entries. Dates listed: Jan/ 8–Feb. 4
31b verso	38	Later list of characters
32	__	Blank page
33a	48	Plot. Oct. 1, 2 and 3
33b	49	Plot. "Memo Drac" (28.12.95, 24/11/95, 17/3/96 and 5/4/96)
34	50	Plot. Chap. 26. "Drac."
34 verso	51	Plot. Chap. 27
35a	1	First list of characters. "Lawyer — Aaronson purchase"
35b	31	Plot. 10–27
35c	32	Plot. 20–27
35 verso a	2	Plot. "Letter to President Incorporated Law Society" (8/3/90)
35 verso b	34	Plot. Books I, II and III (29/2/92)
35 verso c	30	Plot. Chap. 1–9
36a	33	Plot. 17–27
36b	35	Itinerary. Train and coach schedules — "London to Paris"
36b verso	37	_____. — "L. Arr"
36c	36	Train schedules — "Leave Klausenberg"
37	__	**"Dracula" Notes, etc. [II]**[393]

393. Section II (Rosenbach 37 to 47 verso b) consists of handwritten research notes, headed by three pages of notes on the plot.

R#	*EM#*	*Description*
38a	3	Plot. Vampire — Memo 1
38b	4	Plot. Vampire — Memo 2
38c	5	Plot. Vampire — Memo 3
38 verso a	52	Mme. E. de Laszowska Gerard. "Transylvanian Superstitions"
38 verso b	53	_____.
39a	54	_____.
39b	55	_____.
39 verso a	58	Notes from Robert H. Scott. "Fishery Barometer Manual"
39 verso b	59	_____.
40a	60	_____.
40b	61	Note on the "Dimitry"
40 verso	62	Note on Wrecks at Whitby by anon. (Mr. Petherick?)
41a	63	Glossary of Whitby Dialect
41b	64	_____.
41 verso a	65	_____.
41 verso b	66	_____.
42a	67	Note on Whitby: "Three old fishermen" (30/7/90)
42a verso	68	_____.
42b	69	Note on Whitby: "Tonight talked with Coast Guard" (11/8/90)
42b verso	75	Map. Whitby — sketch
42 verso a	70	Note on Whitby: "Grey day" (11/8/90)
42 verso b	71	Note on Whitby: "Whitby cliff 9pm" (18/8/90)
43a	78	List of non-fiction sources — "Baring-Gould Curious Myths"
43a verso	79	_____.
43b	80	Notes on Sir T. Browne. "Necromancy: Divination by the Dead"
43 verso a	56	Notes on S. Baring-Gould. *The Book of Were-Wolves*. Cont. on 43 verso b.
43 verso b	57	Notes on S. Baring-Gould. *The Book of Were-Wolves*. Cont. from 43 verso a.
44[394]	—	Newspaper article. "Vampires in New England." Cont. from 46v.
45a	81, 84	Note on head injuries by Sir William Thornley Stoker — "Memo/Signature"
45b	82, 83	_____. "Sketch/the surgeon opportunity"
45 verso	86	Photograph 1. Whitby Abbey
46	87	Photograph 2. Whitby Abbey
46 verso	85	Newspaper article. "Vampires in New England." Cont. on 44.
47a	74	Map. Whitby — sketch
47b	76	Whitby. Memo. (Dated 15/10/90)
47 verso a	72	Map. Whitby — sketch
47 verso b	73	Map. Whitby — sketch
48	—	**"Dracula" Notes, etc. [III]**[395]
49	88	A Fellow of the Carpathian Society. *Magyarland.*
50	89	_____.
51	90	_____.
52	91	Isabella L. Bird. *The Golden Chersonese.*
52 verso		_____. Contains the first sentence of page 52.
53	92	_____.
54	93	A. F. Crosse. *Round About the Carpathians.*
55	94	_____.
56	95	_____.
57	96	_____.
58	97	_____.
59	98	Major E. C. Johnson. *On the Track of the Crescent.*

394. Originally, this page contained the last paragraph of the newspaper clipping "Vampires in New England." Recently, the Rosenbach moved this to the end of the article on page 46 verso.
395. Section III (Rosenbach 49 to 85) consists of typewritten research notes.

R#	*EM#*	*Description*
60	99	_____.
61	100	_____.
62	101	_____.
63	102	_____.
64	103	_____.
65	104	_____.
66	105	F. C. & J. Rivington. *The Theory of Dreams.*
67	106	_____.
68	107	_____.
69	108	Charles Boner. *Transylvania: Its Products and Its People.*
70	109	_____.
71	110	William Wilkinson. ...*Wallachia and Moldavia.*
72	111	_____.
73	112	_____.
74	113	_____.
75	114	Tombstones — Whitby Churchyard on Cliff. Inscriptions.
76	115	_____.
77	116	_____.
78	117	_____.
79	118	_____.
80	119	_____.
81	120	_____.
82	121	_____.
83	122	_____.
84	123	_____.
85	124	Degrees of Wind: Beaufort's Scale.

Appendix II. Bram Stoker: A Brief Biography

Bram Stoker is remembered today as the author of *Dracula*. The title character of this remarkable novel has been a household word for many years, but its author remained virtually unknown until the 1960s. Harry Ludlam's *A Biography of Dracula* appeared in 1962, to be followed by three more full-length biographies: Daniel Farson, *The Man Who Wrote Dracula* (1975); Barbara Belford, *Bram Stoker* (1996); and Paul Murray, *From the Shadow of Dracula* (2004).[396]

Abraham (Bram) Stoker was born in Clontarf on the outskirts of Dublin, on 8 November 1847. His father, Abraham Stoker, was a clerk with the British civil service in Ireland. His mother, Charlotte Thornley, who was from western Ireland, was an active social reformer. The Stokers were Protestants who attended the Church of Ireland. Bram, the third of seven children, had four brothers (William Thornley, Thomas, Richard and George) and two sisters (Margaret and Matilda).

He was a sickly child, but no explanation for this mysterious illness that kept him bedridden for much of his young life has ever been provided. His mother entertained him with stories and legends from her native Sligo, which included supernatural tales and narrative accounts of death and disease. These stories may have introduced him to some of the motifs to be found in his immortal novel. By the time he entered Trinity College in Dublin in 1864, Stoker was a strong young man who excelled at athletics, especially football, racing and weightlifting. He also received awards for debating and oratory, and became President of the Philosophical Society.

Upon graduating, he followed in his father's footsteps and, in 1870, accepted a position with the Irish civil service. Seven years later he earned a promotion to Inspector of Petty Sessions and, eventually, published a reference for civil servants, *The Duties of Clerks of Petty Sessions in Ireland* (1879). He also wrote theatre reviews and short works of fiction for a local newspaper. His review of *Hamlet* led to a meeting with the actor, Henry Irving, that would change the course of his life. In *Personal Reminiscences of Henry Irving*, Stoker recalled this meeting in glowing terms: "Soul had looked into soul! From that hour began a friendship as pro-

396. The following studies offer fascinating insights into selected parts of Bram Stoker's life: Phyllis Roth, *Bram Stoker* (1982); Peter Haining and Peter Tremayne, *The Un-Dead* (1997); Elizabeth Miller, *Bram Stoker's Dracula: A Documentary Volume* (2005); and Lisa Hopkins, *Bram Stoker: A Literary Life* (2007).

found, as close, as lasting as can be between two men" (v1.33). In 1878, shortly after his marriage to the nineteen-year-old Dublin beauty Florence Lemon Balcombe,[397] Stoker accepted a position as the manager of Irving's new Lyceum Theatre in London. His association with Irving would continue until the actor's death in 1905.

Stoker's responsibilities at the Lyceum included organizing provincial seasons and overseas tours, keeping financial records and acting as Irving's secretary. He organized the Lyceum's eight North American tours, during which he met and became friends with Walt Whitman and Mark Twain. His association with Irving (who was knighted by Queen Victoria in 1895) brought him into contact with many of the leading figures of his day. Alfred Lord Tennyson, Richard F. Burton, Henry Morton Stanley, Lord and Lady Randolph Churchill, and William Gladstone were among his many friends and acquaintances. But the most significant influence on his life was Irving himself.

Except for vacations and periods of work-related travel, Stoker spent the rest of his life in London. His writing was done during any spare time his exceptionally busy schedule allowed. He began what would become *Dracula* in early 1890, and continued to work on it intermittently over the next seven years. The novel was composed against a backdrop of social upheaval. The turn of the century was rife with changes that challenged the fiber of Victorian England and middle-class values: mass immigration from central and eastern Europe, challenges to traditional gender roles, conflicts between religion and the new science, and anxieties about atavism and criminality. Many scholars have pointed out that *Dracula* embraces all of these fears and anxieties.

Henry Irving's death in 1905 left a void in Stoker's life that was accompanied by a gradual decline in his health. He apparently had suffered from Bright's disease since 1897 and, in 1906, suffered the first of two strokes. He died on 20 April 1912. Just as Henry Irving had taken the limelight from him in life, his death was eclipsed by the sinking of the *Titanic*, which had occurred five days earlier. Some writers have claimed that he died of syphilis, but this is debatable; his death certificate is inconclusive. He was cremated and his remains were interred at Golders Green in London.

397. Florence had been courted by Oscar Wilde, while George du Maurier called her "one of the three most beautiful women in London."

Appendix III. Bram Stoker: A Brief Bibliography[398]

Dracula, Bram Stoker's fourth novel, was published in 1897 when he was 49 years old.[399] Most of his novels are sentimental romances in which the hero tries to win the love of a woman. As in *Dracula,*[400] he may be aided by good father figures or menaced by bad ones. By the end of the novel, all of the evil men and evil (or flirtatious) women are punished or destroyed. Following the modest success of *Dracula*, Stoker worked some kind of vampire into *The Jewel of Seven Stars*, *The Lady of the Shroud* and *The Lair of the White Worm*. Unfortunately, he did not invest the time and energy in these works that had made *Dracula* a masterpiece and, since none of them boasted a villain of Count Dracula's stature, they fell far short of the mark he had set in 1897.

1879 *The Duties of Clerks of Petty Sessions in Ireland.* Dublin: Printed for the Author by John Falconer, 1879. 247 p. hb. • Non-fiction.

1881 *Under the Sunset.* London: Sampson, Low, Marston, Searle, and Rivington, 1881. 190 p. hb. illus. by W. Fitzgerald & W. V. Cockburn. Contents: "Under the Sunset." "The Rose Prince." "The Invisible Giant." "The Shadow Builder." "How 7 Went Mad." "Lies and Lilies." "The Castle of the King." "The Wondrous Child." • Collection of eight fairy tales for children. Clive Leatherdale tells us that these stories repeat certain motifs, "familial love, the division of the world into Good and Evil; the horrendous punishments meted out to those who sin; the inevitable triumph of Good; and the mysterious boundary between life and death" (*Novel & Legend* 63).

1886 *A Glimpse of America.* London: Sampson, Low, Marston & Co., 1886. 48 p. pb. • On December 21, 1885, Bram Stoker gave a lecture to the London Institution about the Lyceum Theatre's recent tour of America.

---

398. For a comprehensive list of Bram Stoker's work, including reprints and foreign editions, see Richard Dalby and William Hughes, *Bram Stoker: A Bibliography*. Westcliff-on-Sea, Essex: Desert Island Books, 2004.

399. Mary Wollstonecraft Shelley was 20 years old when the first edition of *Frankenstein; or, The Modern Prometheus* came out; Robert Louis Stevenson was 35 when *The Strange Case of Dr. Jekyll and Mr. Hyde* was published.

400. Robert Tracy contends that "The successful courtship of a beautiful young woman is the most popular of fictional plots. The death of a beautiful young woman, Poe tells us, is the most powerful poetic theme" ("Loving You All Ways" 33).

1891 *The Snake's Pass.* New York: Harper & Bros., 1890. 234 p. pb. • Novel. This romantic adventure which is set in Ireland revolves around a lost treasure.
_____. London: Sampson, Low, Marston, Searle & Rivington, Ltd., 1891. 356 p. hb.

1892 "Lord Castleton Explains" in *The Gentlewoman* 4 (30 January 1892). • Part 10 of the serial novel, "The Fate of Fenella," which was written by 24 different authors.

1894 *The Water's Mou.'* New York: Theo L. De Vinne & Co., 1894. 82 p. pb. • Novel. Romantic adventure set in Cruden Bay. Note: "Mou'" is an abbreviation for "Mouth."
_____. London: A. Constable and Co., 1895. 165 p. hb. & pb.

1895 *The Shoulder of Shasta.* Westminster: Archibald Constable and Co., 1895. 235 p. hb. • Novel. Romantic adventure set in California.

1897 *Dracula.* Westminster: Archibald Constable and Company, 1897. 390 p. hb.[401]
_____. New York: Doubleday & McClure Co., 1899. 378 p. hb. • Amended. There is a crucial change in the fourth chapter. When Count Dracula forbids his consorts to drink Jonathan Harker's blood, the first edition says, "Wait. Have patience. To-morrow night, to-morrow night is yours!" (4:51) but the Doubleday edition states, "Wait! Have patience! To-night is mine. To-morrow night is yours!" (51). This alteration is the only indication that Dracula feeds on men as well as women.
_____. Westminster: Archibald Constable and Company, 1901. 138 p. pb. Cover by Nathan. • Abridged edition. Bram Stoker's revised version of his opus offers us a rare, stereoscopic view of one of the most remarkable novels in literature. Critics either praise this version or detest it.
_____. London: William Rider & Son, Limited, 1912. Ninth edition. 404 p. hb. dj. by Holloway. • Amended. Most British editions use this text.
_____. Garden City, NY: Doubleday, Page & Company, 1927. 354 p. hb. • Amended. Most modern American reprints of *Dracula* use this text.

1898 *Miss Betty.* London: C. Arthur Pearson Limited, 1898. 202 p. hb. • Novel. This historical romance revolves around a young heiress.

1902 *The Mystery of the Sea.* New York: Doubleday, Page & Co., 1902. 498 p. hb. • Novel. Mystery and romance with supernatural elements, including second sight and the spirits of drowned sailors. While on vacation in Cruden Bay, Archibald Hunter decodes a cipher that reveals the location of a lost treasure.
_____. William Heinemann: London, 1902. 498 p. hb.

1903 *The Jewel of Seven Stars.* London: William Heinemann, 1903. 337 p. hb. • Novel. The five thousand year-old mummy of an Egyptian queen is transported to London where it is briefly resurrected. Movie: *Blood from the Mummy's Tomb* (1971); *The Mummy's Shroud* (1976) and *The Awakening* (1980).
_____. New York and London: Harper & Brothers Publishers, 1904. 311 p. hb. dj.
_____. London: William Rider & Son Limited, 1912. 307 p. hb. dj. • Revised, with a new, weaker but happier ending. Most subsequent editions are based on this text.

1905 *The Man.* London: William Heinemann, 1905. 436 p. hb. • Novel. Romance.
_____. Retitled: *The Gates of Life.* New York: Cupples & Leon Company, Publishers, n.d. [1908]. 332 p. hb. Illus. by F. B. Madan. Abridged by the author.

1906 *Personal Reminiscences of Henry Irving.* London: William Heinemann, 1906. 2 vol. 372 + 388 p. hb. • Non-fiction. Biography.
_____. London: William Heinemann, 1907. 1 vol. 480 p. hb. • Abridged.

1908 *Lady Athlyne.* London: William Heinemann, 1908. 333 p. hb. • Novel. Romance.

1908 *Snowbound: The Record of a Theatrical Touring Party.* London: Collier & Co., 1908. 256 p. hb.

401. Hutchinson & Co's colonial edition of 1897 is printed from the same plates as Constable's first edition and may, in fact, precede it.

Contents: "The Occasion." "A Lesson in Pets." "Coggin's Property." "The Slim Syrens." "A New Departure in Art." "Mick the Devil." "In Fear of Death." "At Last." "Chin Music." "A Deputy Waiter." "Work'us." "A Corner in Dwarfs." "A Criminal Star." "A Star Trap." "A Moonlight Effect." • Collection of 15 stories.

1909 *The Lady of the Shroud.* London: William Heinemann, 1909. 367 p. hb. • Novel. Romance, with elements of science fiction. Political intrigues force an East-European princess to pose as a vampire.

_____. London: William Rider & Son, Ltd., 1914. 355 p. hb.

1910 *Famous Imposters.* London: Sidgwick & Jackson, Ltd., 1910. 349 p. hb. Contents: "Pretenders." "Practitioners of Magic." "The Wandering Jew." "John Law." "Witchcraft and Clairvoyance." "Arthur Orton (Tichborne claimant)." "Women as Men." "Hoaxes, etc." "Chevalier D'Eon." "The Bisley Boy." • Non-fiction collection.

1911 *The Lair of the White Worm.* London: William Rider & Son, Ltd., 1911. 328 p. hb. Illustrated by Pamela Colman Smith. Novel. A monstrous white worm that lives in an ancient well can assume the form of a beautiful Lady Arabella March. Movie: 1988.

_____. Retitled: *The Garden of Evil.* New York: Popular Library, 1966. 220 p. pb.

Posthumous Publications

1914 *Dracula's Guest: And Other Weird Stories.* London: George Routledge & Sons, Ltd., n.d. [1914]. 200 p. hb. dj. by Handfurth. Contents: "Preface" by Florence A. L. Bram Stoker. "Dracula's Guest." "The Judge's House." "The Squaw." "The Secret of the Growing Gold." "A Gipsy Prophecy." "The Coming of Abel Behenna." "The Burial of the Rats." "A Dream of Red Hands." "Crooken Sands." • Posthumous collection of nine supernatural stories.

_____. Retitled: *Dracula's Guest.* New York: Hillman-Curl, Inc., 1937. 284 p. hb. dj. by Photo Associates. A Clue Club Mystery.

1986 "Author's Preface" in *Dracula and The Lair of the White Worm* (London: W. Foulsham & Co. Ltd., 1986. Ed. by Richard Dalby) 11–12. • The first English translation of the Bram Stoker's preface for the Icelandic edition of *Dracula* (*Makt Myrkranna* [*The Power of Darkness*], 1901) claims that tragedies in the novel arise from the same source as the notorious murders of Jack the Ripper.

1997 *Dracula; or, The Un-Dead: A Play in Prologue and Five Acts.* Nottingham: Pumpkin Books, 1997. 277 p. hb. dj. Ed. by Sylvia Starshine. Drama. • This dramatized version of *Dracula* was enacted at the Lyceum Theatre on 18 May 1897 to secure the dramatic rights for the novel. This adaptation, in which proof copies of the novel were cut and pasted unto a handwritten manuscript, opens with Harker's arrival at the castle. Among other things, the play leaves no doubt that Dracula was beheaded.

Appendix IV. Bram Stoker's Nonfiction Sources for *Dracula*

Sources Stoker is known to have taken notes from

Baring-Gould, Rev. Sabine. *The Book of Were-Wolves: Being an Account of a Terrible Superstition*. London: Smith, Elder & Co., 1865.
Bird, Isabella L. *The Golden Chersonese*. London: John Murray, 1883.
Boner, Charles. *Transylvania: Its Products and its People*. London: Longmans, Green, Reader and Dyer, 1865.
Browne, Sir Thomas. *Pseudodoxia Epidemica, or Vulgar Errors*. London, 1646.
Crosse, Andrew F. *Round About the Carpathians*. London: Blackwood, 1878.
A Fellow of the Carpathian Society [Nina Elizabeth Mazuchelli]. *Magyarland: Being the Narrative of our Travels through the Highlands and Lowlands of Hungary*. London: Sampson Low, Marston, Searle and Rivington, 1881.
Gerard, Emily. "Transylvanian Superstitions." *The Nineteenth Century* (July 1885). 128–144.
Johnson, Major E. C. *On the Track of the Crescent: Erratic Notes from the Piraeus to Pesth*. London: Hurst and Blackett, 1885.
Rivington, F. C. and J. *The Theory of Dreams*. London: St. Paul's Churchyard, 1808.[402]
Robinson, F. K. *A Glossary of Words Used in the Neighbourhood of Whitby*. London, 1876.
Scott, Robert H. *Fishery Barometer Manual*. London: HMSO, 1887.
Wilkinson, William. *An Account of the Principalities of Wallachia and Moldavia: with various Political Observations Relating to Them*. London: Longman, Hurst, Rees, Orme and Brown, 1820.

Sources listed by Stoker (without any notes)

Baring-Gould, Rev. Sabine. *Curious Myths of the Middle Ages*. London: Rivingtons, 1877.
Baring-Gould, Rev. Sabine. *Germany, Present and Past*. London: Kegan Paul, Trench, 1879.
Bassett, Fletcher S. *Legends and Superstitions of the Sea and of Sailors—In All Lands and at All Times*. London: Sampson Low, Marston, Searle and Rivington, 1885.
Dorman, Rushton M. *The Origin of Primitive Superstitions: And Their Development into the Worship of Spirits and the Doctrine of Spiritual Agency among the Aborigines of America*. London: Lippincott, 1881.
Jones, John. *The Natural and the Supernatural: Or, Man—Physical, Apparitional and Spiritual*. London: Balliere, 1861.
Jones, William. *Credulities Past and Present*. London: Chatto and Windus, 1880.
Jones, William. *History and Mystery of Precious Stones*. London: Richard Bentley & Son, 1880.
Jones, Rev. W. Henry and Lewis L. Kropf. *The Folk-Tales of the Magyars*. London: Elliott Stock, 1889.

---

402. Bram Stoker's notes from Rivington include excerpts from Sir Thomas Browne's *Religio Medici* (1643), Samuel Garth's "The Dispensary" (1706) and George Cheyne's *The English Malady* (1733).

Lea, Henry Charles. *Superstition and Force—Essays on The Wager of Law, The Wager of Battle, The Ordeal and Torture.* Philadelphia: H. C. Lea, 1878.
Lee, Rev. Frederick George. *The Other World: Or, Glimpses of the Supernatural—Being Facts, Records and Traditions.* London: Henry S. King, 1875.
Lee, Henry. *Sea Fables Explained.* London: William Clowes & Sons, 1883.
Lee, Henry. *Sea Monsters Unmasked.* London: William Clowes & Sons, 1883.
Lee, Sarah. *Anecdotes of Habits and Instincts of Birds, Reptiles and Fishes.* Philadelphia: Lindsay Blalmston, 1853.
Maury, L. F. Alfred. [No title cited.]
Mayo, Herbert. *On the Truths Contained in Popular Superstitions—with an Account of Mesmerism.* London: William Blackwood & Sons, 1851.
Pettigrew, Thomas Joseph. *On Superstitions Connected with the History and Practice of Medicine and Surgery.* London: John Churchill, 1844.
Reville, Rev. Albert. *The Devil: His Origin, Greatness and Decadence.* London: Williams and Norgate, 1871.
Spottiswoode, W. *A Tarantasse Journey through Eastern Russia in the Autumn of 1856.* London, 1857.
Spottiswoode, W. "Miscellany."
Thiers, J. B. *Traite des superstitions qui regardent les sacraments.* Paris, 1700–04.

Incomplete entries

Truibs, J. See various headings
Wright, T. See various headings

Appendix V. "Vampire" from the *Encyclopædia Britannica* (1888)[403]

VAMPIRE, a term, apparently of Servian origin (*wampir*), originally applied in eastern Europe to blood-sucking ghosts, but in modern usage transferred to one or more species of blood-sucking bats inhabiting South America.

In the first-mentioned meaning a vampire is usually supposed to be the soul of a dead man which quits the buried body by night to suck the blood of living persons. Hence, when the vampire's grave is opened, his corpse is found to be fresh and rosy from the blood which he has thus absorbed. To put a stop to his ravages, a stake is driven through the corpse, or the head cut off, or the heart torn out and the body burned, or boiling water and vinegar are poured on the grave. The persons who turn vampires are generally wizards, witches, suicides and those who have come to a violent end or have been cursed by their parents or by the church. But any one may become a vampire if an animal (especially a cat) leaps over his corpse or a bird flies over it. Sometimes the vampire is thought to be the soul of a living man which leaves his body in sleep, to go in the form of a straw or fluff of down and suck the blood of other sleepers. The belief in vampires chiefly prevails in Slavonic lands, as in Russia (especially White Russia and the Ukraine), Poland and Servia, and among the Czechs of Bohemia and the other Slavonic races of Austria. It became especially prevalent in Hungary between the years 1730 and 1735, whence all Europe was filled with reports of the exploits of vampires. Several treatises were written on the subject, among which may be mentioned Ranft's *De masticatione mortuorum in tumulis* (1734) and Calmet's *Dissertation on the Vampires of Hungary*, translated into English in 1750. It is probable that this superstition gained much ground from the reports of those who had examined the bodies of persons buried alive though believed to be dead, and was based on the twisted position of the corpse, the marks of blood on the shroud and on the face and hands — results of the frenzied struggle in the coffin before life became extinct. The belief in vampirism has also taken root among Albanians and modern Greeks, but here it may be due to Slavonic influence.

Two species of blood-sucking bats (the only species known)—*Desmodus rufus* and *Diphylla ecaudata*— representing two genera, inhabit the tropical and part of the subtropical regions of

403. 9th edition, vol. 24. 52–53.

the New World, and are restricted to South and Central America. They appear to be confined chiefly to the forest-clad parts, and their attacks on men and other warm-blooded animals were noticed by some of the earliest writers. Thus Peter Martyr (Anghiera), who wrote soon after the conquest of South America, says that in the Isthmus of Darien there were bats which sucked the blood of men and cattle when asleep to such a degree as to even kill them. Condamine, a writer of the 18th century, remarks that at Borja (Ecuador) and in other places they had entirely destroyed the cattle introduced by the missionaries. Sir Robert Schomburgk relates that at Wicki, on the river Berbice, no fowls could be kept on account of the ravages of these creatures, which attacked their combs, causing them to appear white from loss of blood. The present writer, when in South and Central America, had many accounts given him as to the attacks of the vampires, and it was agreed upon by most of his informants that these bats when attacking horses showed a decided preference for those of a grey colour. It is interesting to speculate how far the vampire bats may have been instrumental — when they were, perhaps, more abundant — in causing the destruction of the horse, which had disappeared from America previous to the discovery of that continent.

Although these bats were known thus early to Europeans, the species to which they belonged were not determined for a long time, several of the large frugivorous species having been wrongly set down as blood-suckers, and named accordingly. Thus the name *Vampyrus* was suggested to Geoffrey and adopted by Spix, who also considered that the long-tongued bats of the group *Glossophaga* were addicted to blood, and accordingly described *Glossophaga soricina* as a very cruel blood-sucker (*sanguisuga crudelissima*), believing that the long brush-tipped tongue was used to increase the flow of blood. *Vampyrus spectrum*, a large bat inhabiting Brazil, of sufficiently forbidding aspect, which was long considered by naturalists to be thoroughly sanguivorous in its habits, and named accordingly by Geoffrey, has been shown by the observations of travelers to be mainly frugivorous, and is considered by the inhabitants of the countries in which it is found to be perfectly harmless. Charles Waterton believed *Artibeus planirostris*, a common bat in British Guiana, usually found in the roofs of houses, and now known to be frugivorous, to be the veritable vampire; but neither he nor any of the naturalists that preceded him had succeeded in detecting any bat in the act of drawing blood. It fell to the lot of Charles Darwin to determine one of the blood-sucking species at least, and the following is his account of the circumstances under which the discovery of the sanguivorous habits of *Desmodus rufus* was made: "The vampire bat is often the cause of much trouble by biting the horses on their withers. The injury is generally not so much owing to the loss of blood as to the inflammation which the pressure of the saddle afterwards produces. The whole circumstance has lately been doubted in England; I was therefore fortunate in being present when one was actually caught on a horse's back. We were bivouacking late one evening near Coquimbo, in Chile, when my servant, noticing that one of the horses was very restive, went to see what was the matter, and, fancying he could detect something, suddenly put his hand on the beast's withers, and secured the vampire" (*Naturalist's Voyage Round the World*, p. 22).

Desmodus rufus, the common blood-sucking bat, is widely spread over the tropical and subtropical parts of Central and South America from Oaxaca to southern Brazil and Chile. It is a comparatively small bat, a little larger than the noctule, the head and body about 3 in. in length, the forearm 2½, with a remarkably long and strong thumb; it is destitute of a tail, and has a very peculiar physiognomy. The body is covered with rather short fur of a reddish-brown colour but varying in shade, the extremities of the hairs sometimes ashy. The teeth are peculiar and characteristic, admirably adapted for the purposes for which they are employed. The upper front teeth (incisors), of which there are only two, are enormously enlarged, and in shape obliquely triangular like small guillotines. The canines, though smaller than the incisors, are large and sharp; but the cheek-teeth, so well developed in other bats, are very small and reduced in number to two above and three below, on each side, with laterally compressed crowns rising but slightly above the level of the gum, their longitudinally disposed cutting edges (in the upper jaw) being continuous with the base of the canine and with each other. The lower front teeth (incisors) are small, bifid, in pairs, and separated from the canines, with a space in front. The lower cheek-teeth are narrow, like those in the upper jaw, but the anterior tooth is slightly larger than the others, and separated by a small space from the canines. Behind the lower incisors the jaw is deeply hollowed out to receive the extremities of the larger upper incisors.

With this peculiar dentition there is associated as remarkable a departure from the general type in the form of the digestive apparatus. The exceedingly narrow oesophagus opens at right angles into a narrow, intestine-like stomach, which almost immediately terminates on the right, without a distinct pylorus, in the duodenum, but on the left forms a greatly elongated caecum, bent and folded upon itself, which appears at first sight like a part of the intestines. This, the cardiac extremity of the stomach is, for a short distance to the left of the entrance of the oesophagus, still very narrow, but soon increases in size, till near its termination it attains a diameter quite three times that of the short pyloric portion. The length of this cardiac diverticulum of the stomach appears to vary from 2 to 6 in., the size in each specimen probably depending on the amount of food obtained by the animal before it was captured.

The only other known species of blood-sucking bat, *Diphylla ecaudata*, inhabits Brazil, and appears to be less abundant than *Desmodus rufus*, from which it is distinguished by its slightly smaller size, by the absence of a groove in the front of the lower lip, the non-development of the interfemoral membrane in the center, and the presence of a short calcaneum (absent in *D. rufus*), but more particularly by the presence of an additional rudimentary cheek-tooth (?molar) above and below, and the peculiar form of the lower incisors, which are much expanded in the direction of the jaws and pectinated, forming a semi-circular row touching each other, the outer incisors being wider than the inner ones, with six notches, the thinner incisors with three each.

Thus constituted, these bats present, in this extraordinary differentiation of the manducatory and digestive apparatus, a departure from the type of other species of the family (*Phyllostomidae*) to which they belong unparalleled in any of the other orders of *Mammalia*, standing apart from all other mammals as being fitted only for a diet of blood, and capable of sustaining life upon that alone. Travellers describe the wounds inflicted by the large sharp-edged incisors as being similar to those caused by a razor when shaving: a portion of the skin is shaved off and, a large number of severed capillary vessels being thus exposed, a constant flow of blood is maintained. From this source the blood is drawn through the exceedingly narrow gullet—too narrow for anything solid to pass—into the intestine-like stomach, whence it is, probably, gradually drawn off during the slow process of digestion, while the animal, sated with food, is hanging in a state of torpidity from the roof of its cave or from the inner sides of a hollow tree.

Appendix VI. Possible Literary Influences

Modern vampire literature originated in the eighteenth century. Following a series of plagues and famines, stories about corpses that had risen from their graves circulated throughout Eastern Europe. It is evident today that most of these so-called "resurrections" can be traced to the improper diagnoses of wasting diseases and premature burials but many people once believed that these "revenants" had been reanimated by ritual magic or resurrected by the devil. If a deceased person were suspected of being a vampire, his or her corpse was taken from its grave and staked through the heart, beheaded or burned to ashes. The church, which played the leading role in the prosecution of witches, proclaimed that anyone who died in a state of sin could become a vampire after death. That crucifixes, sacred wafers and holy water are effective weapons against literary and cinematic vampires can be traced to these early beliefs.

The French theologian Dom Augustin Calmet collected many of these accounts in his treatise of 1746. Eventually, poets throughout Europe began to transform the vampire from a moldering peasant wrapped in its burial shroud to a literary device for exploring the themes of life, death and eroticism in daring new ways. Notable examples of this trend include Burger's "Lenore" (1773), Goethe's "The Bride of Corinth" (1797) and Coleridge's "Christabel" (1797).

Bram Stoker's Original Foundation Notes & Data for His "Dracula" list many of his research documents but, surprisingly, they do not mention any of his literary inspirations. With the exception of "Carmilla," it is difficult to pinpoint these sources exactly. For example, Wilkie Collins, who popularized the epistolary form of story telling, has often been cited as a precursor of *Dracula*. The first chapter of *The Woman in White* tells readers that the events in the novel appear "...for the first time, in this place. As the Judge might once have heard it so the Reader will hear it now. No circumstance of importance, from the beginning to the end of the disclosure, shall be related on hearsay evidence" (9). However, *The Moonstone*, which came out eight years later, and other similar works could have ignited Stoker's imagination.

It is as if Bram Stoker read each of the following works and asked himself, "How can I make my vampire novel more terrifying than any of them?"

1819: John Polidori. "The Vampyre."
1836: Theophile Gautier. "La Morte Amoureuse." Trans. "Clarimonde" [1882].[404]
1847: *Varney the Vampyre; or, The Feast of Blood.*

404. There is more than one translation of "La Morte Amoureuse," which has been published as "The Beautiful Dead," "The Beautiful Vampire," "Clarimonda," "The Dead in Love," "The Dead Leman," "The Dead Lover," "The Dreamland Bride" and "Vampire."

1853: "The Mysterious Stranger."
1886: Robert Louis Stevenson. "The Strange Case of Dr. Jekyll and Mr. Hyde."

"The Vampyre"

John Polidori's story, "The "Vampyre," was inspired by a vignette Lord Byron wrote for the famous literary gathering and ghost-story contest in Geneva. Its first appearance in *The New Monthly Magazine* on 1 April 1819 was attributed to Lord Byron. The story caused a sensation because many people believed it to be a self-portrait of the "Satanic Lord." Its unprecedented popularity created the first "vampire craze." Imitations of "The Vampyre" as well as stories and plays about vampiric noblemen spread throughout Europe.

"The Vampyre" transformed the revenant of folklore from a lumbering peasant who returned from the grave to attack family and friends into a nobleman who frequented fashionable clubs and wandered the globe in search of suitable, nubile victims. The story's protagonist, Lord Ruthven invites young Aubrey on a tour of the continent. After killing a woman Aubrey befriends in Greece, he returns to England to prey on Aubrey's sister. *Dracula* follows a similar pattern. However, neither the Notes nor the novel explain how Jonathan Harker's relationship with Count Dracula leads to the vampire's attacks on Lucy and Mina.

"Clarimonde"

Jonathan Harker's initial encounter with three vampire women has much in common with Romuald's affair with the un-dead Clarimonde. In Gautier's story, the vampire is introduced in a rapturous dream-like episode where young Romuald confesses, "Poor country-priest though I was, I led every night in a dream — would to God it had all been a dream..." (66). This motif could have inspired Harker's remark, "In the moonlight opposite me were three young women, ladies by their dress and manner. I thought at the time that I must be dreaming..." (3:38). Later, when Romuald bends over the courtesan's corpse, he states that he "could not deny myself the last sad sweet pleasure of imprinting a kiss upon the dead lips of her who had been my only love" (98), while Harker eventually admits, "I felt in my heart a wicked, burning desire that they would kiss me with those red lips" (3:38).

The incident in which Dracula lunges at Harker's throat after his guest cuts himself while shaving also has a precedent in "Clarimonde." Romuald recalls as follows:

> One morning I was seated at her bedside, and breakfasting from a little table placed close at hand, so that I might not be obliged to leave her for a single moment. In the act of cutting some fruit, I accidentally inflicted rather a deep gash on my finger. The blood immediately gushed forth in a little purple jet; and a few drops spurted upon Clarimonde. Her eyes flashed; her face immediately assumed an expression of savage and ferocious joy such as I had never before observed in her. She ... sprang upon my wound which she commenced to suck with an air of unutterable pleasure [116].

Varney the Vampyre

Varney the Vampyre adds a number of significant features to the emerging stereotype of the vampire. First of all, Varney himself is described as follows:

> The figure turns half round, and the light falls upon the face. It is perfectly white — perfectly bloodless. The eyes look like polished tin; the lips are drawn back, and the principal feature next to those dreadful eyes is the teeth — the fearful-looking teeth — projecting like those of some wild animal, hideously, glaringly white, and fang-like [v1.3].

There are also references to the vampire's appearance after feeding — his lips are "dabbled in blood" and his face "flushed with colour." The neck of his victim — in this case Flora — bears the telltale sign of "two bloody bite marks." Many passages have a familiar ring: mixed reactions of desire and fear, sleepwalking, the ways of destroying vampires, the vampire hunt, a midnight vigil at the tomb of a suspected vampire, a vampire transforming into a wolf, and a chase to the vampire's resting place. All of these features became permanent fixtures of the literary vampire after Bram Stoker used them in his novel.

The staking of Clara could almost be a scene from *Dracula*:

> The blacksmith shuddered as he held the stake in an attitude to pierce the body, and even up to that moment it seemed to be a doubtful case, whether he would be able to accomplish his purpose or not; at length, when they all thought he was upon the point of abandoning his design and casting the stake away, he thrust it with tremendous force through the body and the back of the coffin.
>
> The eyes of the corpse opened wide — the hands were clenched, and a shrill, piercing shriek came from the lips... [v2.843].

At the conclusion of the novel, Varney commits suicide by throwing himself into Mount Vesuvius. This scene may have inspired an early version of the typescript in which Dracula's death is followed by a cataclysmic explosion.

"The Mysterious Stranger"

This story was translated from the German, and the illustrated translation/the October-December issue of *Chambers' Repository* appeared in 1853. This translation was reprinted in *Odds and Ends* in 1860. Greg Cox observes, wryly, that this story "reads like a Dracula rip-off, even though it was written thirty-seven years earlier" (*The Transylvanian Library* 18). "The Mysterious Stranger" is set in the Carpathian Mountains. Its protagonist is a tall, pale, thin aristocratic vampire called Azzo von Klatka. He has superhuman strength, does not eat ordinary food, inhabits a remote castle that is surrounded by wolves under his control, and has an affinity with bats. Furthermore, he can become a cloud of mist, can enter dwellings only after being invited in, inspires a mixture of attraction and repulsion in his victims, produces a state of lethargy in his victims and is pursued by a fearless vampire-hunter. The parallels with *Dracula* are obvious.

"The Strange Case of Dr. Jekyll and Mr. Hyde"

As Robert Mighall observes, "Stevenson's tale put the modern city, and specifically London, firmly on the map of Gothic horror. In this, it had an immediate influence on writers like Oscar Wilde, Arthur Conan Doyle and Arthur Machen, and is perhaps largely responsible for creating the late-Victorian London of our cinematic imaginations: a foggy gas-lit labyrinth where Mr. Hyde easily metamorphoses into Jack the Ripper, and Sherlock Holmes hails a hansom in pursuit of them both" ("Introduction" xxx–xxxi).

In most cases there is no proof that Stoker read a literary work that could have inspired him. However, this is not necessary if the circumstantial evidence is irrefutable. In 1888, the

Lyceum's production of *The Strange Case of Dr. Jekyll and Mr. Hyde* was forced to close because people feared that the play was inspiring the serial killer who had come to be known as "Jack the Ripper." People who had seen the play added to the controversy by wondering if its star, Richard Mansfield, could be descending from the stage to act out his performance in the abyss of Whitechapel. At this time, Bram Stoker had been managing the Lyceum for ten years.

Stevenson's rationalized werewolf tale is narrated by two doctors and a lawyer. Dr. Henry Jekyll's friends fear that his new acquaintance, the loathsome Edward Hyde, has a mysterious hold over him and may, in fact, be blackmailing him. As they compare stories, they discover that Dr. Jekyll and Mr. Hyde are one and the same. Early drafts of *Dracula* read like a detective novel that follows a similar pattern. Entries such as "Strange clues" (p. 8), "The Count suspected" (p. 24) and "Mina suspects Dracula" (p. 8) lead to the conclusion that Dracula is the vampire who attacked Lucy.

In both stories, the monsters are atavistic shape-shifters with extraordinary powers who have lairs in similar parts of London (Soho and the neighboring Piccadilly). One of them is a chemist, the other is an alchemist. In addition, the name of one of the narrators, Richard [R.] Enfield, could have inspired the name Renfield, while Henry Jekyll's string of degrees ("MD, DCL, LLD, FRS, &c.") may have been conferred upon Professor Van Helsing. The fact that Mr. Hyde "had never been photographed, and the few who could describe him differed widely, as common observers will" (24–25) may have inspired the idea that a vampire cannot be photographed (p. 6) and "painters cannot paint him" (p. 4). In addition, a line from Dr. Jekyll and Mr. Hyde, "The door which was equipped with neither bell nor knocker..." (6), could have found its way into *Dracula* with Jonathan Harker's observation as he stood in silence outside of the castle door, "Of bell or knocker there was no sign..." (2:15).

Bram Stoker's many friends and acquaintances included authors such as James M. Barrie, Mary Elizabeth Braddon, Richard F. Burton, Arthur Conan Doyle, William Gilbert, Edward Heron-Allen, Robert S. Hichens, Florence Marryat, Vincent O'Sullivan, and Hesketh and Kate Prichard, who all wrote some form of vampire story. It would be fascinating to know if he had discussed his masterpiece with any of these luminaries and, if so, what they said, but, unfortunately, there is no record of any such conversations.

Appendix VII. Bram Stoker's Library[405]

There is no doubt that Bram Stoker, who was interested in subjects ranging from the classics to horror fiction and occult matters, was widely read. Harry Ludlam mentions that in 1910, Bram and his wife, Florence, discarded hundreds of books when they moved from Chelsea to a smaller house in St. George's Square. After his death, his library was auctioned by Sotheby, Wilkinson and Hodge on 7 July 1913 in their *Catalogue of the Valuable Printed Books Autograph Letters and Illuminated and Other Manuscripts including the Library of the Late Bram Stoker, Esq.* Many of these books were published before 1897 and, hence (provided they were in his possession when he was planning or writing *Dracula*), could have influenced his masterpiece. The most important titles are as follows:

Blair, Robert. *The Grave: A Poem.* London: T. Bensley, 1813. Illus. by Robert Blake.

Budge, A. E. Wallis. *Book of the Dead: The Papyrus of Ani; a Reproduction in Facsimile, with Hieroglyphic Transcript, Translation and Introduction.* London: The Medici Society, 1913. 2 vol.

_____. *The Mummy: Chapters in Egyptian Funeral Archeology.* Cambridge: Cambridge University Press, 1893.

Byron, Lord. *Childe Harold's Pilgrimage: Cantos I–II.* London: John Murray, 1812.

Campbell, J. G. *Superstitions and Witchcraft and Second Sight in the Highlands and Islands of Scotland.*

Dowden, Edward. *Life of Percy Bysshe Shelley.* London: Kegan Paul, Trench, 1886. 2 vol.

Haggard, H. Rider. *Mr. Meesom's Will.* First edition, 1888.[406]

Hoffman, E. T. A. *Weird Tales: A New Translation from the German with a Biographical Memoir by J. T. Bealby.* London: John C. Nimmo, 1885. 2 vol.

Kipling, Rudyard. *The Jungle Book.* London: Macmillan and Co., 1894.

_____. *The Second Jungle Book.* London: Macmillan and Co., 1895.

Lavater, John Caspar. *Essays on Physiognomy.* London: John Murray, 1789. 5 vol. Trans. from the French by Henry Hunter. Lavater's explanation of character on the basis of physical features influenced modern psychiatry.

Leather, Robinson K. and Ried le Gallienne. *The Student and the Body-Snatcher: And Other Trifles.* London: Elkin Mathews, 1890.

MacRitchie, D. *Fians, Fairies and Picts.* London: Kegan Paul, Trench, Trubner, 1893.

Millet, F. D. *The Danube, From the Black Forest to the Black Sea.* New York: Harper & Brothers, 1893.

Shakespeare, William. *The Works of William Shakespeare in Reduced Facsimile from the Famous First Folio Edition of 1632.* London: Chatto & Windus, 1896.

---

405. Christopher Frayling includes a list of "Books in Bram Stoker's library, relevant to the writing of *Dracula*" (346–347), while Leslie Shepard discusses many of these titles in "The Library of Bram Stoker."

406. This was either Harper's edition of 1888 or the Spencer Blackett edition, which was published in London the same year. In this little-known story, a man's last will and testament is tattooed on a woman's skin.

_____. *The Works of William Shakespeare*. London: Gordon Browne, Blackie and Son. 1888–1890. 8 vol. ed. Henry Irving and Frank A. Marshall.
Shelley, Mary W. *Frankenstein, the Modern Man-Demon*. n.d.
Shelley, Percival Bysshe. *Poetical Works, with Memoir by Leigh Hunt*. 4 vol. n.d.
Sikes, William Wirt. *British Goblins: Welsh Folk-Lore, Fairy Mythology, Legends and Traditions*. London: Sampson Low, Marston, Searle & Rivington. 1880.
Stevenson, Robert Louis. *The Works of Robert Louis Stevenson*. Edinburgh: Longmans Green & Co. 28 vol. 1894–1899.
Ward, H. *Five Years with the Congo Cannibals*. London: Chatto & Windus, 1890.
Von Klinger, F. M. *Faustus, His Life, Death and Descent into Hell*. London: W. Simpkin and R. Marshall, 1825. Trans. from the German by George Borrow. A satire of Goethe's *Faust*.
The Yellow Book. Various issues.

Appendix VIII. *Dracula:* The Novel vs. the Notes

The following is a plot summary of *Dracula.* Key events and motifs that are not mentioned in the Notes are highlighted in italics.

1: Jonathan Harker travels to Transylvania to meet his client, Count Dracula, about the purchase of an estate near London. In Bistritz, he is warned about vampires. *A peasant gives him her crucifix.* On St. George's Eve, a rendezvous at the Borgo Pass with a mysterious coachman initiates a terrifying coach ride that terminates at a *ruined* castle.

2: Harker waits outside the castle door until *Dracula greets him with "Enter freely and of your own will!" and "I am Dracula."* When Harker hears wolves outside the castle, *Dracula replies, "Listen to them, the children of the night. What music they make!"* They discuss Dracula's plans for moving to England and *details about his estate in Purfleet (Carfax).* Dracula does not cast a reflection *in Harker's shaving glass. When Harker cuts himself, Dracula lunges at his throat but is thwarted by Harker's crucifix.* Harker realizes he is a prisoner in the castle.

3: Dracula tells Harker about his lineage, recalling ancient battles "*as if he had been present at them all.*" Harker sees his host emerge from a window and *crawl head-first down the wall of the castle. Three* vampire women begin to "kiss" Harker, who is about to succumb when the Count intervenes with "This man belongs to me." *He then gives the women a baby to feast on.*

4: A peasant woman outside the castle who screams, "Monster, give me my child," is slaughtered by wolves. Harker sees great wooden boxes filled with earth. Dracula tells Harker he may leave but wolves stop him from doing so. *Dracula is compared to Judas. Harker finds Dracula asleep in one of his boxes and strikes him with a shovel, leaving a scar. Having learned that Dracula's consorts intend to feed on him once Dracula has left for England,* Harker gathers his courage and executes a daring escape from the castle.

5: In England, we are introduced to Harker's fiancée (Mina Murray) and Lucy Westenra who has received three proposals of marriage in one day — from Dr. Jack Seward, Quincey Morris from Texas, and Arthur Holmwood (a.k.a. Lord Godalming)—*and has accepted Holmwood's proposal.* Seward notes that his new patient, *R. M. Renfield,* has peculiar eating habits.

6: In Whitby, Lucy and Mina meet an old sailor named *Mr. Swales who ridicules the belief that the physical body is resurrected after death. Renfield* eats flies and spiders. *Mina is worried, for she has not heard from Jonathan* while Lucy has resumed her old habit of walking in her sleep.

7: Dracula sails to Whitby on the *Demeter,* which crashes into the harbor during a fierce storm. Its crew is missing; the captain's corpse is tied to the wheel. Dracula leaps from the wreckage in the form of a large dog (or wolf).

8: Mina discovers that Lucy is not in her bed. She finds her in her nightgown in the churchyard, with "something dark" bending over her. There are two wounds on Lucy's neck. Lucy is plagued by nightmares; her health deteriorates. Mina receives a letter from Sister Agatha's hospital in Budapest, saying Jonathan is safe, but he is recovering from a brain fever. *Renfield* is excited about the coming of his "Master."

9: Mina rushes to Budapest. Jonathan gives her his journal before they are married. A bat appears at Lucy's window. Dr. Seward calls in his friend and teacher, Professor Abraham Van Helsing, *a Dutch specialist in obscure diseases,* to diagnose Lucy's mysterious illness. He realizes her condition is *a matter of "life and death, perhaps more."*

10: Van Helsing tries to save Lucy with a blood transfusion. Her relief is short-lived. Another transfusion follows. Van Helsing tries to protect Lucy with garlic.

11: After Mrs. Westenra removes the garlic, Lucy deteriorates again. A third transfusion follows. A bat appears at Lucy's window. A newspaper reports that a wolf has escaped from the London Zoo. *Renfield rants, "The blood is the life!"* A wolf *crashes* through Lucy's bedroom window. Mrs. Westenra dies.

12: Lucy is worse. Quincey Morris becomes the fourth and final blood donor. Dracula's boxes arrive at Carfax, next to Seward's asylum. Renfield raves incoherently. *When Lucy asks Arthur for a kiss, Van Helsing pulls them apart.* Lucy dies.

13: Lucy is buried. Van Helsing investigates the cause of her death. Harker sees Dracula in London *during the day; he has grown younger.* A beautiful lady *(the "bloofer lady")* is attacking children on Hampstead Heath.

14: Mina reads Jonathan's journal and makes a typewritten copy for Van Helsing. Van Helsing suspects that Lucy is the fiend who is attacking children.

15: Van Helsing and Seward break into Lucy's tomb and pry open her coffin; it is empty. *They keep watch outside her tomb and see a white figure carrying a child. Van Helsing claims that Lucy is now "Un-Dead."*

16: The men return to Lucy's tomb and *confront her, she vanishes into her tomb. The next day, they enter the tomb again and Arthur is chosen to drive the "mercy-bearing" stake through her heart. Upon Lucy's "true" death, her beauty and innocence are restored.* The vampire hunters vow to find the cause of this tragedy and eliminate him.

17: Jonathan and Mina join the vampire hunters. Mina collects, collates and types various records.

18: *Mina comforts Renfield. Van Helsing credits Mina with "a man's brain" and "a woman's heart."* Van Helsing informs the others about vampires' strengths and weaknesses. *Renfield begs to be set free, claiming he is a "sane man fighting for his soul." The hunters set out to find Dracula's boxes and sterilize them.*

19: The men break into Dracula's house at Carfax where *they are surrounded by rats.* They find some of the boxes he has scattered throughout London. Dracula enters Mina's bedroom in mist form. The next day, Mina is restless and tired.

20: The hunters find several of Dracula's lairs, *including one that he purchased under the alias "Count de Ville."*

21: *Dracula attacks Renfield. On his deathbed, he tells the men that Dracula is now preying on Mina. The men break into Mina's bedroom where they find that Count Dracula has drunk Mina's blood and is now forcing her to drink his. They drive him off with their crucifixes.*

22: *Mina reveals that Dracula had fed on her twice before; he plans to extract revenge on the vampire hunters by turning her into his un-dead slave.* When Van Helsing blesses Mina, a sacred wafer burns into her forehead. The men pledge allegiance to Mina, *who declares herself "Unclean!"*

23: Van Helsing provides more details about Dracula, who "*was in life a most wonderful man,*" but now has a "child's brain." The men find and destroy all but one of Dracula's boxes. They confront Dracula at his house in Piccadilly and, as he escapes, he turns and taunts them with, "*You think to baffle me, with your pale faces all in a row*" and "*My revenge is just begun!*" *Mina reminds the men to do their duty with compassion for their enemy, who is "the saddest case of all."* Mina asks Van Helsing to hypnotize her; her psychic link to Dracula reveals that he has boarded a ship.

24: Dracula flees to Transylvania via Varna aboard the *Czarina Catherine*. The vampire hunters, who now include Mina, vow to follow Dracula back to his homeland and destroy him, ending Mina's curse.

25: Mina's transformation continues. *At her request, the men agree to slay her if she becomes a vampire or endangers them in any way. The vampire hunters read the Burial Service for her.* Van Helsing uses Mina's psychic link to Dracula to track his movements.

26: The chase continues by land and by sea. *When they arrive in Varna, they learn that Dracula's box was unloaded in Galatz. Mina outlines three routes Dracula may take*, and they split up into three groups.

27: *As Van Helsing and Mina near the castle, Dracula's brides call out to their "sister." Van Helsing protects Mina within a holy circle. Entering the castle, Van Helsing stakes the vampire women.* The vampire hunters converge on Dracula and his gypsy retinue. As the sun sets, Dracula rises from his box with a look of triumph in his eyes but *Harker and Morris slay him with their knives. Dracula dies with a "look of peace" on his face.* Mina's scar disappears. Morris dies a hero.

Note: *Seven years later, the Harkers return to Transylvania. They now have a son named Quincey.*

Appendix IX. *Dracula*: The Novel We Could Have Read

Had Bram Stoker adhered to his initial plans for his masterpiece and dashed it off with the same haste that marks other works, *Dracula* would have been a very different novel. In *The Un-Dead* (or *The Dead Un-Dead*) a German professor, Max Windshoeffel, would have confronted Count Wampyr from Styria, Lucy Westenra would have been engaged to Dr. Seward, while one of the vampire hunters (probably Mina) would have been slain by a werewolf.

Assorted plots and characters are deleted. After the first draft, ten unnamed characters disappear abruptly:

- a philosophic historian (1)[407]
- an undertaker (1)
- an undertaker's man (1)
- a lawyer's shrewd, skeptical sister (1)
- a crank (1)
- a maid who is engaged to the undertaker's man (1)
- an auctioneer (7,[408] 8)
- a silent man, Count's servant in London (1, 7)
- a deaf mute woman, Count's servant in London (1, 7)
- doctor at Dover custom house (3)

Other characters are dignified with a name before they are dispatched:

- Francis Aytown, a painter (7)
- Cotford, a detective inspector (1, 7)
- Alfred Singleton, a psychical research agent (7)
- William Young, a lawyer (7)
- Kate Reed, friend and former schoolfellow of Lucy and Mina (7, 9)
- Trollope, receives visit from Dracula (45)
- Pickford, to whom Dracula writes a letter (45)

Other characters blossom into familiar faces:

---

407. The page numbers refer to the Eighteen-Bisang/Miller numbers.

408. The names on page 7 appear to have been inserted at a later, unknown date. Therefore, where applicable, we have also cited the next appearance of each character on this page.

- Lawyer, Abraham Aaronson = Arthur Abbott = John = Peter Hawkins (1, 2, 7,[409] 9)
- Lawyer's clerk who goes to "<Ge> [Germany]" Styria = a trustworthy lawyer who does not speak German = young man = Jonathan Harker (1, 2, 7, 9)
- Mad doctor, who loves girl = Doctor of madhouse = Seward (1, 5, 7, 13)
- His beloved = Lucy Westenra (1, 7, 9)
- Mad patient, with theory of perpetual life = fly patient = Flyman (1, 7, 8, 32)
- German professor (of history) = Max Windshoeffel = Professor Abraham Van Helsing (1, 7, 29)
- Old dead man made alive = Old Count = Count Wampyr = Count Dracula (2,[410] 7, 9, 19)
- girls; one tries to kiss young man not on lips but throat = woman = women (2, 12, 41)
- Wilhelmina Murray (called Mina) = (7)
- A Texan, Brutus M. Marix = Quincey P. Adams = Quincey P. Morris (7, 38, 41)
- Hon. Arthur Holmwood — son of Viscount Godalming (38)

Originally the novel opened with a series of letters between a foreign Count and his lawyers about the purchase of an estate in London (1, 2, 8, 9). Consequently, Jonathan Harker was sent to Styria (1, 8).

Harker's adventures in Munich:

- he travels from London to Munich via Paris (37, 40)
- he stays at Quatre Saisons hotel (10, 40)
- "adventure snow storm and wolf" (30, 40)
- he visits the Pinakothek Museum (10)
- he attends the opera, the "Flying Dutchman" (40)
- he visits a Dead House where he thinks old man on bier is dead but he is not. A corpse vanishes; he has seen the corpse but does not take part in a discussion about it (2, 3, 10, 30, 41)

Harker's stay at Castle Dracula:

- an encounter with a "wehr wolf" (14)
- shrieks from a grave, sights of terror and falling senseless, with someone or something being found by the Count (14)

Count Dracula:

- despises death and the dead (4)
- can tell if bodies are dead or alive (6)
- can banish good thoughts, create evil thoughts and destroy will (4)
- is affected only by relics that are older than he is (4)
- cannot be painted [à la Dorian Gray], any portrait looks like someone else (4, 6)
- cannot be photographed, photographs come out black or like a skeleton corpse (4, 6)
- insensitive to music (4, 6)
- cannot cross thresholds without assistance, stumbles on threshold (3, 6, 20)
- can determine and prove if people are sane (28)
- leeches are attracted to him, then repulsed (89)
- can pick out murderers (97)

Events in (or originating in) England:

- Dracula lands at Dover (3)
- coffins selected to be taken over, wrong one brought (3)

409. Any or all of the familiar names on page 7 may have been added to the first draft on a subsequent, unknown date.
410. The words "Count" and "Count's" on page 1 are probably emendations.

- at the zoological gardens, Dracula enrages eagles and lions but intimidates wolves and hyenas (4, 6)
- a dinner party where 13 guests tell a series of stories is joined by Count (5, 7, 8)
- the Count disappears, i.e., cannot be found (8, 29, 34)
- Seward and Lucy are engaged (7)
- the men find a secret, blood-red room in Dracula's house (7, 8, 15, 27, 34)
- Quincey Morris to go to Transylvania, to act as a scout (8, 25, 26, 29, 34)
- doctor sees man in coffin and restores him to life (5)
- Mina is married in London, Lucy attends the wedding (8, 19)
- Lucy visits asylum and affects the mad patient (15)
- Lucy is curious about the neighboring estate, Seward promises he will get permission to show it to her (15)
- The Count is suspected (24)
- a visit to the Count (27)
- Count Dracula returns; he is angry about the intrusion which, however, is "explained" by the capture of the fly patient (28)
- new light on Dracula (29)
- Harker sees the Count who, he realizes, is the man in the Munich dead house (29, 31, 34)

Whitby:

- Lucy finds strange brooch on shore and puts it on, leading to wound in throat & brooch covered with blood (18, 34)
- Seward visits Whitby (19)
- Lucy attends Mina's wedding (19, 34)
- Count Dracula tries to get into Lucy's room in various forms, he finally covers her window with a mass of blood, but she is guarded by some spell (20)
- wolf captured near Lucy's house (20)
- Lucy tries to bite Seward (21)

Conclusion (Transylvania):

- someone is killed by a "wolf—(wehr)" (8)
- flyman and Texan and ___ (34)
- at the castle, figures vanish in the river (49)
- volcano (49)[411]
- Quincey comes to the rescue with a maxim gun (51)
- the wild whirling figures of the women on the tower of the castle are obliterated by lightning (51)

411. After Dracula's death, Mina records that "The Castle of Dracula now stood out against the red sky, and every stone of its broken battlements was articulated against the light of the setting sun" (27:388). The typescript continues with the deleted material:

"As we looked there came a terrible convulsion of the earth so that we seemed to rock to and fro and fell to our knees. At the same moment, with a roar that seemed to shake the very heavens, the whole castle and the rock and even the hill on which it stood seemed to rise in the air and scatter skywards in fragments while a mighty cloud of black and yellow smoke volume on volume in rolling grandeur was shot upwards with inconceivable rapidity. Then there was a stillness in nature as the echoes of that thunderous report seemed to come as with the hollow boom of a thunder clap — the long reverberating roll which seems as though the floors of heaven shook. Then down in a mighty ruin falling whence they rose came the fragments that had been tossed skyward in the cataclysm.

"From where we stood it seemed as if the one fierce volcano burst had satisfied the need of nature and that the castle and the structure of the hill had sunk again into the void. We were so appalled with the suddenness and the grandeur that we forgot to think of ourselves" (539).

Works Cited

Auerbach, Nina. "Mayhem and Maidens: The Romance of the Victorian Freud" in Lynne Pykett, ed. *Reading Fin de Siècle Fictions*. London: Longmans, 1996. 22–38.

Baedeker, Karl. *Southern Germany and Austria, Including Hungary and Transylvania*. 6th ed. London: Dulau, 1887.

Barber, Paul. *Vampires, Burial, and Death: Folklore and Reality*. New Haven, CT: Yale University Press, 1988.

Barclay, Glen St. John. *Anatomy of Horror: The Masters of Occult Fiction*. London: Weidenfeld and Nicolson, 1978.

Baring-Gould, Sabine. *The Book of Were-Wolves: Being and Account of a Terrible Superstition* [1865]. New York: Causeway Books, 1973.

_____. "Margery of Quether" [1884]. Rpt. in *Margery of Quether: And Other Weird Tales*. Mountain Ash, Wales: Sarob Press, 1999. ed. Richard Dalby.

Belford, Barbara. *Bram Stoker: A Biography of the Author of Dracula*. New York: Alfred A. Knopf, 1996.

Bierman, Joseph S. "The Genesis and Dating of *Dracula* from Bram Stoker's Working Notes" in Carter. 51–55.

Boucher, Anthony. "Introduction" in *Dracula*. New York: The Limited Editions Club, 1965. v–xi.

Bram Stoker's Dracula: A Centennial Exhibition at the Rosenbach Museum & Library. Philadelphia: Rosenbach Museum & Library, 1997.

Byron, Glennis, ed. *Dracula*. Peterborough, ON, Canada: Broadview Press, 1998.

Carter, Margaret L., ed. *Dracula: The Vampire and the Critics*. Ann Arbor, MI: UMI Research Press, 1988.

Chitimia, Silvia. "Les traces de l'occult dans le folklore roumain" in *Le Défi Magique*, vol. 2. Presses Universitaires de Lyon, n.d. 135–148. French text.

Collins, Wilkie. *The Woman in White* [1860]. London: Penguin, 2003. ed. Matthew Sweet.

Cox, Greg. *The Transylvanian Library: A Consumer's Guide to Vampire Fiction*. San Bernadino, CA: The Borgo Press, 1993.

Dalby, Richard. "Introduction" in Bram Stoker. *The Primrose Path*. Westcliff-on-Sea: Desert Island Books, 1999. 6–10.

_____, and William Hughes. *Bram Stoker: A Bibliography*. Westcliff-on-Sea: Desert Island Books, 2004.

Dickens, David B. "The German Matrix of Stoker's *Dracula*" in Miller, 1998. 31–40.

Douglas, John, and Mark Olshaker. "Jack the Ripper" in *The Cases that Haunt Us*. New York: Pocket Star, 2001. 1–92.

Du Maurier, George. *Trilby: A Novel*. New York: Harper & Brothers, 1895.

Eighteen-Bisang, Robert. "Dracula, Jack the Ripper and a Thirst for Blood" in *Ripperologist* 60 (July 2005). 3–12.

Emerson, Joel H. *The Un-Dead: The Dracula Novel, Rewritten to Include Stoker's Deleted Characters and Events*. www.xlibris.com: Xlibris, 2007. Rev. 2007.

Farson, Daniel. *The Man Who Wrote Dracula: A Biography of Bram Stoker*. London: Michael Joseph, 1975.

Fontana, Ernest. "Lombroso's Criminal Man and Stoker's *Dracula*" in Carter. 159–165.

Frayling, Christopher. *Vampyres: Lord Byron to Count Dracula*. London: Faber and Faber, 1991.

"From Ponkapog to Pesth" in *The Atlantic Monthly* January 1877.

Frost, Brian J. *The Essential Guide to Werewolf Literature*. University of Wisconsin Press, 2003.

Gautier, Theophile. "Clarimonde" ["La Morte Amoureuse" 1836] in *One of Cleopatra's Nights: And Other Romances*. New York: R. Worthington, 1882. Trans. from the French by Lafcadio Hearn. 66–125.
Gerard, Emily. *The Land Beyond the Forest*. London: Blackwood, 1888.
_____. "Transylvanian Superstitions" in *Nineteenth Century* (July 1885). 130–150.
Griffin, Gail B. "Your Girls That You All Love Are Mine: *Dracula* and the Victorian Male Sexual Imagination" in Carter. 137–148.
Haining, Peter. *The Dracula Scrapbook*. Stanford: Longmeadow, 1987.
_____, ed. *The Vampire Omnibus*. London: Artus Books, 1995.
Haining, Peter, and Peter Tremayne. *The Un-Dead: The Legend of Bram Stoker and Dracula*. London: Constable, 1997.
Harker, Joseph. *Studio and Stage*. London: Nisbet, 1924.
Hopkins, Lisa. *Bram Stoker: A Literary Life*. London: Palgrave Macmillan, 2007.
Hughes, William. *Beyond Dracula: Bram Stoker's Fiction and Its Cultural Context*. London: Palgrave Macmillan, 2000.
Johnson, Major E. C. *On the Track of the Crescent: Erratic Notes from the Pireus to Pesth*. London: Hurst and Blackett, 1885.
Kline, Salli J. *The Degeneration of Women: Bram Stoker's Dracula as Allegorical Criticism of the Fin de Siècle*. Rheinbach-Merzbach, Germany: CMZ-Verlag, 1992.
Leatherdale, Clive. *Dracula: The Novel & the Legend: A Study of Bram Stoker's Gothic Masterpiece*. Wellingborough, UK: Aquarian Press, 1985.
_____. *The Origins of Dracula*. London: William Kimber, 1987.
_____, ed. *Dracula Unearthed*. Southend-on-Sea: Desert Island Books, 2006.
Le Fanu, Joseph Sheridan. "Carmilla" [1872]. Rpt. in Ryan. 71–137.
Levi-Strauss, Claude. "The Structural Study of Myth" [1958] in *Structural Anthropology*. New York: Basic Books, 1968. 206–231.
Lovecraft, H. P. Letter to Robert Barlow. 10 December 1932. Rpt. in McNally and Florescu, 1979. 24.
Ludlam, Harry. *A Biography of Dracula: The Life Story of Bram Stoker*. London: W. Foulsham, 1962.
Martens, Lorna. *The Diary Novel*. Cambridge: Cambridge University Press, 1985.
Mayo, Herbert. *On the Truths Contained in Popular Superstitions* [1851]. Westcliff-on-Sea: Desert Island Books, 2003.
McKee, Robert. *Story: Substance, Structure, Style, and the Principles of Screenwriting*. New York: Regan, 1997.
McNally, Raymond T. *A Clutch of Vampires: These Being Among the Best from History and Literature*. Greenwich: New York Graphic Society, 1975.
_____, and Radu Florescu, eds. *The Essential Dracula*. New York: Mayflower, 1979.
_____, and _____. *In Search of Dracula: A True History of Dracula and Vampire Legends*. Greenwich: New York Graphic Society, 1972.
Mighall, Robert. "Introduction" in Stevenson, 2002. ix–xxxviii.
Miller, Elizabeth. *Dracula: Sense & Nonsense* [2000]. Southend-on-Sea: Desert Island Books, 2006.
_____, ed. *Bram Stoker's Dracula: A Documentary Volume*. Farmington Hills, MI: Thomson Gale, 2005. Dictionary of Literary Biography # 304.
_____, ed. *Dracula: The Shade and the Shadow*. Westcliff-on-Sea: Desert Island Books, 1998.
Moretti, Franco. *Signs Taken for Wonders*. Trans. From the Italian by S. Fischer, D. Forgacs and D. Miller. New York: Verso, 1988.
Morrison, Ronald D. "Reading Barthes and Reading *Dracula*: Between Work and Text" in *Kent Philological Review* 9 (1994). 23–28.
Murray, Paul. *From the Shadow of Dracula: A Life of Bram Stoker*. London: Jonathan Cape, 2004.
"The Mysterious Stranger" [1853]. Rpt. in Ryan. 36–70.
Nizet, Marie. *Le Capitaine Vampire*. Paris: Auguste Ghio, 1879. French text. Translated from the French by Brian Stableford. *Captain Vampire*. Encino, CA: Black Coat Press, 2007.
Perkowski, Jan L. *The Darkling: A Treatise on Slavic Vampirism*. Slavica: Columbus, OH, 1989.
Polidori, John. "The Vampyre" [1819]. Rpt. in Ryan. 7–24.
Richardson, Maurice. "The Psychoanalysis of Count Dracula" [1959]. Rpt. in Frayling. 418–422.
Roth, Phyllis A. *Bram Stoker*. Boston: Twayne, 1982.
Ryan, Alan, ed. *Vampires: Two Centuries of Great Vampire Stories*. Garden City, NY: Doubleday, 1987.
Saberhagen, Fred. *The Dracula Tape*. New York: Warner, 1975.
Sage, Victor. *Horror Fiction in the Protestant Tradition*. New York: St. Martin's Press, 1988.

Seed, David. "The Narrative Method of *Dracula*" in *Nineteenth Century Fiction* 40:1 (1985). 61–75.
Senf, Carol A. *Between Tradition and Modernism*. New York: Twayne, 1998.
Shelley, Mary. "Introduction" [1818] in D. L. Macdonald and Kathleen Scherf, ed. *Frankenstein*. Peterborough, ON, Canada: Broadview Press, 1999. 47–48.
Shepard, Leslie. "The Library of Bram Stoker" in Carol Margaret Davison, ed. *Bram Stoker's Dracula: Sucking Through the Century, 1887–1997*. Toronto: Dundurn, 1997. 41–44.
Skal, David J. *Hollywood Gothic: The Tangled Web of Dracula from Novel to Stage to Screen*. New York: W. W. Norton, 1990.
Stenbock, Stanislaus Eric (Count). "The True Story of a Vampire" [1894]. Rpt. in *Studies of Death*. London: Durtro Press, 1997. 73–89.
Stevenson, Robert Louis. "The Strange Case of Dr. Jekyll and Mr. Hyde" [1886]. Rpt. in *The Strange Case of Dr. Jekyll and Mr. Hyde: And Other Tales of Terror*. London: Penguin Books, 2002. ed. Robert Mighall.
Stoddard, Jane ("Lorna"). "Mr. Bram Stoker: A Chat with the Author of *Dracula*" [1897] in G. Byron. 484–488.
Stoker, Bram. "Author's Preface" [1901]. Rpt. in *Bram Stoker Society Journal* 5 (1993). 7–8.
_____. *Dracula*. London: Archibald Constable and Company, 1897.
_____. *Dracula*. London: Archibald Constable and Company, 1901. Revised edition.
_____. *Dracula*. New York: Doubleday & McClure, 1899. Amended edition.
_____. *Dracula*. London: William Rider & Son, n.d. [1912]. Amended edition.
_____. *Dracula; or, The Un-Dead: A Play in Prologue and Five Acts* [1897. Unpublished]. Nottingham, UK: Pumpkin Books, 1997. ed. Sylvia Starshine.
_____. "Dracula's Guest" in *Dracula's Guest: And Other Weird Stories*. London: George Routledge & Sons, Ltd., n.d. [1914]. 1–18.
_____. "The Judge's House" [1891] in *Dracula's Guest*, 1914. 19–44.
_____. Letter to William Gladstone. 24 May 1897. Rpt. in Miller, 2005. 274.
_____. *Personal Reminiscences of Henry Irving*. 2 vol. London: Heinemann, 1906.
_____. "The Squaw" [1893] in *Dracula's Guest*, 1914. 45–62.
_____. *The Un-Dead*. Original typed manuscript, on the rectos of 529 pages. [1897.] Unpublished.
Stoker, Florence A. L. Bram. "Preface" in Bram Stoker, *Dracula's Guest*, 1914. n.pag.
Sugden, Philip. *The Complete History of Jack the Ripper*. New York: Carroll & Graf, 2002.
Summers, Montague. *The Vampire: His Kith and Kin* [1928]. New York: University Books, 1960.
"A Thirst for Blood" in *The East London Advertiser* 6 (October 1888).
Todorov, Tzvetan. *The Fantastic: A Structural Approach to a Literary Genre*. Ithaca, NY: Cornell University Press, 1975.
Tracy, Robert. "Loving You All Ways: Vamps, Vampires, Necrophiles and Necrophilles," in *Sex and Death in Victorian Literature*, ed. Regina Barreca. Bloomington: Indiana University Press, 1990. 32–59.
Tropp, Martin. *Images of Fear: How Horror Stories Helped Shape Modern Culture (1818–1918)*. Jefferson, NC: McFarland, 1990.
Tusan, Michelle. "Inventing the New Woman: Print Culture and Identity Politics during the Fin-de-Siècle" in *Victorian Periodicals Review* (Summer 1998).
Twitchell, James B. *The Living Dead: A Study of the Vampire in Romantic Literature*. Durham, NC: Duke University Press, 1981.
The Undead: The Book Sail 16th Anniversary Catalogue. Orange, CA: McLaughlin Press, 1984. ed. John McLaughlin.
Varney the Vampyre; or, The Feast of Blood. [1847]. Rpt. New York: Dover, 1972. 2 vol. Attributed to James Malcolm Rymer. ed. E. F. Bleiler.
Warren, Louis S. *Buffalo Bill's America: William Cody and the Wild West Show*. New York: Alfred A. Knopf, 2005.
Weissman, Judith. "Women as Vampires: *Dracula* as a Victorian Novel" in Carter. 69–77.
Wicke, Jennifer. "Vampiric Typewriting: *Dracula* and Its Media" in *ELH* 59:2 (1992). 467–493.
Wilson, A. N., "Introduction" in *Dracula*. Oxford: Oxford University Press, 1983. vii–xix.
Wolf, Leonard, ed. *The Annotated Dracula*. New York: Clarkson N. Potter, 1975.

Index of Bram Stoker's Original Notes

This is an index to Stoker's original material, as transcribed.

Index of Editors' Annotations

This is an index to the editors' annotations, including other scholars' comments about Stoker, his Notes and related matters.